MARY,
GOD-BEARER TO A WORLD IN NEED

MARY,

God-Bearer to a World in Need

edited by
MAURA HEARDEN
and VIRGINIA M. KIMBALL

foreword by
Bertrand Ruby

PICKWICK Publications · Eugene, Oregon

MARY, GOD-BEARER TO A WORLD IN NEED

Copyright © 2013 Wipf and Stock Publishers. All rights reserved. Except for brief quotations in critical publications or reviews, no part of this book may be reproduced in any manner without prior written permission from the publisher. Write: Permissions, Wipf and Stock Publishers, 199 W. 8th Ave., Suite 3, Eugene, OR 97401.

Pickwick Publications
An Imprint of Wipf and Stock Publishers
199 W. 8th Ave., Suite 3
Eugene, OR 97401

www.wipfandstock.com

ISBN 13: 978-1-61097-026-6

Cataloging-in-Publication data:

Mary, God-bearer to a world in need / edited by Maura Hearden and Virginia M. Kimball ; foreword by Bertrand Ruby

xxiv + 178 p.; 23 cm—Includes bibliographical references.

ISBN 13: 978-1-61097-026-6

1. Mary, Blessed Virgin, Saint. I. Hearden, Maura. II. Kimball, Virginia M. II. Ruby, Bertrand. III. Title.

BT610 .M38 2013

Manufactured in the USA.

Scripture texts marked NAB are taken from the *New American Bible, revised* edition © 2010, 1991, 1986, 1970 Confraternity of Christian Doctrine, Washington, D.C. and are used by permission of the copyright owner. All Rights Reserved.

Scripture texts marked NRSV are taken from the *New Revised Standard Version Bible: Catholic Edition*, copyright 1989, 1993, Division of Christian Education of the National Council of the Churches of Christ in the United States of America. Used by permission. All rights reserved.

A previous version of chapter 2, "Mary and the Truth about Life," by Fr. José Granados, PhD, appeared in *Anthropotes* 23 (2007) 101–30. This chapter by Fr. Granados is published here with permission from *Anthropotes*.

Portions of chapter 6, "Mary's Song: The *Magnificat*," by Sr. Mary Catherine Nolan, OP, STD, have been excerpted from her book *Mary's Song: Living Her Timeless Message*, copyright 2001 by Ave Maria Press, Inc., PO Box 428, Notre Dame, IN, 46556, www.avemariapress.com with permission from Ave Maria Press. All rights reserved.

This book is dedicated to the Mother of Our Lord, her faithful servants, and all who are in need of her motherly care.

Contents

List of Contributors · ix
Foreword: The God-Bearer for a World in Need
    by Bertrand Buby · xiii
Editors' Preface · xxi
Abbreviations · xxiii

1 Mary of Galilee, Mother and Mystic: Prophet to a World in Need · 1
   by Virginia M. Kimball

2 Mary and the Truth about Life · 23
   by José Granados

3 What Can the Holy Family Teach Us About Marriage? · 42
   by Marianne Lorraine Trouvé

4 Mary: Mirror of Justice · 57
   by Christopher M. Carr

5 The Marian Dimension of the Church and the Economic Order · 77
   by Nicholas J. Healy Jr.

6 Mary's Song: The *Magnificat* (Luke 1:46–55) · 91
   by Mary Catherine Nolan

7 The Virgin Mary, a Model of Encounter: The Relevance of
   the Qur'ānic Mary to Christian-Muslim Dialogue · 110
   by Rami Wakim, with support from
   His Beatitude Gregorios III, Melkite Patriarch

8 The Blessed Virgin Mary—Our Educator · 125
   by Danielle M. Peters

9   Currents and Contentions: Authentic Devotion
    to the God-Bearer at the Dawn of the Third Millennium · 144
    by Kenneth F. Yossa

10 Mary and the Communal Nature of Salvation · 161
    by Maura Hearden

Contributors

Christopher M. Carr, PhD, is an assistant professor of religious studies at Misericordia University in Dallas, Pennsylvania. He is a member of the Catholic Theological Society of America and has presented at the Ecumenical Society of the Blessed Virgin Mary-USA.

Fr. José Granados, DCJM, STD, is the vice president of the Pontifical John Paul II Insitute for Studies on Marriage and Family at the Lateran University, Rome, where he teaches as an associate professor of Sacramental Theology. He is also a visiting professor at the Pontifical Gregorian University (Rome). Fr. Granados has lectured at the different sessions of the Pontifical John Paul II Institute in Washington, DC; Melbourne, Australia; the Philippines; and at the Catholic University of Santiago de Chile. He has published, among other works: *Called to Love: Approaching John Paul II's Theology of the Body* (2009), with Carl A. Anderson; *Los misterios de la vida de Cristo en Justino Mártir* (2005), awarded the Bellarmino Prize; *Teología de los misterios de la vida de Jesús* (2009); and *Teología de la carne: el cuerpo en la historia de su salvación* (2011).

Nicholas J. Healy Jr., DPhil, is an assistant professor of philosophy at the Pontifical John Paul II Institute for Studies on Marriage and Family in Washington DC. He is an editor and frequent contributor to the journal *Communio: International Theological Review* and the author of *Being in Communion: The Eschatology of Hans Urs von Balthasar* (2005).

Maura Hearden, PhD, is an assistant professor of theology at DeSales University in Center Valley, PA, where she teaches Mariology and a variety of other theological courses. Dr. Hearden is a member of the Mariological Society of America and a board member of the Ecumenical Society of the Blessed Virgin Mary-USA. Her work has been published in *Mary for* the Love and Glory of God; Pro Ecclesia; The Journal of Ecumenical Studies; American Catholic Studies; and Spiritual Life.

Virginia M. Kimball, STD, is an adjunct professor of theology at Assumption College, teaching biblical and theological courses online in Continuing and Career Education, in Worcester, MA. She is a member and former president of the Mariological Society of America, and is currently president of the Ecumenical Society of the Blessed Virgin Mary. Her work is published in *Mary for the Love and Glory of God*; *Mary for Time and Eternity*; *Marian Studies*; *Liturgical Illuminations: Discovering Received Tradition in the Eastern Orthros of Feasts of the Theotókos*; *Society of Biblical Studies* (online journal); and she is a contributor to the *Mary Page* (www.marypage.org) and *Catholic Web* (www.catholicweb.net).

Sr. Mary Catherine Nolan, OP, STD, is a Roman Catholic Dominican Sister who holds a Doctor of Sacred Theology degree from the International Marian Research Institute, the American branch of the Roman Pontifical Theological Faculty Marianum. She is author of *Mary's Song: Living Her Timeless Message* and has contributed a chapter, "Mary and Islam," in the ESBVM publication *Mary for the Love and Glory of God*, as well as articles for *Marian Studies*, the Mariological Society of America journal. She is a writer, lecturer, spiritual director, and retreat director.

Sr. Danielle M. Peters, ISSM, STD, is a member of the Secular Institute of the Schoenstatt Sisters of Mary and serves as an official of the Congregation for the Doctrine of the Faith. A former professor and coordinator of academic programs at the pontifical International Marian Research Institute (IMRI) in Dayton, OH, she continues to collaborate with IMRI as student advisor and occasional guest lecturer. She is a member of the Mariological Society of America and of the Catholic Theological Society of America.

Sr. Marianne Lorraine Trouvé, FSP, is a member of the Daughters of St. Paul, a religious congregation serving the Church through communications media. She has an MA in theology with a concentration in Marian studies from the University of Dayton. Since 1994 she has served as an editor for Pauline Books & Media, specializing in titles related to Mary and to the theology of the body. She is the author of *St. Clare of Assisi*; *Angels: Help from on High*; and *St. Catherine Labouré and Our Lady of the Miraculous Medal*; and is a contributor to *Ask a Catholic Nun* (https://www.facebook.com/AskACatholicNun).

Rami Wakim, MTh, a doctoral student at the Jesuit's Centre-Sèvres in Paris, is an assistant professor of patristics at St. Paul's Institute in Lebanon. He works as an academic counselor at St. Anne's Patriarchal Seminary where he teaches church history and liturgical theology. Deacon Wakim is secretary to H. B. Gregorios III, Patriarch of the Greek Melkite Catholics of Antioch and all the East. His work is published in *Le Lien* and *Al-Maçarra*.

Fr. Kenneth F. Yossa, PhD, is a priest of the Byzantine Catholic Church. He earned his doctorate (Marquette University) in systematic theology and has recently served at Franciscan University of Steubenville and Ocean County College (Toms River, NJ) as an adjunct lecturer. He has authored a number of works, including *Common Heritage, Divided Communion* (2009), which treats of ancient and contemporary relations between the Oriental and Eastern Orthodox communions.

Foreword

The God-Bearer for a World in Need

This book, which shows the role that Mary plays in addressing the many needs and issues of our world, is a superb implementation of the principles promulgated by the Second Vatican Council (1962–1965) in the eighth chapter of the Dogmatic Constitution of the Church. Specifically, section 65 states:

> For Mary, who since her entry into salvation history unites in herself and re-echoes the greatest teachings of the faith as she is proclaimed and venerated, calls the faithful to her Son and His sacrifice and to the love of the Father. . . . Hence the Church, in her apostolic work . . . justly looks to her, who, conceived of the Holy Spirit, brought forth Christ, who was born of the Virgin that through the Church He may be born and may increase in the hearts of the faithful also. The Virgin in her own life lived an example of that maternal love, by which it behooves that all should be animated who cooperate in the apostolic mission of the Church for the regeneration of men.

The theologians, educators, and Scripture scholars who wrote this book have collaborated in fulfilling the spirit of that paragraph by demonstrating the role of the God-Bearer (*Theotókos, Mater Dei,* Mother of God) in "the apostolic mission of the Church for the regeneration of men," which includes attention to the pressing needs of the world as well as ultimate questions of eternal salvation. The ten authors have given us a gift, which comes from their careful research, deep reflections, and penetrating "reading of the signs of our times." They weave a golden thread through their theological writings, presenting Mary as the God-Bearer, the life-giver for the many needs of contemporary society and the world. Each author speaks in a clear and compelling way from his or her professional knowledge about issues of faith, justice, family life, economic concerns, spirituality, prayer, interreligious dialogue, and human dignity, all issues which desperately need Mary's presence in a "culture of life" over against a "culture of death." Finally, in keeping with the vision of Vatican II, the authors never lose sight of the fact that the title "God-Bearer" is seen primarily as a christological one and an ecclesial one. Mary is never separated from her son nor from us who are the people redeemed by her son Jesus.

Permit me to simply and succinctly present a trajectory of the book and how it is a mosaic of unity without confusion as each scholar weaves the details of his or her topic around the golden thread of the image of the God-Bearer.

Chapter 1 is done by editor Dr. Virginia Kimball, a renowned scholar in ecumenical circles. She shows us the importance of prayerful and mystical faith that young adults are yearning for in beauty, community, spirituality, and justice. Mary has a prophetic role in helping people to understand what it means to be Christian. This mother has been given to us by God (Gal 4:4–5). As one who trusted God completely, she shows us that we must not make God an afterthought. As mother, mystic, and prophet, she demonstrates for Christians all the fruits given by God, which provide true joy. Mary was as human as we are and her mystical experience of God can be ours.

Chapter 2 is written by Fr. José Granados, DCJM, who helps us discern the false notions of life over against the Gospel of Life. The title of his chapter is clear and direct and carried out within the pages of this essay, "Mary and the Truth about Life." He interprets for us *Gaudium et Spes* of Vatican II (#22) while relating it to *Evangelium Vitae*, the "Gospel of Life"(#44). In the false view of life there is the absolutizing of an autonomy that forgets its relational character with the world, with others, and with God, thus losing the broader context of life's origin and destiny, without which life itself is meaningless. Mary sheds light and offers guidance in this situation, by redefining life in the light of relationship (with nature, our neighbors, and God) as originally received from another and called to be given to others in a fruitful way. Incarnational theology is both christological and mariological. It is relational through the Church.

Chapter 3 is presented by Sr. Marianne Lorraine Trouvé, FSP, who describes the needs of marriage and family life through a study of what the Holy Family of Jesus, Mary, and Joseph can teach us. She is a learned student of the thought of Pope John Paul II on the theology of the body and on his *Role of the Christian Family in the Modern World*. Within the

Christian family, Sr. Trouvé observes that there is need for greater development of interpersonal relationships, a renewed awareness of the dignity of women, and attention to the education of children. The golden thread is woven into this chapter as the author notes that an awareness of the Holy Family precisely as family adds an important element to Marian devotion. Other forms of Marian devotion portray Mary as a solitary figure, or more often, with her son Jesus. But seeing Mary as part of the Holy Family involves another important figure: Joseph. We see Mary as a married woman and the Holy Family as a model of married relatedness.

Chapter 4 is titled "Mary: Mirror of Justice" and is authored by Dr. Christopher M. Carr. He returns us to the sources of what justice really is, since in the West it has been forgotten. He states,

> [Mary is] a kind of mirror that reflects what justice generically means and entails through the specific things we know about her from Scripture and Tradition. All the essential characteristics of justice are variously manifested in Marian doctrines or the events from her life.

Relying on Thomas Aquinas, the following essential definition of justice is given—"the habitual strength of will whereby one affirms another's human dignity by giving that person that which is due." Furthermore, Dr. Carr points out that justice is the only one of the four cardinal virtues that is relational! "[T]he essence then of justice is the willingness to give another person what that person is entitled to have precisely as a person." Mary as Mirror of Justice is a concrete example of the way in which this relational virtue could be lived.

Chapter 5 presents the "Marian Dimension of the Church and the Economic Order," by Dr. Nicholas J. Healy Jr., of the Institute for Studies on Marriage and the Family, Washington, DC. His sources are the Congregation for the Doctrine of the Faith, "Instruction on Christian Freedom and Liberation" and the World Day of Peace, January 1, 2000, "Message for the Celebration of the World Day of Peace," delivered by Pope John Paul II. The two citations from these documents are the focus of this chapter. The former states,

> Mary is totally dependent on her Son and completely directed towards him by the impulse of her faith; and, at his side, she is the most perfect image of freedom and of the liberation of humanity and of the universe. It is to her as mother and model that the

Church must look in order to understand in its completeness the meaning of her own mission.

John Paul's message contains the following: "An economy which takes no account of the ethical dimension and does not seek to serve the good of the person—of every person and the whole person—cannot really call itself an 'economy.'" Pope Benedict XVI adds to the thought of both quotations saying, "Mary is the personal concretization of the Church…the Church in person and as a person. [Mary] is the most perfect image of freedom and of the liberation of humanity and of the universe." Dr. Healy's entire chapter is an excellent study of the Church's recent teachings in the area of the economic order and serves to weave the golden thread of Mary into her deep relationship to the Church as her spiritual mother. He suggests three areas in which the Marian illumination of human nature and activity helps us (re)discover the deepest meaning of economic life as an aspect of life lived in communion with God and one another: (1) creation as a gift; (2) creaturely receptivity; and (3) participating in the good. Scripture is the starting point (Luke 1:46–47) offering us a window to the soul of Mary. The content of this chapter complements the theological thought offered on justice in chapter 4.

Chapter 6 is the work of Sr. Mary Catherine Nolan, OP, STD, whose doctorate analyzed the *Magnificat* of Mary (Luke 1:46–56) and reflected upon it in the light of the mission of her Dominican community. This chapter is a further development of her research and adds to her popular book on the *Magnificat* published by Notre Dame Press. The development springs also from the liturgical use of the *Magnificat* in the Eastern Christian Churches for Morning Prayer while in the West it is always said, chanted, or sung at Vespers. The *Magnificat* consists of two phases: (1) the wholesomeness and total magnanimity of Mary's praise of God and then (2) Mary's focus on the actions of God whose benevolence is to the lowly, to the hungry, to the poor and to the powerless. Sr. Nolan shows us that Scripture truly is the soul of Marian theology through this clear and concise presentation of Mary's Song. God remembers all through merciful kindness (*hesed*), which leads to healing and gratitude. People who have received God's loving kindness are invited to extend mercy, kindness and forgiveness to others. Thus, the message of Mary's *Magnificat* is that God is acting in our lives and in the events of history to bring about the reign of justice, the reign of right relationships, and therefore the reign of peace.

Chapter 7 shows us the Virgin Mary as a "Model of Encounter" in "The Virgin Mary, a Model of Encounter: The Relevance of the Qur'ānic Mary to Christian-Muslim Dialogue." This outstanding chapter was encouraged by His Beatitude Gregorios III and entrusted to the author, Deacon Rami Wakim, Secretary for the Melkite Greek Catholic Patriarchate. We learn how Mary is venerated by the Muslims, and how she is mentioned in almost forty places within the Qur'an—her name appears thirty-four times! In certain sacred places both Christians and Muslims gather in prayer at chapels or shrines dedicated to Mary. This article helps us to see that Mary is certainly a bridge of peace in our dialogue with our Muslim brothers and sisters. Solidarity and peace are what we all pray for with Mary's presence in our respective Scriptures. Mary shows us the path of being truly religious, blessed by God, and of bearing the fruit of peace to the world. Sheikh Mahassine sums up the portrait of Mary in the Qur'an in this way: "She is especially chosen and purified, she is a model of faith in God and natural return to Him, of compliance to His will (the meaning of Islam), of devotion, of modesty, of piety and contemplation, of silence, and of prayer and fasting." Contained within that citation of the Sheikh are three of the five pillars of Islam (the five pillars are: faith in the oneness of God and the finality of the prophet, Muhammad; daily prayer; almsgiving; fasting; and pilgrimage to Mecca). There is much belief about the person of Mary that Islam and Christianity hold in common.

Chapter 8 is the work of Sr. M. Danielle Peters, ISSM, STD. It presents the Blessed Virgin Mary as our Educator. This theme proceeds from a doctoral study presented to the International Marian Research Institute in Dayton, Ohio. She prefaces her study with a quotation from Pope John Paul II: "No human mother can limit her task solely to the procreation of human beings; she must also undertake the task of nourishing them and educating them." Mary teaches in order to educate. This is the task of all teachers and mothers, as well. Sr. Peters explains how we are to understand Mary's motherhood in the "order of grace." Mary has a singular and unique cooperation with the Savior in the entire work of redemption. As spiritual mother, Mary gives birth to Christians and nurtures them spiritually. Her ongoing maternal role includes a formative and educational influence on every child of God. Since the overall goal of education is "promoting the Christian transformation of the world by which natural values, viewed in the full perspective of humanity as redeemed by Christ, may contribute to the good of society as a whole." Sr. Peters develops the chapter through the anthropological paradigm of our vocation to holiness. Our Lady educates us through her example, and as our spiritual mother, she mediates for us the graces needed to grow in holiness. We all are challenged to enter into "Mary's School."

Chapter 9 is the contribution of Fr. Kenneth F. Yossa, PhD. His chapter is called "Currents and Contentions: Authentic Devotion to the God-Bearer at the Dawn of the Third Millennium." Theologians are not apt to speak or write about devotions. Here we have an outstanding exception in the theological thought of Fr. Yossa, who makes a good case for devotion to the God-Bearer as an aid for confronting the problems and issues of the present day. The Catholic Church has been challenged from within by questions of how and to what extent (if any) authentic devotion to Mary ought to have a place in the life of Christians. The devotions to Mary took quite a plunge in the years after Vatican II, especially in popular expressions such as novenas, May devotions, and even the Rosary. Recently, however, there has been a slow but sure growth in an interest in scriptural talks about Mary, in a revival among the young Catholic college students for the recitation of the Rosary and certainly in the development of liturgical Masses (*Collection of Masses of the Blessed Virgin Mary* consisting of a Sacramentary and Lectionary). The latter were designed to deepen the theology of Mary and serve as a source for reviving Saturdays in honor of Mary. Fr. Yossa confirms the importance of the great encyclical on Marian Devotions (*Marialis Cultus*, by Paul VI) and concludes his essay with an important excerpt from paragraph 57:

> Contemplated in the episodes of the Gospels and in the reality which she already possesses in the City of God, the Blessed Virgin Mary offers a calm vision and a reassuring word to modern man, torn as he often is between anguish and hope, defeated by the sense of his own limitations and assailed by limitless aspirations, troubled in his mind and divided in his heart, uncertain before the riddle of death, oppressed by loneliness while yearning for fellowship, a prey to boredom and disgust. She shows forth the victory of hope over anguish, of fellowship over solitude, of peace over anxiety, of joy and beauty over boredom and disgust, of eternal visions over earthly ones, of life over death.

Chapter 10 is written by one of the editors of this book, Dr. Maura Hearden. Her topic is "Mary and the Communal Nature of Salvation." She starts with this striking sentence of Alexander Schmemann: "The world is a fallen world because it has fallen away from an awareness that God is all in all.... Even the religion of this fallen world ... has accepted the all-embracing secularism which attempts to steal the world away from God." Dr. Hearden reminds us that "the human race is bonded at the very core of our being: in our common origin, existence, and destiny in God." She further explains that the process of transformation into the deeper communion with God that is required for salvation is a communal enterprise. While secularism may attempt to "steal the world away from God" and us from one another, "Mary can anchor the Christian mind firmly in a Christian worldview as a sea of secular contradictions storms against it." The author then brilliantly links the mystery of sacramental communion with the dogmas of the Blessed Virgin Mary, showing how one dogma helps explain another and how the dogmas need to be seen in an organic and ever-growing manner. She states,

> Even the so-called "Marian privileges," those gifts that seem to set Mary apart from the rest of the human race, actually depend upon and exemplify our unity with each other and God.... The Church (which consists of a hierarchical institution as well as a Mystical Body) is often described as a "sacramental communion." It is "sacramental" in the sense that Christ is truly present in and working through it. It is a "communion" because the presence of the Holy Spirit is a bond uniting all the members of the Body.

Her summary is an excellent synthesis of the entire book:

> The Marian doctrines discussed throughout this essay are ultimately woven into a single truth about Mary's role in salvation history: Mary's mission as the Bearer-of-God, the *Theotókos*, is made possible by the divinely bestowed bond of the Immaculate Conception and consummated by her glorious Assumption into Heaven. These cosmic events mediated Christ Himself, and thus His grace, to the world—the saving grace of perfect communion with and in God. Mary's life makes strikingly evident the communion that we already share as well as the communion to which we aspire. We are materially and spiritually interdependent creatures, our brothers' keepers in this life and for the next.

In concluding, I would like to share with you my joy in making this journey with Mary with these ten theologians. For me, it carries out the express purpose of the chapter on Mary in the *Constitution on the Church* in such a way that all of the paths of theology are seen as leading to an appreciation of the guiding light and presence of Mary on this journey of faith. The dogmas of Mary are developed in connection with the issues and needs of our time, as well as a source for our personal appreciation for who Mary is or who she can come to be in our lives. The book is a good example of how our faith always needs to search for deeper understanding through our own study and pondering (*fides quarens intellectum* of St. Anselm).

This book is perfect for an appreciation of the work of Marian theologians who realize the importance of Holy Scripture as the soul of Marian theology. It is appropriate for use in college classrooms and in seminaries. It is an excellent work for those unfamiliar with Marian thought to be brought up to date and to appreciate how important Mary's role in the history of salvation is.

Having had personal contact with four of the theologians both in classes I taught and in their continuing work for the Church, I especially experienced great joy in reading their recent theological and Marian thought on the Virgin Mary as God-Bearer to the needs of our time.

Rev. Bertrand Buby, SM
Professor of Scripture at the International
   Marian Research Institute in Dayton, Ohio
June 30, 2012, Feast of the Holy Martyrs of Rome

Editors' Preface

> "Mary is totally dependent on her Son and completely directed towards him by the impulse of her faith; and, at his side, she is the most perfect image of freedom and of the liberation of humanity and of the universe."[1]

Everyone yearns for freedom—freedom from political oppression, poverty, disease, crime, war, and misery in all its forms. Yet as history progresses, the prize seems desperately elusive. Oppressive regimes topple, but still we are not free. Technological innovation increases productivity in ways that stagger the imagination, but still we are not free. In many ways the social demons from which we've fled have multiplied and grown stronger so that, despite tremendous efforts, the world still groans in pain.

Why can't we find the freedom we're looking for? Why is the prize so elusive? As many a great thinker has observed, it is not enough to seek freedom from something; we must also seek freedom for something. When we turn away from that which enslaves us, we must be certain that we are turning toward that which will free us. For when one power structure topples, another rises to take its place, and freedom depends upon the character of the latter. To whom and what will we give ourselves? This is the question upon which the future depends.

The Blessed Virgin Mary gave herself without reserve to the One, Almighty Source of all the goodness that we truly crave, and so became the vessel through which her son entered the world, offering salvation to it—salvation from eternal death and the earthly misery that inevitably occurs when ultimate wisdom, truth, and goodness are rejected or ignored. The God who saved all humanity from eternal doom is the same God who

---

1. Joseph Ratzinger, *Instruction on Christian Freedom and Liberation*, §97, online: http://www.vatican.va/roman_curia/congregations/cfaith/documents/rc_con_cfaith_doc_19860322_freedom-liberation_en.html.

saved Israel from slavery in Egypt and lovingly turned water into wine at the wedding feast of Cana.

Attempting to resolve the world's crises apart from the power of its Creator condemns the world to the woeful inadequacy of its own finitude, but the abandonment of self to the love of that Creator opens the world to possibilities never before imagined. Whatever hope the world has of peace and prosperity in the here and now rests with its ability to abandon itself to God, as Mary of Nazareth so clearly did. The editors of this book suggest that all who strive for freedom and true happiness solicit the motherly help and example of this remarkable woman who received the Holy Spirit into her heart and body more fully than any mere creature has or will in human history.

The essays in this book explore the relationship between Mariology and a wide variety of topics, from mysticism to economic justice. The variety is purposeful, for this-worldly goals such as economic justice depend upon other-worldly goals, namely mystical communion with God. It was Mary's freely willed communion with the divine that made her the *Theotókos* (the God-Bearer) to the world. Let us pray that each of us might, in our own unique way, bear God to this world which is in such need of Mary's divine son, so that one day we may dare to say that the Father's will *is* done on earth as it is in Heaven.

Maura Hearden

Virginia M. Kimball

Abbreviations

AAS	*Acta Apostolicæ Sedis*
Adv. Haer.	*Adversus Haereses*
CCC	*Catechism of the Catholic Church*
CCL	*Corpus Christianorum Series Latina*
CL	*Christifideles Laici*
CV	*Caritas in Veritate*
DS	Denzinger-Schönmetzer, *Enchiridion Symbolorum, definitionum et declaration de rebus fidei et morum* (1965)
EE	*Ecclesia de Eucharistia*
EV	*Evangelium Vitae*
FC	*Familiaris Consortio*
GS	*Gaudiem et Spes*
LG	*Lumen Gentium*
MC	*Marialis Cultus*
MD	*Munificentissimus Deus*
NAB	*New American Bible*
NMI	*Novo Millennio Ineunte*
NRSV	*New Revised Standard Version of the Bible*
PG	*Patrologia Graeca*
PL	*Patrologia Latina*
RC	*Redemptoris Custos*

RM	*Redemptoris Mater*
RV	*Rosarium Virginis*
SM	*Signum Magnum*
ST	*Summa Theologica*
VS	*Veritatis Splendor*

1

Mary of Galilee, Mother and Mystic
Prophet to a World in Need

VIRGINIA M. KIMBALL

". . . and his mother kept all these things in her heart" (Luke 2:51 NAB)

St. Gregory Palamas once described the Virgin Mary as one whose profound sanctity can only be understood as mystical.[1] In referring to the vision of a seraphic angel touching the mouth of prophet Isaiah with tongs holding burning coals carried from the altar of God (Isa 6:6–7), and of the great vision of Moses in the Burning Bush on Mt. Sinai (Exod 3:2), Gregory wrote the following:

> Surely everyone is aware that the Virgin Mother is both that burning bush and those tongs, as she conceived the divine fire without being consumed by fire.[2]

---

1. St. Gregory Palamas (1296–1359), known as a deeply mystical saint, composed among his writings well-known homilies on the Entrance of the Mother of God into the Temple. He described Mary the mother of Christ as the archetype of the hesychastic way of life, a way of spiritual "stillness," referring to Psalm 46:11: "Be still and know that I am God" (NAB).

2. Palamas, "On the Entry of the Mother of God into the Holy of Holies I," in *Mary the Mother of God: Sermons by Saint Gregory Palamas*, trans. and ed. Christopher Veniamin (South Canaan, PA: Mount Tabor, 2005), 35.

Today, understanding Mary, mother of Christ, in a spiritual and mystical way is usually absent from modern-day thinking by many Christians, although it has become evident that young adults are, indeed, yearning for beauty, community, spirituality, and justice.[3] However, such understanding is the key to the full embrace of Christian life and the vibrancy of God's call to everyone. Mary is apt to be seen more in a picture book manner —at Christmastime in a bucolic nativity scene or again on Good Friday as the sorrowful mother who knelt at the foot of the cross weeping for her dying son. These may be the only glimpses that most Christians have of Mary, the woman who is so important in understanding what it means to be Christian. Today, in this world of self-indulgence, self-centeredness, and materialistic goals,[4] many find their daily existence devoid of any spiritual awareness of this mother given by God to humanity.

Yet, more and more today, Christians yearn for deep spiritual connections with God. Such a quest stands in opposition to today's tendencies: worrying about jobs and careers, houses, cars, places to live comfortably, and attainment of numerous secular goals. Often, in our society, God is a mere afterthought. It is a challenge to remember that happiness is not to be found in earthly accomplishments and the possession of things alone. Jesus promised joy, happiness, and eternal life. Once Jesus is embraced, life on earth is filled with God's spirit, and filled with true happiness and joy—an experience that grows and lasts forever! To the Samaritan woman at the well, Jesus said: "Whoever drinks the water I shall give will never thirst; the water I shall give will become in [her or] him a spring of water welling up to eternal life" (John 4:14 NAB).[5] In an ancient Christian hymn, composed in the fifth century, we find words describing the mother of Christ herself as the "well" of that living water, meaning that her child Jesus is the "living

---

3. The author is grateful to Rev. Dr. Joshua Genig for pointing this out and recommending N. T. Wright, *Simply Christian: Why Christianity Makes Sense* (New York: HarperCollins, 2010).

4. There is a movement back to God, however, in the face of persistent atheism and secularism. People are once again turning back to Christianity and learning its value. See David Bentley Hart, *Atheist Delusions: The Christian Revolution and Its Fashionable Enemies* (New Haven, CT: Yale University Press, 2009). Hart describes the society that we live in: "We live in an age whose chief value has been determined, by overwhelming consensus, to be the inviolable liberty of personal volition, the right to decide for ourselves what we shall believe, want, need, own, or serve" (21–22).

5. In the Sermon on the Mount, Jesus preached the Beatitudes, axioms of what it means to experience the joy of God and the true meaning of "happiness": "Joyful are those who hunger and thirst for righteousness, for they shall be satisfied" (author's wording).

water": "O *Theotókos*, living and abundant fountain. . . . Rejoice, O Lady, never empty fount of living water."[6] We, too, should pause, reflect, and contemplate the urgency of lifting ourselves up to Jesus, thereby realizing the profound gifts that these waters of life and joy provide.

Christianity truly speaks of life and joy! Mary, the young engaged but unmarried woman, who bore God's Son into the world, was and is the loving mother who knew God, carried and bore God to our world, and exists now with God to bring us to ever increasing joy. According to God's plan, she lives in eternity—dedicating herself to the welfare of her son's people. She is the way to her son, to life and joy. She was and continues to be mother and mystic—loving and trusting God and, in this way, being a prophet to a world in great need.

To help us conceive of Mary as the young woman touched on the lips by the burning coals of heaven and a human who was so filled in her own body with the Holy Presence of Almighty God, we turn to St. Ephrem's description: "Hail, you who did fold in your bosom, and hold in your arms Him whom no space can contain."[7] Mary, as mother, holds the all-powerful Creator of the Universe in her womb. To think that "God is a consuming fire" (Heb 12:29 NAB) and dwelt in the young woman's body leaves one speechless. The only explanation possible is that anything is possible with God (Matt 19:26), accomplished in the mystery of God!

The following pages on Mary as mystic, mother, and prophet will offer tastes of wisdom and guidance from Scripture and Tradition. With these few examples offered, it becomes evident that the mystical path of Mary can be our path if we, too, want to know true joy. The topics to be considered are: Mary as prophet; Mary as mystic; and Mary in Tradition, looking at Mary in early liturgy and daily prayer; understanding the words "joy," "happiness," and "blessed" as they originated in the New Testament; Marian iconography; and Mary in Scripture.

Mary, as Prophet

Mary's life as we discern it from the Bible and tradition—her motherhood and her mystical heart—reveal Mary as a prophet who has much to tell

---

6. *Akathist Hymn and Small Compline*, trans. N. Michael Vaporis (Needham, MA: Themely, 1992), Ode 3, vv. 8–9. Most scholars think this hymn was composed by Romanos the Melodist in the fifth century.

7. Thomas Livius, *Blessed Virgin in the Fathers of the First Six Centuries* (New York: Benziger, 1893), 298. St. Ephrem of Syria lived in the years ca. 306–373.

the world about her son. A prophet (Hebrew *nabi'*, Greek *prophētēs*) is "a person who serves as a channel of communication between the human and divine worlds."[8] Mary's prophecy, then, is realized in her mediation with God. Mary, a prophet, is a woman who communicates God's word and interprets God's will and covenant for the faithful. The *Catechism of the Catholic Church* describes prophets, including the women of the Bible:

> God forms his people in the hope of salvation, in the expectation of a new and everlasting covenant intended for all, to be written on their hearts. The prophets proclaim a radical redemption of the People of God, purification from all their infidelities, a salvation which will include all the nations. Above all, the poor and humble of the Lord will bear this hope. Such holy women as Sarah, Rebecca, Rachel, Miriam, Deborah, Hannah, Judith, and Esther kept alive the hope of Israel's salvation. The purest figure among them is Mary.[9]

As prophet, Mary once sang joyfully of her dedication to God, in a song we now call the "Magnificat." She was visiting her cousin Elizabeth, also pregnant in her advanced years through a miraculous gift of life given by God. Mary, who was carrying Christ in her womb, sang forth with the radiance of a pregnant and tender young mother. It was a scene of two women unusually pregnant with life, proclaiming not only joy over their own sons, but expressing a profound reconnection with the God of Life for their people. In this, there is clear witness to Mary's strong prophetic voice:

> My soul proclaims the greatness of the Lord;
> my spirit rejoices in God my savior.
> For he has looked upon his handmaid's lowliness;
> behold, from now on will all ages call me blessed.
> The Mighty One has done great things for me,
> and holy is his name.
> His mercy is from age to age to those who fear him.
> He has shown might with his arm,
> dispersed the arrogant of mind and heart.
> He has thrown down the rulers from their thrones but lifted up the lowly.
> The hungry he has filled with good things;

---

8. Paul J. Achtemeier, ed., *HarperCollins Bible Dictionary* (San Francisco: Harper SanFrancisco, 1996), 884.

9. CCC §54.

the rich he has sent away empty.
He has helped Israel his servant, remembering his mercy,
according to his promise to our fathers,
to Abraham and to his descendants forever (Luke 1:47–55 NAB).

Mary's song is strikingly similar to Hannah's song in 1 Samuel 2:1–10, singing praises to God for sending a son to her with these words: "My heart exults in the LORD" (1 Sam 2:1). Mary, in her song, proclaims: "My soul proclaims the greatness of the Lord" (Luke 1:46). It should be pointed out that the relationship of "heart" (*leb* in Hebrew) and "soul" (*nefesh* in Hebrew, *psychē* in biblical Greek) in these two songs are evidently interconnected. The Greek word for "soul" echoes the Hebrew meaning of *nefesh* by indicating an experience of joy and love. In Luke 1:46 "the *psychē* is the subject of praise of God; the presence of *pneúma* shows that this is God's gift and work."[10] Layered upon this meaning in the Greek are the interweaving Hebrew concepts of soul and heart: "When the soul is said in OT fashion to praise and love God, the meaning is very close to that of heart."[11] The evident connection between Mary and Hannah is that both women placed total trust in God, received a son destined to be a king, and dedicated their precious child back to God. Hannah sang in Hebrew: "My heart exults in the LORD; my strength is exalted in my God" (1 Sam 2:1 NRSV). Correspondingly, Mary—the young Jewish woman—sings in the Greek of the New Testament: "My soul magnifies the Lord, and my spirit rejoices in God my Savior" (Luke 1:46–47 NRSV). In Hebrew, the "heart" is the place of God's dwelling and life giving in the human person. There is no duality of body and soul in the anthropological understanding of Hebrew, as embraced in Jewish culture of the first century. In the Greek of the New Testament, the word "soul" represents the connection of the human with God. The relationship of these two words, the Hebrew *nefesh*, and Greek *psychē*, portray the deep and expansive relationship this young woman Mary has with God. Her whole being grows (seen in the Greek *megaleion*, in Latin *magnificat*) with God. God is with her and yet ever expansive. It is not "greatness" in importance but a depth of life and of relationship with God that she experiences. In reality, according to a dynamic translation of these two phrases (the Hebrew and then the Greek—the original language

---

10. Geoffrey W. Bromiley, *Theological Dictionary of the New Testament* [hereafter: *TDNT*], abr. in one vol., ed. Gerhard Kittel and Gerhard Friedrich (Grand Rapids: Eerdmans, 1985), 1348.

11. Ibid.

of the New Testament), we see that Mary repeats Hannah's words but with profound, mystical dimension.

Mary as Mystic

When God called this young woman of Galilee some two thousand years ago to be the human mother of God's son, Jesus—coming to the world to heal a deep rupture of love and relationship between God and humanity—the communication was announced by the angel Gabriel. This announcing (Annunciation) of God's plan to reconnect with humanity was a direct and mystical experience for the young woman whose Hebrew name was Miriam (Luke 1:28).

Mysticism is a term that has many contours, but its meaning is simply understood as "the direct intuition or experience of God; and a mystic is a person who has, to a greater or less degree, such a direct experience."[12] Noted scholar on mysticism, Evelyn Underhill, describes mysticism as "the science of the Love of God" and adds that the mystic pursues a "life which aims at union with God."[13] This union, which aptly describes Mary and her life, is expressed in the following way by St. Augustine: "My life shall be a real life, being wholly full of Thee."[14] Referring to one writing in *The Philokalia*, Abba Philimon (ca. 600 CE) described the life of the mystic:

> The saints were people of this kind. They were totally severed from the ways of the world, and by keeping the vision of heaven unsullied in themselves they made its light shine by observing the divine laws. And having mortified their earthly aspects (Col 3:5) through self-control and through awe and love for God, they were radiant with holy words and actions. For through unceasing prayer, and the study of the divine scriptures the soul's noetic eyes are opened, and they see the King of celestial powers, and great joy and fierce longing burn intensely in the soul; and as the flesh, too, is taken up by the Spirit, man becomes wholly spiritual.[15]

Mysticism is known to grow within a person in three stages, originally identified as "three grades of purification, enlightenment, and union," as

---

12. Evelyn Underhill, *Mystics of the Church* (Eugene, OR: Wipf & Stock, 2002), 9.
13. Ibid., 20.
14. Ibid., 10.
15. Bernard McGinn, *Essential Writings of Christian Mysticism* (New York: Modern Library, 2006), 127–28.

described by St. Clement of the early church.[16] Mary is the epitome of this description. She recognizes the message of the angel due to her knowledge of Scripture and her intense prayer life (purification); she embraces the message and call sent by God (enlightenment), and she takes action in her remarkable *fiat* ("let it be done"), pledging to bear God's Son (union). Mary's mystical union with Christ, the Son of God, has been portrayed— as seen in Ephrem and Palamas—in ancient Christian iconography as the "burning bush" encountered by Moses on Mt. Sinai. She received God, who is burning with divine love, within her body; but, Mary is not consumed. St. John of Damascus wrote:

> The prophecies concerning you have been fulfilled, O chaste Virgin! A prophet prefigures you as a gate of Eden turned toward the East, through which no one passed except the Maker of you and of all the universe. [Referring to Ezek 44:2] Another saw you as a bush engulfed in flames [referring to Exod 3:2]: the flames, in fact, of the deity took up residence in you and did not consume you.[17]

Mary's *enlightenment* or *illumination* as a mystic came when the angel Gabriel approached her, bringing news of God's plan, so truly mystical as she heard God's call and then responded in the wisdom of the Holy Spirit who overshadowed her. How was she to be a mother without a man? With God's illumination she responded in humility and trust: "Behold, I am the handmaid of the Lord. May it be done to me according to your word" (Luke 1:38 NAB). We see the unity of Mary and God reaching completion: in the incarnation and birth of her son, and throughout her life with him for eternity.

After the incarnation of her son, pregnant and certainly somewhat afraid, Mary ventured across the hills of Galilee to visit her cousin Elizabeth, as mentioned. When she met her cousin, aged and pregnant because of God's mercy, Elizabeth's child leapt in her womb. In this mystical moment, Elizabeth proclaimed: "Blessed are you who believed that what was spoken to you by the Lord would be fulfilled" (Luke 1:45 NAB). We take note that she knew Mary as one truly oriented in the word of God, an important aspect in the life of a mystic. Elizabeth's response is to call Mary "blessed." Elizabeth proclaimed: "Most blessed are you among women, and

---

16. Underhill, *Mystics*, 55.

17. John Damascene, *Dogmatic Writings on the Theotókos*, in *Testi Mariani del Primo Millennio* [hereafter: TM], 2 §546, as quoted in Giovanna Parravicini, ed., *Mary Mother of God: Her Life in Icons and Scripture* (Ligouri, MO: Ligouri/Triumph, 2004), 13.

blessed is the fruit of your womb" (Luke 1:42 NAB). The word "blessed," we will discover, is derived from the Greek word for "joy." Mary's life as it was blessed will be witnessed in her life of trials faced with trusting faith, as she persisted in her experience of God, evidencing "joy" in the face of serious and sad obstacles. She demonstrates in her life the possibility for true joy and God's sustaining gift of life to all Christians who come to her son.

For the mystic, taking action for God initiates the entire relationship with God, which was for Mary her call to be a mother.[18] When the night of Jesus' birth came, Mary gave birth in a cave and the sky was filled with angels.[19] Heaven was celebrating the coming of God's Son to earth so that God could be with humanity again in a close relationship (Emmanuel). "All this took place to fulfill what the Lord had said through the prophet: 'Behold, the virgin shall be with child and bear a son, and they shall name him Emmanuel' which means 'God is with us'" (Matt 2:22–23 NAB). Mary's pregnancy and giving birth is evidence of taking action for God, the essential aspect for a mystic.

When Mary and Joseph took their son to the temple in Jerusalem for the traditional sacrifice and dedication of their baby son, we find that the priest Simeon prophesies Mary's future: "Behold, this child is destined for the fall and rise of many in Israel, and to be a sign that will be contradicted (and you yourself a sword will pierce) so that the thoughts of many hearts may be revealed" (Luke 2:34–35 NAB). The prophet Isaiah had warned:

> But with the LORD of hosts make your alliance—for him be your fear and your awe. Yet he shall be a snare, an obstacle and a stumbling stone to both the houses of Israel, a trap and a snare to those

---

18. Underhill, *Mystics*, 10: "The Christian mystic therefore is one for whom God and Christ are not merely objects of belief, but living facts experimentally known first hand; and mysticism for him becomes, in so far as he responds to its demands, a life based on this conscious communion with God."

19. Ancient tradition affirms that Jesus was born in a cave. In the region of Bethlehem, there were limestone caves that people used as places to keep their livestock. In this there is a mystical meaning that is portrayed in the traditional Byzantine icon of the Nativity, the Creator of Earth and Heaven descends to earth and is born in a dark cave, often known to be the place of the dead. The God of Life descends into the world of death. In this icon is also seen the baby Jesus, wrapped in linen cloths—appearing to be swaddling clothes of an infant but symbolizing the linens of the shroud that would wind his body after the crucifixion. Constantly, God's Son represents life, coming to trample down death by death itself. The traditional Nativity icon may be seen in Alfredo Tradigo, *Icons and Saints of the Eastern Orthodox Church* (Los Angeles: Getty Museum, 2006), 105.

who dwell in Jerusalem; And many among them shall stumble and fall, broken, snared, and captured (Isa 8:13–15 NAB).

Mary, who had given birth to a son who was both human and divine, was going to find her life full of challenge and oppressive, dangerous action by enemies of Christ, her son. But with faith, she persists and dedicates her discipleship in a prophetic way for generations to come.

We learn of a significant moment of fear and trial for Mary, which happened when Jesus was twelve years old. After journeying to Jerusalem to celebrate the Feast of the Passover, as the family did each year, Mary and Joseph suddenly discovered as they traveled home that Jesus was missing. We hear of how Mary, terrified that he was lost, pondered her son's response when she and Joseph finally found him in the temple speaking with rabbis.[20] We learn from this account in Luke that Mary's response was to trust God and treasure it all in her heart. The text tells us, "And his mother kept all these things in her heart" (Luke 2:51 NAB).

"Heart" and "soul" in Hebrew anthropology, as we have seen, are concepts that are closely bound together and provide a rather different idea than contemporary definitions. The place of the heart, the life source of the person, is the place of the soul. If we examine the definition of the Greek word used in Luke's text for "kept" followed by the phrase "in her heart," we are struck with the paradox of such wording.[21] In contemporary reflection on the result of Mary finding Jesus in the temple, "and his mother kept all these things in her heart" (Luke 2:51), the use of the word "kept" here would be associated with memory and the intellect, and "heart" merely to the idea of "feeling." But paradox assists us in an understanding of the mystical aspect of Mary's life, in its Hebrew and biblical Greek context. Paradoxical accounts are the best way to approach the mystery of God when there is no rational explanation. Considering aspects that do not make rational sense—the paradox—can actually be the only way for any comprehension at all. Keeping these moments and pondering them in her

---

20. "After three days they [Mary and Joseph] found him in the temple, sitting among the teachers, listening to them and asking them questions. And all who heard him were amazed at his understanding and his answers. When his parents saw him they were astonished; and his mother said to him, 'Child, why have you treated us like this?' . . . He said to them, 'Why were you searching for me? Did you not know that I must be in my Father's house?'" (Luke 2:46–49 NRSV).

21. The word for "kept" or "stored up" used in Luke 2:51 is *diaterein*, derived from *diatereo*, "for 'keeping' or 'storing up' in the memory" (*TDNT*, 1176). And yet, the text states these things were stored up "in her heart."

heart is a mystical reality of Mary's relationship to God. The actual definition of the Hebrew word "heart" sheds some light:

> There is in the NT a rich usage of *kardia* for a. the seat of feelings, desires, and passions (e.g., joy, pain, love, desire, and lust); . . . b. the seat of thought and understanding; . . . c. the seat of the will (e.g., Acts 11:23; 2 Cor 9:7, [Luke] 21:14); and d. the religious center to which God turns, which is the root of the religious life, and which determines moral conduct; . . . as the heart of the sinner; . . . as the heart of the redeemed.[22]

Thus, the Greek of the New Testament does not imply a dichotomy of "body and soul" assumed in today's culture, for no such dichotomy was found in the Hebrew culture of Mary.

If we turn to the Hebrew context of the word "heart," we find a direct connection with the biblical Greek word for heart, *kardia*. The Hebrew words *leb* and *lebab* have the literal meaning of "breast" and "physical vitality."[23] However, figuratively, and the ancients are not shy of symbol and metaphor, the heart is used:

> a. for courage (2 Chr 17:6) in various expressions, b. for the seat of rational functions ([Deut] 29:3), c. for the place of willing and planning (Jer 23:20), and d. for the source of religious and ethical conduct (1 Sam 12:20).[24]

This means that the Hebraic "heart and soul" and the Greek "heart" are true equivalents. We must understand that the "soul" of Mary, the *nephesh*—meaning the very spirit of God who gives her life and denoting "her total person, what [he or] she is"[25]—is intimately connected to what she holds in her heart. In Mary's world, God's relationship with humans exists in the heart: "The LORD looks on the heart" (1 Sam 7b NRSV). The great command, respected to this day by Jewish people, is the Great Shema. Mary is truly one who took her Hebrew heritage "to heart": "Hear, O Israel: The LORD is our God, the LORD alone. You shall love the LORD your God with all your heart, and with all your soul, and with all your might" (Deut 6:4–5 NRSV). And, to this God adds: "Keep these words that I am commanding you today in your heart" (Deut 6:6 NRSV). We see Mary doing exactly this.

22. *TDNT*, 416.
23. Ibid., 415.
24. Ibid.
25. Ibid., 1344.

The root of the Hebrew word for soul, *nephesh*, means "to breathe" in its biological sense. "Breathing is a decisive mark of the living creature; its cessation means the end of life. The root then comes to denote 'life' or 'living creature.'"[26] This reminds us of the creation of the earthling, Adam. "Then the LORD God formed man from the dust of the ground, and breathed into his nostrils the breath of life; and the man became a living being" (Gen 2:7 NRSV). The person's heart is "like breathing, it has an ebb and flow. . . . God tests it (Ps 17:3), knows it (Ps 33:15), purifies it, and unites it with himself (Kgs 8:16)."[27] And now, we find that both *nephesh* and "heart" relate to "spirit" in Hebrew anthropology.[28] These close relationships between the words "heart," "soul," and "spirit" give us insight into how Mary "kept" all the words and events she experienced "in her heart." We can only say it is mystical.

By God's intent, Mary is a close and loving mother for all; she is mother of the Mystical Body—the body of the faithful who are the Body of Christ, her son, in the world. Christ said this, himself:

> Abide in me as I abide in you. Just as the branch cannot bear fruit by itself unless it abides in the vine, neither can you unless you abide in me. I am the vine; you are the branches. Those who abide in me and I in them bear much fruit, because apart from me you can do nothing (John 15:4–5 NRSV).

Mary abides in Christ and directs all cares for those who are hurting, needy, sick, and sorrowful directly to her son. There is an ancient icon that depicts Mary as leading the faithful to her son. It is called the *Hodegetria* (leading the way, sometimes called "Mary, the Directress") and shows Mary holding her son and pointing to Him. This work of mediation pertains to her role as prophet. Mary's help gives resounding joy to a world in dire need, not because she herself answers prayers but because she directs all concerns and needs to her son.

---

26. Ibid., 1343.

27. Ibid., 1345.

28. The Hebrew word *nephesh* generally means "breath," inferring the breath of God and of life. "The Hebrew term which [*psyche* in Greek] renders is a fluid and dynamic one which is hard both to define and to translate" (*TDNT*, 1343). "In spite of parallels, a distinction remains between 'spirit' and both [*nephesh*] and heart, although spirit and heart are virtually identical in Ezek. 11:5 and Jer. 3.17" (*TDNT*, 1345).

For Mary, her discipleship was a complete immersion into the covenant of God's love.[29] Imagine the mystical aspect of this: Mary was a human being whose womb held the human child Jesus who was at the same time always God, the Lord who is beyond our comprehension—Creator of the Universe, the All Knowing (Omniscient), Everywhere Present (Omnipresent), All Powerful (Omnipotent) One! From the ancient days of Christianity, Mary is described as *Platytera,* a Greek word meaning "wider than the heavens"—her human body mystically wider than imaginable, containing the Uncontainable who is God Almighty. And yet ... Mary was and is every bit as human as all women! Consider an icon in the ancient tradition called "The Mother of God, the Stone Not Broken Off by Human Hand." This iconographic subject uses symbolism closely connected to the prophecy of Daniel:

> "A rock broke off from the mountain, but not by the hand of man ... and it became a great mountain that filled all the region." The rock that in Nebuchadnezzar's dream smashes to pieces the statue of the giant is Christ, while the Virgin is symbolized by the sky that sends down the rock. In fact, the mountain appears on the breast of the Mother of God [in the icon], along with other symbols of Old Testament prophecies: the rainbow (sign of alliance between God and humans), Gideon's fleece covered with dew, and Jacob's ladder, a symbol of the union of heaven and earth realized through the Incarnation.[30]

Early Christian writing and iconography often used symbolic parallelism to try and represent the mystical aspects in the Incarnation and Mary's continuing role in God's plan.

At a time in the first centuries when people thought of gods and pictured a mother of a god as a goddess, Christians were quite careful to profess that Mary was the absolutely human woman "who bore" God into the world. The special name given Mary from as early as the second or third century was *Theotókos*. This Greek word combines the word for God, *Theos*, with a form of the verb that means to bear, *tokos*. The term *Theotókos* carefully distinguishes Mary as the birth-giver of Jesus who was truly God and truly man, her mysticism nothing akin to being a goddess. For, as St. Paul in writing to new Christians in Galatia was careful to point out: "When the fullness of time had come, God sent his Son, born of a woman, born under

---

29. See Marie Azzarello, *Mary, the First Disciple: A Guide for Transforming Today's Church* (Toronto: Novalis, 2004).

30. Parravicini, *Mary Mother of God*, 26–27.

the law" (Gal 4:4 NAB). In other words, she does not possess her son's divine nature in her own right, but has a share in that nature, mystically, as his mother.

Sources from Tradition

From as early as the late first and second centuries, a number of texts developed which were Bible-like but never recognized as inspired by God, like those which were eventually gathered into the canon, or list of books we now call the Bible. These writings are called the apocryphal writings. The one writing which offers the most tradition about Mary outside the Bible is the *Proto-Gospel of James*. The multiple apocryphal accounts of the Dormition of Mary, the Falling Asleep or Death of Mary, also form an important corpus of Marian tradition which became sources for the Feast of the Dormition for the Eastern Church and the dogma of the Assumption of the Virgin Mary in Catholic Mariology.[31] Details in the *Proto-Gospel of James* are filled with the mystical aspect of Mary's dedication to God in the temple as a small child, her engagement to Joseph, the Annunciation, the birth, and later details in her life. The Dormition traditions establish that Mary died and was then taken both body and soul to Jesus, her son, in heaven, demonstrating Mary's death as prophetic—showing the faithful that we too will be resurrected at the end of time and taken both body and soul to be with Christ in heaven.

These apocryphal texts are not always literally historical and are often symbolic or highly mystical. Evidence of acceptance and regard for the apocryphal texts, and especially that of the *Proto-Gospel of James* and the Dormition traditions, are represented in Christian sacred images: in catacomb art; in early icons known as "liturgical art" because they were and are used in worship, representing a "writing" of revelation (in much the same sense as the written words of the Bible); in images including stained glass windows; altar pieces; illuminated manuscripts from the Middle Ages; in the artistic work of the Renaissance and Baroque painters and sculptors; and in folk art around the world. This demonstrates that early and medieval

---

31. Other apocryphal writings included in the Marian tradition are: Pseudo-Matthew; the Infancy Gospel of Thomas; Acts of Pilate / Gospel of Nicodemus; the Gospel of Philip—one of the Nag Hammadi documents; the Apocryphal Acts of the Apostles; the Gospel of Peter; and the Sibylline Oracles, which included texts written in Greek hexameter and included material from gnostic, Jewish, and Christian origins.

Christianity perhaps embraced more the mystical aspects of Mary and her life, aspects which perhaps were later lost as art became more human centered, attempting to portray Mary more in a sense of pageantry and through cultural details of the artist's time.

The feast of Mary's entry into the temple is an ancient tradition documented in the *Proto-Gospel of James*.[32] This writing was first thought to be a heretical, Gnostic document but scholars now have evidence that it reflects life for Mary from a viewpoint portraying first century Jewish mysticism.[33] Based on the *Proto-Gospel of James*, are details related to several of the significant feasts in the life of the early church, known as the Twelve Major Feasts. The interpretation of the feast day of Virgin Mary's Entry into the Temple as a very small child is understood mystically as Mary herself who is entering the temple, who is sustained in the company of angels, and who eventually will be embracing in her body the presence of God, making her then the very temple to hold God within her body.[34]

> By associating the Temple with the *Theotókos*—the very presence of Holy God within its inner sanctuary, and her association with angels having climbed the 15 steps of ascent, we are illumined by her purity—her presence in the Presence of the Transcendent God, her preparation at the hands of angels, her care in the gifts of God, her steadfast faith, and her all-holiness.[35]

Mary's father, Joachim, was an esteemed member of the temple and went to make his yearly offering in the holy of holies. However, he was sent away because of the fact that he had no children, and fell into disgrace in the eyes of the temple community. He and his wife, Anna, turned to Yahweh

---

32. Also called the *Protoevangelium of James*, or similar titles.

33. Tim Horner, "Jewish Aspects of the *Protoevangelium of James*," *Journal of Early Christian Studies* 12 (2004) 335.

34. Traditionally, the Twelve Feasts include the Nativity of the *Theotókos* (September 8); Exaltation of the Cross (September 14); Presentation of the *Theotókos* in the Temple (November 21); Nativity of Christ (December 25); Baptism of Christ/Theophany (January 6); Presentation of Jesus in the Temple (February 2); Annunciation (March 25); Entry into Jerusalem/Palm Sunday (Sunday before Pascha); Ascension of Christ (40 days after Pascha); Pentecost (50 days after Pascha); Transfiguration of Christ (August 6); and the Dormition/Assumption of the *Theotókos* (August 15).

35. Mary is symbolized as the "Daughter of Zion" in the account of her entry into the temple. See Virginia M. Kimball, "Entrance of the Theotokos into the Temple: Daughter of Zion Dwells in Heaven's Presence," in *Mary for the Love and Glory of God,* ed. Maura Hearden and Virginia M. Kimball (Bloomington, IN: AuthorHouse, 2011), 98.

in prayer[36]—Joachim who had withdrawn to the desert to fast and pray, and Anna who remained home to pray and trust in God. Then, Anna and Joachim became pregnant. Many details about Mary's birth, her entry into the temple, her betrothal to Joseph, and the birth of her child are all chronicled in this non-canonical document with many descriptions that are not in the Bible.[37]

Multiple non-biblical sources relate early tradition describing Mary's death: "The Lord embraced her, and he took her holy soul and placed it in Michael's [the archangel] hands. . . . And we, the apostles, beheld the soul of Mary as it was given into Michael's hands."[38] Pseudo-Dionysius the Areopagite of the fifth to the sixth century describes the transferal of Mary to be one with her son at her death, traditionally called the "Feast of the Dormition"—meaning "she fell asleep in the Lord":

> But when they opened the tomb that had contained the sacred body, they found it empty and bare of the mortal spoils. Even though they felt sorrow, they managed to understand that, after the heavenly chants had ended, the holy body had been removed by the very ethereal powers, after having been predisposed in a supernatural manner to the dwelling of honor, of light, and of glory hidden to the visible and carnal world, in Jesus Christ Our Lord, to whom be given glory and honor for all eternity. Amen![39]

When Pseudo-Dionysius states that Mary was "predisposed in a supernatural manner to the dwelling of honor, of light, and of glory" in heaven, he means that through her free will she has lived close to God and therefore has become totally receptive to oneness with her son who is her God. This is the stage of union in mysticism.

---

36. Anna and Joachim would use the Hebraic name *Yahweh* for God, a name so profound in meaning that it was not pronounced aloud. The inherent meaning of the name *Yahweh* is "The One" (often simply just *El*) called "Who Is!" This name reveals its meaning—the Author of Life.

37. Frederica Mathewes-Green, *Lost Gospel of Mary: The Mother of Jesus in Three Ancient Texts* (Brewster, MA: Paraclete, 2007), 26–81. See also "Infancy Gospel of James," Early Christian Writings, online: http://www.earlychristianwritings.com/infancyjames.html.

38. An ancient account of Mary's death—her "dormition," or falling asleep in the Lord, according to Stephen J. Shoemaker, "The Earliest Greek Dormition Narrative," in *Ancient Traditions of the Virgin Mary's Dormition and Assumption* (New York: Oxford University Press, 2002), 365.

39. Pseudo-Dionysius the Areopagite, *To Titus*, in TM 1 §627, as quoted in Parravicini, *Mary*, 120.

Early Liturgy and Daily Prayer

The ancient liturgy and daily prayer of the church, evidence of a tradition of faith from as early as the fifth century, and celebrated in the Eastern Catholic Church and Eastern Orthodox churches, declares the mystical aspect of Mary's life, especially on the Feast of the Annunciation:

> Gabriel called out from heaven to her who is holy and pure: "Hail! For in your womb you shall conceive the pre-eternal God, who by His word has set together the ends of the earth!" Mary answered, "I know not man: how can I bear a Son? Who has ever seen a birth without seed?" Disclosing God's purpose, the angel said to the *Theotókos* and Virgin, "The Holy Spirit shall come upon you, and the Power of the Most High shall overshadow you!"[40]

The early liturgical and prayer texts reveal the establishment of faith about Mary, the mother of Christ, using a *lex orandi, lex credendi* principle ["the law of prayer, the law of belief," meaning that the way Christians pray reveals what Christians believe].[41]

A very early hymn asking the help of the Virgin Mary is called the *Sub Tuum Praesidium*. Scholars have determined that this hymn dates back to the third century, and perhaps even the second century. It has powerful wording that indicates the belief by Christians that Mary could take their needs to her son. "This is the first instance of a prayer to Our Lady, expressing belief in her intercessory power, applying to her the word *rysai* [Greek], (deliver) of the *Pater Noster* ['Our Father' in Latin], Matt 6:13. The text contains the word *Theotókos* in the vocative case."[42]

> We fly to thy patronage, O Holy Mother of God [*Theotókos*]
> despise not our petitions in our necessities,
> But deliver us always from all dangers.
> O glorious and blessed Virgin. Amen.[43]

---

40. *March Menaion*, Service Books of the Byzantine Churches (Newton, MA: Sophia, 1985), 73. A sessional hymn for Orthros [Matins], Tone 3.

41. Virginia M. Kimball, "*Liturgical Illuminations: Discovering Received Tradition in the Eastern Orthros of Feasts of the Theotókos*" (PhD dissertation, International Marian Research Institute, University of Dayton, 2010), 65–73.

42. Michael O'Carroll, *Theotokos: A Theological Encyclopedia of the Blessed Virgin Mary* (Collegeville, MN: Liturgical, 1990), 336.

43. Kimball, "*Liturgical*," 520.

No doubt this prayer, chanted in community, indicates that from the earliest of times the Christian faithful turned to Mary, mother and mystic, as their mother, in a sense clutching her hand as she led them to her son.[44]

Other magnificent liturgical hymns from the ancient church include the *Paraklesis*,[45] a series of chanted petitions to Mary;[46] the *Akathistos*, a hymn chanted standing up and commemorating the Annunciation as a way to enlist Mary's help—traditionally sung during Lent especially in Eastern Catholic and Eastern Orthodox churches;[47] and the beautiful hymns in Latin Gregorian chant including the *Ave Maria*, the *Magnificat*, *Stabat Mater*, *Regina Caeli*, and *Salve Regina*.[48] Eventually, in the late Middle Ages of Europe, as an accompaniment to the Psalms of daily prayer, the Rosary was developed.[49] Also, popular from the time of the Middle Ages was the *Angelus*, also a prayer commemorating the Annunciation of the angel to Mary.[50]

Marian Iconography

Spiritual depictions of Mary known as icons, which technically are not art but "writings" of God's revelation, also point to Mary as mother, mystic

---

44. It is important to note also that the term *Theotókos* appears in this ancient hymn.

45. See Virginia M. Kimball, "Language of Mediation in Eastern Liturgical Prayer," *Marian Studies* 52 (2001) 183–218.

46. This hymn, usually chanted throughout the Lenten weekdays before the Feast of the Dormition/Assumption in Eastern churches and Eastern Catholic churches, is thought to have originated between the eighth and tenth centuries; these chanted petitions are sometimes combined with Vespers.

47. Probably composed by Romanos the hymn composer in the fifth century and later adapted by other hymnists in the eigth century. Set as an acrostic with verses that reflect on the Annunciation and the Incarnation, especially Mary's role in God's plan, the well-known refrain is constantly given throughout this hour-long chanted prayer: "Rejoice, Bride Unwedded."

48. There are numerous versions, but as an example, for words and brief sheet music, see: http://interletras.com/canticum/eng/translation_virgin.html.

49. See O'Carroll, *Theotokos*, 313: "In the development of the Rosary there was a fusion of different elements. One was the desire to give the laity a form of common prayer which would be modeled on monastic prayer. As this was based on 150 psalms, the faithful were encouraged to recite 150 Paternosters [the Our Father prayer]; they were given beads to help them." In addition, the *Aves* [Hail Mary prayer] were added and still later mysteries as small chaplets of meditative prayer.

50. See ibid., 379: "This custom probably dates from the eleventh century. Pope Gregory IX (d. 1241) ordered the ringing of the bell to remind people to pray for the crusades. We find St. Bonaventure in 1269 asking that the faithful be urged to follow the Franciscan custom of saying three Hail Marys as the bell rang in the evening."

and prophet. In the catacombs, there is perhaps the first image we have of Mary from the Catacomb of Priscilla. This shows a mother cradling a baby in her arms, representing Mary's central prophetic role, bringing God to the world. Above her head is what scholars think is the prophet Balaam pointing to a star, a popular symbol in catacomb art to represent the messiah. The early Christian patristic writers interpreted the following biblical passage to mean a prophecy of Christ because Christ was understood to be the "light" of God and the "staff" of Israel. Balaam spoke: "I see him, though not now; I behold him, though not near: A star shall advance from Jacob, and a staff shall rise from Israel."[51] The other common image of Mary in the catacombs is that of *orans,* meaning the praying figure which shows Mary standing in prayer (the manner in which early Christians prayed) and lifting her arms to God.

Once icons began to be "written," tradition having it that Luke the evangelist authored the first image of Mary, there developed three major themes for these icons that were repeated and repeated over the ages: the *Eleousa,* mother of the tender touching; *Hodegetria,* mother showing the way; and *Deesis,* the praying and petitioning mother of Christ. The *Eleousa* depicts the *Theotókos* tenderly touching her child, sometimes coming cheek to cheek with him. This type of icon represents the humanity of Jesus as he comes into human contact with his mother. The *Hodegetria* icon, mentioned previously, depicts the *Theotókos* pointing to her son, indicating that He is the way (the Greek word for "the way" is incorporated in the name of this icon.) This type of icon shows the divinity of Christ as his mother leads us to Him. Both of these types are seen in the Virgin of Vladimir.[52] The third type of icon, also repeated for centuries is the *Deesis,* with the *Theotókos* bending her head toward her Child and extending her arms in prayer. This is the only icon from early Christianity which shows Mary without Jesus. It is, however, usually stationed on the icon screen where she is bending toward the Eucharistic table on the altar, or in an icon where she is standing at the foot of the cross. In this type, she is praying to her son.[53] The themes of these three themes (typologies) give us the earliest of

---

51. Num 24:17 NAB. A color image of this fresco painting from the catacomb of Priscilla in Rome can be seen in a color plate in the *Catechism of the Catholic Church.*

52. To see the Virgin of Vladimir image along with a brief description, see: http://tars.rollins.edu/Foreign_Lang/Russian/byzant.html.

53. Ivory was often the material used for icons in early Christianity. One such example is seen in the collection of the Metropolitan Museum of Fine Arts in New York City, depicting the Deesis. Many times the formula for a deesis theme showing the foot

understanding about Mary. She was the loving, physical mother of Jesus; the prophet who leads the faithful to her son who is God; and she is herself a praying disciple of her son.

Old Testament Typologies of Mary

The early church looked to the Old Testament, as well, to find mystical symbols of Mary, known as typologies. The use of these typologies—actually poetic metaphors and similes—are used frequently in patristic writing, the early writers and theologians of Christianity.

Mary as the cloud covering the ark as it was carried through the desert

Exodus 13:21–22

Mary described as Mt. Sinai because she is the physical place where God descends

Exodus 19:16–19

Mary as the burning bush where Moses encountered God on Mt. Sinai

Exodus 3:1–8

Mary the new Eve—Genesis 3:6 [disobeyed God] / Luke 1:38 [said "yes" to God]

Mary the woman of Zion   Zephaniah 3:14–17

Other Old Testament passages often are used in reference to Mary, such as:

Genesis 3:15	Mary will be the woman to crush the head of Satan
Genesis 28:10–17	Jacob's ladder, Mary is the one who connects humanity with God
Isaiah 7:14	Young woman who is a virgin who will bear a son

With careful reflection and meditation, these Old Testament typologies reveal mystical dimensions of Mary evident throughout God's revelation in the Bible. The Bible's texts, inspired by God, prophesied that Mary was to be a real woman, a human mother giving her son, the Son of God,

---

of the cross includes John the Baptist. See the Met online: http://www.metmuseum.org/toah/works-of-art/17.190.133.

his human life. It is clear through the Old Testament typologies that Mary cooperated fully with God's plan—as mystic; as prophet leading all the faithful to God; and primarily as mother who lovingly gave birth to and nurtured her son.

Revelation in the New Testament

In the book of Revelation, we find a mystical account: "A great sign appeared in the sky, a woman clothed with the sun, with the moon under her feet, and on her head a crown of twelve stars. She was with child and wailed aloud in pain as she labored to give birth" (Rev 12:1–2 NAB). She is called the Woman of Zion. Scripture scholars interpret this woman as representing all the faithful of God. Also, the passage can be interpreted to mean Mary with her son, a profound expression of her as mother and prophet. In this final book of the New Testament, we are met with a deeply mystical image of Mary, who bore Christ into the world. She is Christ's mother. She is mother of the faithful, Christ's Mystical Body. She represents the faithful who will fill the final city of God, Zion, living with the God who is Life forever in joy.

Conclusion

What is the wisdom that we glean from the life of Mary? She is the young woman who had many things to "ponder" in her heart. As a mystic called to God, she agreed to dedicate her whole being (heart, soul and body) to God's plan. In her discipleship she is prepared and illumined with the Son's presence. At the end of her life, she is transferred to heaven to be one with her son, a unity that all Christians are called to experience. As prophet, her life speaks the joyful life of living with Christ. Her way was quiet, but always seeking to say "yes" to God. We can see that she opened her heart to God's way, even when she was frightened. She is the mother who was meant to nurture the body of her son in the world as a mother. She is Daughter of Zion, a mystical prophet who can hardly be described while at the same time she is a very earthly mother.

Mary, as mother, mystic and prophet, demonstrates for Christians all the fruits given by God which provide true joy! The angel recognized Mary's joy in the greeting, "Rejoice [hail], Mary full of God's joy [grace]." The original Greek words of the New Testament give us this understanding of "joy" in the Lukan passage with "rejoice" as *chaire* and the word "joy" or "grace" as *charis*—two words derived from the root meaning "love" or "joy." We can see the application of St. Seraphim of Sarov's words: "When the Spirit of God descends on a man, and envelops him in the fullness of his presence, the soul overflows with unspeakable joy, for the Holy Spirit fills everything he touches with joy."[54] Mary experienced this joy from the Holy Spirit to the fullest, prompting Christians in prayer to recognize her as "blessed," which means in the original biblical language "filled with happiness."

When we think of the true goal of love that God has for humanity, having made man and woman in the image and likeness of God, we see that it is *theosis*, a deification—being made holy in absolute union with God, that is the hope of Christians. "He who is joined to the Lord is one spirit with Him" (1 Cor 6:17 NAB). Mary, Christ's mother, demonstrates for all of us the inherent beauty in God's plan, intended for all and shining brightly in her life, for the "power of the Most High has overshadowed her." For Irenaeus (ca. 115 CE):

> There is a constant reference to the phrase that humanity was created "according to the image and likeness of God" ([*ikon*] and [*omoiosis*]) a description he finds in Genesis 1:26. For Irenaeus, the terms are often synonymous but then delineated, in the sense that with the Fall, humanity maintains the "image" but loses the "likeness." When Irenaeus decribes salvation, he paints a picture that could easily form a paradigm for the relationship between the Virgin Mary and God at the Annunciation.[55]

Irenaeus conceived that Christ, "being assimilated to humankind and assimilating humankind to himself," came "in order that humankind might become more dear to the Father, due to their likeness with the Son."[56] Mary as a true disciple demonstrated her likeness with her son. She was not alone. All Christians are called to grow to *theosis*, to fulfill their lives as Mary was called to fulfill hers, seeking the will of God in order to find true happiness and joy in God's covenant . . . forever!

54. Harry M. Boosalis, *Joy of the Holy* (South Canaan, PA: St. Tikhon's Seminary Press, 1993), 82. St. Seraphim of Sarov, a Russian Orthodox monk and mystic, lived from the mid-eighteenth to the mid-nineteenth century.

55. Virginia M. Kimball, "Immaculate Conception in the Ecumenical Dialogue with Orthodoxy," in *Mary for Time and Eternity*, ed. William McLoughlin and Jill Pinnock (Herefordshire, UK: Gracewing, 2007), 200.

56. St. Irenaeus, *Adversus Haereses* [Against Heresies], 5.16.1.

As Christians grow closer to the mother of Christ, it will always be obvious that the mystery of God is at work. Mary was as human as we are and her mystical experience of God can be ours. In an ancient prayer composed by St. Symeon Metaphrastes, to be prayed after one receives the Eucharist, we find the elements of Mary's life which are offered by God to all Christians.[57] In receiving the Most Precious Body and Blood of Jesus at Holy Communion, we hold within ourselves what Mary held in her body and pray:

> Freely, Thou God hast given me Thy Body for my food, O Thou Who art a fire consuming the unworthy. Consume me not, O my Creator, but instead enter into my members, my veins, my heart. Consume the thorns of my transgressions. Cleanse my soul and sanctify my reasonings. Make firm my knees and body. Illumine my five senses.... Always protect, guard, and keep me from soul-destroying words and deeds. Cleanse me, purify me, and adorn me. Give me understanding and illumination. Show me to be a temple of Thy One Spirit.... For Thou art the only Sanctification and Light of our souls, O Good One, and to Thee, our Master and God, we ascribe glory day by day.[58]

From the ancient *Paraklesis* prayer service are chanted these mystical verses, demonstrating the wondrous paradox of Mary's mystical and prophetic life as a mother:

You are a tower adorned with gold,	[Mystic united with God]
A city surrounded by twelve walls,	[Daughter of Zion]
A shining throne touched by the sun,	[Mother who bore the Uncontainable God]
A royal seat for the King,	[A remarkable prophet]
O unexplainable wonder,	[Incomprehensible is the Incarnation]
How do you nurse the Master?[59]	[Earthly mother who nursed her babe]

---

57. St. Symeon Metaphrastes lived in the latter half of the tenth century, being known for his compilation of the *Menaion*, the festal prayers and traditions of the daily feasts of the entire liturgical year.

58. "A Prayer by Saint Simeon Metaphrastes," Orthodox Daily Prayers, Christian Classics Ethereal Library, online: http://www.ccel.org/ccel/anonymous/orthodoxpray.c9.html.

59. Concluding verses, Tone 3, *Service of the Small Paraklesis to the Most Holy Theotokos* (Brookline, MA: Holy Cross Orthodox Press, 1984), 38.

2

Mary and the Truth about Life[1]

JOSÉ GRANADOS

The Child, "whom Mary brought forth 'in the fullness of time' (Gal 4:4) . . . is also a figure of every person, every child . . . because—as the Council reminds us—'by his Incarnation the Son of God has united himself in some fashion with every person.'"[2]

The current violations of the dignity of human life represented, for example, by abortion or euthanasia are not only isolated cases of lack of respect for the human person. What is at work is a whole logic of understanding human life that ends up destroying life itself, and has been called by John Paul II a "culture of death." Overall there is a misleading view of life as absolute autonomy that forgets its relational character (with the world, with others, and with God), thus losing the broader context of life's origin and destiny, without which life itself is meaningless. This chapter addresses how the figure of Mary is able to shed light and offer guidance in this situation, by redefining life in the light of relationship (with nature, our neighbors, and God) as originally received from another and called to be given to others in a fruitful way.

---

1. A previous version of this article was published in: "Mary and the Truth About Life," *Anthropotes* 23 (2007) 101–30.

2. EV §104. The conciliar text referenced is GS §22.

Our departure point will be theological, based on the Christian definition of life and its potential to illumine human experience. In fact, both at the beginning and end of his encyclical *Evangelium Vitae* (EV §2; EV §104), John Paul II quotes a text from the Second Vatican Council's *Pastoral Constitution on the Church in the Modern World, Gaudium et Spes*: "By his Incarnation the Son of God has united himself in some fashion with every person" (GS §22). It is as if the late Pope wished for his encyclical on human life to be understood against this background; as if only the mysterious bond between Christ and all of humanity could allow us to grasp the fullness of the dignity belonging to each single human life.[3]

When he comments on the quote from *Gaudium et Spes* 22 in *Evangelium Vitae*, John Paul II underscores the role of the Virgin Mary.[4] Because of her closeness to the incarnation, she helps us to understand how the union between Christ and every human being is accomplished. By approaching the figure of Mary, then, new light can be shed over the meaning of life in order to understand its dignity. After a brief analysis of the culture of death and of the Christian proposal of a culture of life, we will develop in depth the role played by Mary for the understanding of human life.

The Ambiguity of the Culture of Death

One of the traits of the "culture of death," according to *Evangelium Vitae*, is that its threat against life is not overt but hidden, that it is not always an outspoken manifestation against life.[5] To the contrary, this approach attempts to define itself in terms of its appreciation of life, even up to the point of developing a sort of religion of life. This sentence in Tolstoy's *War and Peace*, "Life is God . . . to love Life is to love God," is quoted with appreciation, together with other expressions such as "celebrate life," "the importance of life," and even "life is sacred."[6] It has been said that "the culture of death

---

3. We find the same idea in EV §81: "This involves above all proclaiming the core of this Gospel. . . . It is the proclamation that Jesus has a unique relationship with every person, which enables us to see in every human face the face of Christ."

4. See in this regard Angelo Amato, "Maria, madre della vita," in *Evangelium Vitae: Commento all'Enciclica sulla Bioetica*, ed. Giovanni Russo (Torino: Editrice elledici, 1995), 283–91.

5. EV §8: "Cain tries to cover up his crime with a lie. This was and still is the case, when all kinds of ideologies try to justify and disguise the most atrocious crimes against human beings"; See also EV §11.

6. An example of this ambiguity is the voice of Don Cupitt in *Life, Life* (Santa Rosa, CA: Polebridge, 2003), 128: "Traditional religious believers are lovers of death. For them

understands itself not as a culture of death but as a culture of life: life in the sense of delight in the senses, delight in beauty, delight in companionship, delight in activities, knowledge, work, sport, eating and drinking, and conversation."[7] To this description we need to add something essential to our culture's definition of life: these goods are to be possessed and enjoyed in an autonomous fashion; life consists mainly in freedom, understood as the absence of restraints to one's action. In this context, biological life is considered merely the support that makes this enjoyment possible. This is why it can be suppressed when we are no longer able to have an autonomous possession of these goods, as in euthanasia; this is why it is deemed unworthy for a newborn to come into this world with a disability.

To understand the paradox of the current cultural situation it is helpful to consider a judgment C. S. Lewis makes regarding love. Lewis accepts that, according to St. John, God is love; but then he adds: "Love begins to be a demon the moment he begins to be a god."[8] Similarly, we could say that, according to the Christian gospel, God is life; but, if life becomes our god, it ends up being a demon. All the values affirmed by our culture regarding life are also affirmed by the Church; but in the Christian vision they are put within a broader context, in which life has a beginning and a final goal. Life comes from another and is called to be given to another, and only in this movement finds its ultimate meaning and sense. As we will show, an affirmation of life that loses all reference to an original source from which life itself springs and a transcendent source towards which life moves, ends up being a destruction of life, and the foundation of the culture of death.

---

the core self is the subjectively conscious self, the immortal soul, which is distinct from the body and is oriented towards the hope of final salvation in the world to come after death.... Modern Westerners, by contrast, are lovers of life and of the pleasures of the world."

7. See Arthur Madigan, "Comprehensive Ethic of Life: Some Observations on Evangelium Vitae," in *Prophecy and Diplomacy: The Moral Doctrine of John Paul II; A Jesuit Symposium*, ed. John J. Conley and Joseph Koterski (New York: Fordham University Press, 1999), 311.

8. See C. S. Lewis, *Four Loves* (New York: Harcourt Brace Javanovich, 1960), 6–7: "St. John's saying that God is love has long been balanced in my mind against the remark of a modern author (M. Denis de Rougemont) that 'love ceases to be a demon only when he ceases to be a god'; which of course can be re-stated in the form 'begins to be a demon the moment he begins to be a god.' This balance seems to me an indispensable safeguard. If we ignore it the truth that God is love may slyly come to mean for us the converse, that love is God." Ibid., 22: "This love, when it sets up as a religion, is beginning to be a god—therefore to be a demon. And demons never keep their promises. Nature 'dies' on those who try to live for a love of nature."

What we have said makes clear that the battle for a culture of life is also a battle of concepts and words, a battle in the world of thought and understanding of reality. At stake are the ideas of man, of the world, and of God (see EV §12), ideas that have practical consequences. The problem is not only that some moral laws have been broken, but a redefinition of the meaning of life. Therefore, it is not enough to defend life against these abuses. In the first place we have to clarify the truth about life. The first question that needs to be raised concerns the meaning and definition of human life.

What is the gospel's definition of life and how does it differ from the vision we have just described? In the following, we will try to find an answer to this question.

Christian Vision of Life

What is life? The Christian's answer to this question is rooted in the center of the Easter faith: the mystery of life's complete victory over death, because of the resurrection of Jesus. The gospel of life is built upon this overabundance of life experienced at Easter. Based on this event, St. John could speak of the "Word of Life" that has been revealed to us (1 John 1:1) and call Christ "the Living One" who has the keys of Death and Hades: "I was dead and look—I am alive for ever and ever" (Rev 1:17–18). It is in the presence of this new life received by Christ from the Father that the question regarding the Christian definition of life finds its adequate context.

The Easter event, however, was not an isolated fact. The first Christians understood its significance from the background of Old Testament anthropology. In Israel's scriptures, life is understood as relationship: relationship with the world, with the rest of the people, and with God. From this perspective, it is difficult to grasp the existence of life after death, since death seemed to be the end of all relationship: "For it is not the nether world that gives you thanks, nor death that praises you. Neither those who go down into the pit await your kindness. The living, the living gives you thanks, as I do today" (Isa 38:18–19).[9]

Israel's consciousness regarding the meaning of life matured as its history progressed. Because of God's decision to stay at the side of his people, Israel came to understand that its relationship with God was so powerful that not even death was able to destroy it. As an example we can think of

---

9. See Paul Beauchamp, *Psaumes nuit et jour* (Paris: Editions du Seuil, 1980).

the prophet Elijah, who at Mount Carmel (1 Kings 18–19), compares the activity of Yahweh, who is called in this context "God of Abraham, God of Isaac, God of Jacob," with the inactivity of the false gods: "Call louder for he is a god and may be meditating, or may have retired, or may be on a journey. Perhaps he is asleep and must be awakened." In contrast, Yahweh is the living God who is so involved in human history as to associate his name to the name of concrete persons: the God of Abraham, Isaac, and Jacob. Because of this association, as Jesus will remind the Pharisees, these people are alive and not dead (Matt 22:31–32).

In this latter text, Jesus gives the definitive interpretation of the Old Testament regarding the essence of life: to live is to be in relationship with God. When the human being separates from this source, his creator and sustainer, he dies. Easter is the final confirmation of this truth. At this moment, the filial relationship of Jesus with the Father is revealed as the true spring of life. The partial understanding that was present in the Old Testament disappears in this perfect equation of life and relationship to God.

The entire life of Jesus is a witness to this truth. He is the one who came to do the Father's will, whose being consists in accomplishing this will. This total commitment to his mission led him to face death on a cross. Against this backdrop, Easter is the confirmation that the life Jesus led on earth was the true life; that the one who lives from the Father and towards the Father has such a fullness of existence that it cannot be conquered by the power of death. Jesus' life is indestructible because it has been offered up to the Father in obedience and love, and thus has been received back from him, from God, who is the inexhaustible fountain of life.

We can conclude, then, that in light of Easter, to live is to be in relationship with God, who is the fountain of life. That's why the New Testament connects the idea of life with that of "being born" from above (see John 3:3), and thus, with becoming God's child, with filiation (sonship). Christian life is life inasmuch as it is received and accepted in love, in the image of the Risen Christ.[10]

---

10. See on this regard, Joseph Ratzinger, *Eschatology, Death, and Eternal Life* (Washington, DC: Catholic University Press, 1988), 94: "How can we describe that moment in which we experience what life truly is? It is the moment of love, a moment which is simultaneously the moment of truth when life is discovered for what it is. The desire for immortality does not arise from the fundamentally unsatisfying enclosed existence of the isolated self, but from the experience of love, of communion, of the Thou. It issues from that call which the Thou makes upon the I, and which the I returns. The discovery of life entails going beyond the I, leaving it behind."

Let us add, as another feature of this life, its fruitfulness, the fact that it can be transmitted to others. The life of the Risen One is the foundation of Christian life. The believers in Christ, as St. John puts it, have life, the life that comes from him (John 20:31: "life in his name"). Because life appears as relational with regard to the Father, it can also be relational with regard to Christ's brothers and sisters, who receive from Jesus a new filiation, a new birth.

In order to understand the newness of this understanding of life, it is interesting to compare it with the Greek understanding. According to Aristotle, life is characterized by self movement.[11] Whereas dead bodies can be moved only from the outside, a living being finds the principle of movement in itself; it possesses life in itself. Along these lines, we can read the definition of eternity as the full "possession of life" given by Boethius and accepted afterwards by the Christian tradition.[12] This possession is absolute only in God and relative to every other instance of life, which cannot embrace life in its entirety because of being immersed in the course of time.

This definition as possession or self-movement had to be enriched in order to grasp the whole of life's mystery: it had to be completed along the lines of Jesus' filiation, with the idea of receptivity. Immortality doesn't consist only in possession, but first of all in receiving life from God as a gift. For Irenaeus of Lyons, the first to use the expression "Gospel of life,"[13] life is a possession that depends on a continuous relationship; it is received by the contemplation of God, and we attain it inasmuch as we stay in his presence.[14] "The friendship of God imparts immortality to those who embrace it," says the bishop of Lyons.[15] The mystery of life, according to the

---

11. Aristotle, *De Anima* II, 2.

12. Boethius, *De consolatione philosophiae* V, VI, as referenced in PL 63:858A.

13. The expression "*Evangelium vitae*" appears in Irenaeus of Lyons in a text where he is discussing the figure of Christ as new Adam and Mary as new Eve. See Irenaeus, *Adv. Haer.*, 3.22.4.

14. See on this regard, Justin Martyr's critique of the definition of life given by Plato. The soul is not immortal by nature, but because of participation in God's life. Life is understood as dependence on God (*Dialogue with Trypho*, 5: "Now, that the soul lives, no one would deny. But if it lives, it lives not as being life, but as the partaker of life; but that which partakes of anything, is different from that of which it does partake. Now the soul partakes of life, since God wills it to live"). It is the same sense that we find in the famous sentence of Irenaeus of Lyons: *vita hominis visio Dei* (*Adv. Haer.* 4.20.7). On this issue, see Ysabel de Andia, *Homo vivens: Incorruptibilité et divinisation de l'homme selon Irénée de Lyon* (Paris: Études Augustiniennes, 1986).

15. Irenaeus, *Adv. Haer.* 4.13.4.

words of John Paul II in *Evangelium Vitae* §81, belongs to the mystery of relationship.

Mary and Life

The life received by Jesus at Easter was the key for the Christian interpretation of life. The perception of this new life, however, was not obvious. It was easy to misunderstand its meaning and importance, and it was precisely in order to preserve the truth about this life that the presence of Mary was required. As we will see in the following, the figure of Mary helped preserve the full truth about the Life announced at Easter.

How was the primitive Church experience that the newness of this life announced at Easter, so recently received from the Lord, threatened? Some interpreted the life of the risen Jesus, communicated to the Christians, as the life of a ghost, a spiritual life not linked with everyday history (see Luke 24:39). According to the gnostic heretics, this life (understood as merely spiritual) was a divine sparkling that dwelled in the human being awaiting its liberation from the oppression of its existence in the body. Real life was the life of the divine spirit that did not enter into this world and its mutable events. This was not only a theoretical attitude; the practical consequences were manifest when facing death at the moment of martyrdom. If this hour arrived, the gnostic didn't feel obliged to pronounce his confession for Christ, for this was only an external, unnecessary sign. For him, it was enough to live the new life received internally, which a merely external betrayal was not able to affect.[16]

Others, on the opposite end of the spectrum, interpreted the resurrection as the coming back to earthly life. For the Ebionites the new life was immortal, but consisted of the continuation of life on earth. According to St. Irenaeus of Lyons, they rejected the commixture of the heavenly wine and wished it to be water of the world only.[17]

The primitive Church found that the most natural way to preserve the true meaning of Christian life was the figure of Mary, the Mother of Jesus. This fact already reveals to us the importance of Mary regarding the culture

---

16. On the issue, see H. Campenhausen, *Die Idee des Martyriums in der alten Kirche* (Göttingen: Vandenhoeck & Rurecht,1936); Antonio Orbe, *Los primeros herejes ante la persecución*, Estudios Valentinianos 5 (Roma: Apud aedes Universitatis Gregorianae, 1956).

17. Irenaeus, *Adv. Haer.* 5.1.3.

of life. In the Christian tradition, she appears in a moment in which the true meaning of life is obscured.[18] The Virgin, who was invoked in the old breviary as defeater of all heresies, was the defeater of all threats against the truth of the gospel of life, crystallized in her Risen Son. In the following we will describe the ways in which Mary stands at the service of life's truth.

Mary Defends the True Meaning of the New Life of Her Son

At Easter it became evident for the disciples that Jesus had a new life that came from the Father. This coming of Jesus from the Father was an event of such absolute significance that it explained not only the new state of Christ, but also the meaning of all reality since the foundation of the world: Jesus was confessed as the eternal Son in which the world was created.

What was the role of Mary in this regard? First, because she was the true mother of Jesus, she made it clear that the indestructible life Jesus now possessed (Heb 7:16) was not a kind of ghostly existence alien to this world, but remained rooted in his earthly history, which started at Bethlehem. Second, because of the mystery of Christ's virginal conception and birth, Mary made clear that Jesus' life had its roots in the eternal Father, from whom Christ came, and was not to be explained only according to earthly coordinates. In short, Mary's virginal motherhood testifies to and defends the true meaning of Easter.[19]

On the one hand, the *true motherhood* of Mary made clear that Jesus was not a ghost. His birth was in continuity with the previous generations of mankind, and in this way inserted in time, in the common history shared by all human beings. Only in this way, by sharing in our history of memories and expectations, could his life be true life, significant for the lives we, too, live.

---

18. The fact that the role of Mary is that of providing the balance and the true understanding of faith is pointed out by Joseph Ratzinger, *Ratzinger Report* (San Francisco: Ignatius, 1985), 106: "It is necessary to go back to Mary if we want to return to that 'truth about Jesus Christ,' 'truth about the Church' and the 'truth about man' that John Paul II proposed as a program to the whole of Christianity when, in 1979, he opened the Latin American episcopal conference in Puebla. The bishops responded to the Pope's proposal by including in the first documents . . . their unanimous wish and concern: Mary must be more than ever the pedagogy, in order to proclaim the Gospel to the men of today."

19. This parallelism is attested to by the infancy narratives, with the constant allusions to Easter, a fact which is especially evident in Luke. Moreover, the first developments of Patristic theology go in the same direction.

On the other hand, the *virginity* of Mary pointed to the newness of the life born in Bethlehem, in accordance with the fullness of life that will appear at Easter. The virgin birth shows, through the action of the Holy Spirit upon Mary, that Jesus' life comes from the Father, and that his life has its origin from above. By so doing, it protects the idea of life as a mystery. That life is a mystery does not mean, of course, that it is a dark force belonging to the realm of the irrational. Instead, the vision of life as a mystery highlights the fact that life is not reducible to technical measurements, and that science cannot exhaust the meaning of life. To say that life is a mystery is to state that life transcends life itself, that it points to something greater, to an origin and a goal beyond itself.

In sum, the presence of Mary witnesses to the defense of the truth about Christ's life, to the fullness of the Easter experience. From this point of view, the comparison between the resurrection of Christ from *Sheol* and his birth from Mary that we find in the writings of several church fathers, is theologically well grounded.[20] In this regard, let us quote, for example, a text by Ephrem the Syrian:

> The womb and *Sheol* shouted with joy and cried out / about your resurrection. The womb that was sealed, / conceived You; *Sheol* that was secured, / brought You forth. Against nature / the womb conceived and *Sheol* yielded. / Sealed was the grave which they entrusted / with keeping the dead man. Virginal was the womb / that no man knew. The virginal womb / and the sealed grave like trumpets / for a deaf people, shouted in its ear. / The sealed womb, the secured stone / among the slanderers the conception is slandered, / that it was human seed, and the resurrection, / That it was human robbery. Seal and signet / refute and convince that He was a heavenly one.[21]

Once again, this vision of life appears as the fulfillment of different threads scattered in the Old Testament tradition. First, we find the idea of women as mothers of the living (see Gen 3:20). In Scripture, women are the place where God reveals himself, in the midst of the material world, as the Lord of Life, as the one who gives life; they are the places where he accomplishes his promises. Since the joyful cry of Eve: "I have conceived a child with the help of the Lord" (Gen 4:1), motherhood points to life's

---

20. See José A. Aldama, *Virgo Mater: Estudios de Teología Patrística* (Granada: Facultad de Teología, 1963), 249–85.

21. Ephrem the Syrian, *Hymns on the Nativity*, 10, 7–9, trans. Kathleen E. McVey (New York: Paulist, 1989), 129–30.

coming from the Father through the chain of generations. Jesus' bodily Resurrection was the fulfilled confirmation of this claim. At Easter, life appeared fully in the world as a gift received, as the Father's action, and as a new birth.

In this way, the resurrection means the final completion of a second thread that is present throughout the scriptures of Israel and deals with the problem of immortality, as we have noticed above. This line from Genesis explains life as relationship with God. Immortality is possible because God is the God of life and wants to be as well "God with us," the God of Abraham, Isaac and Jacob. Because God wanted his life and ours to be in relationship, our life can partake in his immortality.

Now, the relationship between Mary and the resurrection confirms the unity of these two Old Testament threads, relationship with God as foundation of true life, and motherhood as the place where God reveals himself in the midst of history as origin of life. This has a very concrete consequence: the consideration of life as relationship cannot be made merely on a spiritual level that affects only the elevated summits of the soul. The very birth of Jesus from Mary, the biological fact of this birth, is also included as well in this definition. This means that God's covenant with life stands not only as the guarantee of life after death, but is present also at the very origin of life. Relationship with God gives life, not only the life of ghosts or spirits, the life of shadows, but the concrete life of history, the life that is formed in the womb of each mother.[22] That is why we can say, with Joseph Ratzinger, that Mary is the woman "in which 'biology' is 'theology'—that is, motherhood of God."[23]

The embodiment of life is said to be, in *Evangelium Vitae* §81, an essential trait of the culture of life. This fact is not without importance and can serve as a crucial clue to characterize the culture of life in contrast to

---

22. Let us recall, in this regard, the idea of the church fathers that the womb of Mary is the place in which we have been regenerated to a new life: see Irenaeus, *Adv. Haer.* 4.33.11: "*Vulvam eam quae regenerat homines in Deum*" ("That pure womb which regenerates men unto God"), with the exegesis of J. A. Aldama, *María en la patrística de los siglos II y III* (Madrid: Editorial Católica, 1970), 305–9.

23. Joseph Ratzinger, "Thoughts on the Place of Marian Doctrine and Piety in Faith and Theology as a Whole," *Communio* [USA] 30 (2003) 147–60: "And the Woman in whom 'biology' is 'theology'— that is, motherhood of God—is in a special way the point where paths diverge." And also: "Mary's virginity, no less than her maternity, confirms that the 'biological' is human, that the whole man stands before God, and that the fact of being human only as male and female is included in faith's eschatological demand and its eschatological hope" (158).

the culture of death. If we go to the roots of the culture of death, we will find a separation between biological life, on one side, and the life of freedom, knowledge and social relationships, on the other, the former being only a basis on which the latter can be built up. Rights are denied to the unborn because his or her life is reduced to the biological. A right to die is claimed when the life of the sick is understood as merely biological. The conception of biological life is that of a relative value, even an instrument that can be used for higher goals, without an intrinsic relationship with real life.[24]

This interpretation is possible because biological life is explained in the light of a mechanical movement of organized particles, and thus reduced to a particular case of physics. Following the analysis of philosopher, Hans Jonas, we could say that the culture of death is the opposite of the animist conception, for which life was the main explanation of reality and death was the exception, the problem to be solved. In our modern conception, death (dead matter) is the principle of the scientific explanation of the whole universe, and life is the exception, the enigmatic problem to be resolved (in other words, scientists know well how the material universe goes, but are puzzled by the question of how life is possible). From this viewpoint we understand that the culture of death is a worldview unable to integrate biological life with the life of consciousness and freedom, proper to the human being.

In fact, this culture is built, in the last analysis, on the divide between these two realms, the material (objectively studied by natural science) and the spiritual (the subjective realm of consciousness and freedom).[25] Conceptually, life is explained as a quantified process that can be measured and predicted; existentially, life is lived as not having much to do with nature

---

24. See the comments by A. R. Madigan in "Comprehensive Ethic of Life," in *Prophecy and Diplomacy: The Moral Doctrine of John Paul II* (New York: Fordham University Press, 1999), 307: "The culture of death distinguishes sharply between merely biological life and any other sense of the term 'life.' Merely biological life has no value in itself. It has instrumental value inasmuch as it is the necessary condition for goods (2) through (6) [knowledge, play, aesthetic experience, sociability or friendship, practical reasonableness]."

25. Hans Jonas, *Phenomenon of Life: Toward a Philosophical Biology* (Evanston, IL: Northwestern University Press, 2001), 7–9: "When man first began to interpret the nature of things . . . life was to him everywhere, and being the same as being alive. . . . In such a world-view, the riddle confronting man is death: it is the contradiction to the one intelligible, self-explaining, 'natural' condition which is the general life. . . . Modern thought which began with the Renaissance is placed in exactly the opposite theoretical situation. Death is the natural thing, life the problem."

and creation. Conceptually, freedom is out of place because it doesn't fit in the categories of our world; existentially, freedom is absolute, not determined by the biological sciences, depending only on the desire of the individual. This opposition contains a paradox, which explains why we can, at the same time, exalt freedom as a style of life and deny it from the viewpoint of our evolutionary science.

For its part, the development of a culture of life needs to reflect on biological life, on the meaning of biology. What we know about biology needs to be considered part of our knowledge about the human being, including our description of consciousness and freedom, because our incarnate condition is a decisive part of being human. Biological life testifies precisely to the gift—character of life, to the fact that it has first to be received, and that it is rooted always in primordial receptivity.

Mary, in the connection between her virginity and her motherhood, shows that life starts with a concrete action of God in history that touches not only the soul, but also the body.[26] The following text of the Fathers is a witness of how the new Christian conception of life was made extensive to all of creation. The reason for this extension is found in the incarnation, through which the whole of the world was transformed and united to the Word of God. The fact that the text comes from a sermon on a Marian feast makes evident the connection about which we have just spoken:

> She gave birth into the world the treasury of all the good things. ... Yes, for the Creator transformed into something better all of the creation through him, being the human nature the mediation. Since man is the medium between matter and mind, and the link between what is visible and what is invisible, when the Word of God, Creator of all things, was united to the human nature, he was united to every creature through it. That is why we must celebrate today the end of human sterility, because the hindrance that prevented all good things to happen has been cancelled.[27]

Openness of Life and the Possibility of a Culture of Life[28]

The text just quoted reminds us of the sentence in *Gaudium et Spes* that appears at the beginning and end of *Evangelium Vitae*. After stating the

---

26. See Ps 139:13: "For you formed my inmost being" (as quoted in EV §44).
27. John Damascene, *Homily on the Nativity of Mary*, in PG 96:662, 842.
28. See GS §22.

possibility for every human being to acknowledge the sacred value of human life, John Paul II says that this holds true especially for the believers in Christ since "by the Incarnation the Son of God has united himself in some fashion with every human person" (GS §22; EV §2; EV §104). At the end of the encyclical, forming an overarching inclusion, the sentence appears again, and its meaning is now further developed:

> Mary thus helps the Church to realize that life is always at the centre of a great struggle between good and evil, between light and darkness. The dragon wishes to devour "the child brought forth" (see Rev 12:4), a figure of Christ, whom Mary brought forth "in the fullness of time" (Gal 4:4) and whom the Church must unceasingly offer to people in every age. But in a way that child is also a figure of every person, every child, especially every helpless baby whose life is threatened, because—as the Council reminds us—"by his Incarnation the Son of God has united himself in some fashion with every person." It is precisely in the "flesh" of every person that Christ continues to reveal himself and to enter into fellowship with us, so that rejection of human life, in whatever form that rejection takes, is really a rejection of Christ. This is the fascinating but also demanding truth which Christ reveals to us and which his Church continues untiringly to proclaim: "Whoever receives one such child in my name receives me" (Mt 18:5); "Truly, I say to you, as you did it to one of the least of these my brethren, you did it to me" (Mt 25:40).[29]

The quote of the Council appears as the definitive light that the Christian receives regarding the truth of life. We know that there is a union of Christ with every believer, a union that comes about through faith, but the statement of *Gaudium et Spes* §22 goes further. It says that this union takes place between Christ and every human being. The link is understood here in the light of the incarnation as an event that precedes the actual exercise of freedom and is linked to the "flesh of every person."

This union of Christ with every human being reveals an important truth about human life: life is opened to others; it is never isolated in itself. The critics of the "culture of life" fail to see precisely this point, when they write: "It [the culture of life] is an empty suit of a phrase, absent an individual to give it shape. There is no culture of life. There is the culture of your life and the culture of mine."[30] On the contrary, *Gaudium et Spes* §22

---

29. EV §104.
30. Anna Quindlen, "Culture of Each Life," *Newsweek*, April 4, 2005.

announces that the particular fact of Jesus' life was not confined to the life of an individual, but was able to embrace all of humanity as a life given up for the world. The incarnation of Christ reveals the inner truth of every birth that takes place on earth, and its solidarity towards all of history. Life, which is always concrete, can never be a merely private issue.

How is this connection between Christ and every human person possible? To give a complete answer we would need to consider the whole of Christ's life. The presence of the Spirit in Jesus' life and the Spirit's activity in the Resurrection would have to be considered. But an essential part of the answer already lies in the mystery at Nazareth, the incarnation of the Son of God, and is particularly connected to Mary.

It was common among ancient philosophers to explain the brotherhood among all human beings in the fact that all of them have a rational soul. The newness of Christianity, in continuity with the Old Testament, is that the reason for this brotherhood is put also in the flesh, in the common origin that links us to earth. The union that is based only on the rational soul, and the communion that is established in purely spiritual values, ends up becoming an abstract communion, far away from the personal history of every human being on earth. What Christianity announced is that this communion is possible at the concrete level of everyday life.

Because of her closeness to the incarnation, Mary witnesses to the significance of Jesus' birth for the rest of humankind. This fact is attested to in the Gospels (especially in Luke and John), where Mary is seen as a type of Israel and the Church, as Daughter Zion (see LG §55; see also Luke 1:26–56; John 19:25–27). Thus, she is the woman who is never alone because her history is the history of the people of God, which embraces all of humanity. The entire history of the Church is lived by Mary in her history; her time is open to all and embraces all. Notice that this is not at all an abstraction: in Mary everything is made concrete; this concreteness means there is no separation from others, but the offering to others of being included in her following of Jesus. Because of the openness of her life to every other life it is possible to speak of a culture of life, not as an abstract concept that oppresses the individual, but as the building together of a common existence.

This link between the incarnation and every human being allows for Mary to be called the mother of humanity, and not only the mother of all Christians.[31] What happened in the birth of Christ becomes significant to

---

31. See LG §54: "The Mother of God, who is mother of Christ and mother of men, particularly of the faithful"; the constitution had stated before, quoting St. Augustine:

every human birth in the world, and can illumine the dignity of every human life. Every life is thus open to others, responsible for them, and able to be shared with them. In Mary, the question of Cain, "Am I my brother's keeper?" (Gen 4:9), is answered with a resounding "Yes," because she is made more than the keeper, she is the mother of every human life on earth.

Life and Freedom: Mary's Maternity and Freedom as Fruitfulness

Mary's motherhood did not consist only of a physical fact, but was lived out with the full participation of her person. Augustine formulated this idea in a famous sentence: Mary conceived Christ first in her mind and then in her womb.[32] Thus, Mary's motherhood involves her whole person and can illumine this essential aspect for developing a culture of life: its connection with freedom.

We recall the answer she gave to Gabriel: "Be it done to me according to thy word." This "yes" of Mary is an expression of her freedom, of her human participation in the begetting of Jesus' life. It has been argued that Luke is interested here in showing only God's mysterious action in Jesus' birth, but a close analysis of the text of the Annunciation shows that it is patterned according to the vocation scenes of the Old Testament (as, for example, Gideon's vocation to become a judge of Israel in Judg 6:11–24). The Annunciation scene is not only an announcement of God's intervention in the birth of a child, but also the narrative of Mary's personal "yes."[33]

Why is it so important to highlight the close link between life and freedom we find in Mary? Today's culture tends to present an opposition between freedom and life, which becomes evident in the distinction "pro life" / "pro choice."[34] Certainly, a person who declares herself "pro choice"

"She is the mother of the members of Christ . . . having cooperated by charity that the faithful might be born in the Church, who are members of that Head"; see also LG 54: Mary "occupies a place in the Church which is the highest after Christ and yet very close to us."

32. St. Augustine, *Sermo* 215, 4; PL 38:1074.

33. See Klemens Stock, "Die Berufung Marias (Lk 1:26–38)," *Biblica* 61 (1980) 457–91.

34. EV §96: "The first and fundamental step towards this cultural transformation consists in forming consciences with regard to the incomparable and inviolable worth of every human life. It is of the greatest importance to re-establish the essential connection between life and freedom. These are inseparable goods: where one is violated, the other also ends up being violated. There is no true freedom where life is not welcomed and loved; and there is no fullness of life except in freedom. Both realities have something

will not admit that she denies the value of life, but the fact is that she considers life as something positive only inasmuch as it doesn't enter into conflict with personal freedom. Life, real life, equals freedom, understood mainly as limitless autonomy, as the freedom of choice, and as the self-determination of each subject. If life is no longer free in this sense, if it lacks initiative and depends too much on others and the environment, then it is not worth living. Again, biological life is here seen as a mere precondition or basis that allows the exercise of freedom understood as autonomy. When this basis becomes a hindrance to freedom (for example, in the case of a disabling disease) any attempt to overcome or suppress this limit seems worthy and proper to a human being.

Mary's motherhood, as an image of freedom, shows us another way of describing the connection between life and freedom. For freedom can be understood along the lines of creative fecundity using, for example, the analogy of art. How does an artist describe his freedom? It is not a question of the absence of limitations. In fact, these limitations are necessary for him to express beauty (think for example of the resistance of the sculptor's stone). An artist sees his freedom always in the context of something greater, of the beauty he tries to express, which he shares through inspiration. Limitations are intrinsic to this freedom: he is free inasmuch as he is able to use the material world in order to mould it according to this vision of beauty.[35]

This analogy allows us to describe freedom as a superabundance of life, in the context of a greater frame of reference. Mary listens to God's voice and obeys it. God's commandment is not an oppressive voice, but a voice that inspires and calls her to collaboration. The creativity of an artist always starts by listening to this voice. In this sense, to be free is primarily to be called by beauty, to receive one's inspiration from another. Freedom can be compared, as the first Christians did, with a condition of sonship, to a new birth.[36]

---

inherent and specific which links them inextricably: the vocation to love. Love, as a sincere gift of self, is what gives the life and freedom of the person their truest meaning."

35. See Tomás Spidlik, "Per una mariologia antropologica," *Marianum* 41 (1979) 491–506.

36. See Justin Martyr, 1 *Apologia* I, 61: "Since at our birth we were born without our own knowledge or choice, by our parents coming together, and were brought up in bad habits and wicked training; in order that we may not remain the children of necessity and of ignorance, but may become the children of choice and knowledge, and may obtain in the water the remission of sins formerly committed, there is pronounced over him who

Mary exemplifies the meaning of freedom as fruitfulness because the fruit of her womb is the fullness of life, the Life that is source of all life, the one that goes beyond any possible expectation. It was impossible for Mary alone to generate the child of God; her conception was only possible as a gift from God. In addition, Mary makes clear that the fruitfulness we are referring to here is the fruitfulness of love, the love of the Father who sends his Son, the love of Mary who accepts in obedience her vocation and mission. Only in this frame does freedom have a meaning. Only here can freedom be liberated from the search towards "efficiency" by the grace of love. In Mary it becomes clear that love provides the adequate understanding for the connection between freedom and life.

As an example, let us consider the scene of the flight to Egypt, which is shaped against the backdrop of freedom. The concept of freedom as power and dominion is represented by Herod who forces the weak into submission by making them run away to the land of slavery, Egypt. In this exile, however, a different kind of freedom appears, the freedom that God wants to give to his people as a gift, rescuing them from oppression. This new freedom is understood as service to God, as a new birth (see Matt 2:15, quoting Hos 11:1: "Out of Egypt I called my son"). It is a freedom that has to be learned in the limited conditions of the desert; a creative freedom that will lead the people to a fruitful land flowing with milk and honey. When Matthew provides this context to explain the life of Mary and Jesus, he is presenting the motherhood of Mary (named five times together with Jesus: "the child and his mother")[37] as part of this journey of freedom.

In the current battle between two different concepts of freedom and life, Mary's maternity helps us present freedom as the freedom of fruitfulness, and not as mere absence of limitations. For human life to be fruitful it needs to be in connection with something greater than the human being, it needs to be in connection with the presence of God. This presence does not diminish the value of the person, but makes it greater. Moreover, this freedom appears "precisely" in the limitations, in the dependence upon time and matter, and not "despite" this limitation and dependence.

---

chooses to be born again, and has repented of his sins, the name of God the Father and Lord of the universe; he who leads to the layer the person that is to be washed calling him by this name alone."

37. See Matt 2:11; 2:13; 2:14; 2:20; 2:21.

Conclusions

Following *Evangelium Vitae*, we have deepened the connection between Mary and life. The link was provided by a sentence from *Gaudium et Spes* §22 that serves as an inclusion for the whole encyclical. It states that through the incarnation, the Son of God has united himself with every human being. The way in which that happens was not developed by the Council. John Paul II points out the presence of Mary in this mystery and its connection with the flesh of Christ.

We have tried to understand this sentence by underscoring the connection between Mary and the mystery of Easter. The life that comes from Christ to every human being has been made manifest in the Risen One. The resurrection brings to fulfillment the understanding of human life as relationship; we live inasmuch as we love and remain in contact with God, the source of all life. Moreover, this life is not the private life of a single individual, but can be communicated to every human person. The openness of this life, the fact that it is fruitful, is no longer limited to the specific acts of procreation. Fecundity is a permanent dimension of life, because life continually transcends itself and grows beyond itself.

The life of the Risen One serves as a key to interpret human life from the beginning to the end. The role of Mary consists of providing a correct understanding of this life, of safeguarding its profound meaning, its truth. What results from that is a different account of human existence on earth. Life appears as a unity; since Mary is the true mother of this life, it is not only spiritual, but it encompasses nature and the biological, and is also connected with concrete history and the passing of generations; since Mary is a virgin, this life is understood in relationship with a greater mystery, the mystery of the Father, who is the origin and eternal destiny of the living.

Far from reducing the importance of freedom, our considerations lead us to a richer vision of it. Looking at Mary, the form of freedom acquires the form of maternity and, thus, of creativity. On one side, the virginity of Mary is the sign of the presence of God in human history. It witnesses to the transcendence to which life is called. In contrast to the "choice" that is opposed to life, real freedom becomes creative, able to give a fruit that transcends itself. Freedom fulfills itself in the moment in which it accepts the possibility of growing above itself, and renounces this isolation that resembles death.

On the other hand the limits, material and temporal, that human life has to face, the inseparable connection of freedom and the biological realm, are not seen as aggressions against freedom, but as the ground in which a creative answer can stand, as the canvas for the painter or the stone for the sculptor, as the previous gift that allows an answer of love. The true maternity of Mary attests to this connection.

The answer of the Church in the face of a culture of death is a witness to life. This effort is, first of all, a task for the Christian families. The representatives of the culture of death speak of the right that everyone has to bear his or her own burden and to decide if this burden is bearable or not. In contrast, Christian witness takes precisely the form of bearing the burdens of others, of being ready to bear these burdens no matter how heavy they are. This witness also testifies to the humility and courage of being borne as well by others in all these moments of our life in which we are not strong enough to stand on our own feet.

In this respect, the presence of Mary in the Church is crucial. The fact that the Virgin was included in *Lumen Gentium* meant not only a change for Ecclesiology, but also a transformation of ecclesiology. With Mary, the Church becomes a family and every family is opened to the presence of the Church.[38] Mary's answer and the Church's answer remain the answer of joy in the face of life, of all life, even in the midst of suffering and in the face of death. It is the greatness of this joy that is the best witness of Mary in the Church. As St. Ignatius of Antioch put it, in a well-known sentence: "Christianity, when it is hated by the world, is not a matter of persuasion, but a matter of greatness."[39] Like Mary, ours is the task of bearing witness to the greatness of true life.

---

38. EV §92: "It is above all in raising children that the family fulfills its mission to proclaim the Gospel of life. By word and example, in the daily round of relations and choices, and through concrete actions and signs, parents lead their children to authentic freedom, actualized in the sincere gift of self, and they cultivate in them respect for others, a sense of justice, cordial openness, dialogue, generous service, solidarity and all the other values which help people to live life as a gift. In raising children Christian parents must be concerned about their children's faith and help them to fulfill the vocation God has given them. The parents' mission as educators also includes teaching and giving their children an example of the true meaning of suffering and death. They will be able to do this if they are sensitive to all kinds of suffering around them and, even more, if they succeed in fostering attitudes of closeness, assistance and sharing towards sick or elderly members of the family."

39. See Ignatius of Antioch, *Romans* 3, 3, English translation in Bart D. Ehrman, *Apostolic Fathers*, vol. 1, Loeb Classical Library (Cambridge, MA: Harvard University Press, 2003).

3

What Can the Holy Family Teach Us about Marriage?

MARIANNE LORRAINE TROUVÉ

> From the outset [Mary] accepted and understood her own motherhood as a total gift of self, a gift of her person to the service of the saving plans of the Most High.[1]

What can the Holy Family teach us about marriage? It might seem odd at first to ask the question. Doesn't the Catholic Church teach that Mary was always a virgin? So what does her relationship with Joseph say to married couples today? This essay will explore that question, and in the process, will offer some ideas that can help married couples today not only stay together, but fall deeper in love. Because of its importance in both civil society and the Church, marriage has always occupied a crucial place in both arenas.

In his document *On the Role of the Christian Family in the Modern World*, Pope John Paul II looks at the situation of the family today. Among the positive factors he mentions are a greater development of interpersonal relationships, a renewed awareness of the dignity of women, and attention to the education of children.[2] Nevertheless, marriage as an institution has been faltering. High rates of divorce, cohabitation, children born outside

---

1. RM §39, online: http://www.vatican.va/holy_father/john_paul_ii/encyclicals/documents/hf_jp-ii_enc_25031987_redemptoris-mater_en.html.
2. FC §6.

of marriage, and teenage pregnancies in particular have become commonplace. While various studies have documented these trends,[3] probably most people have firsthand experience of this reality in their own circle of relatives and friends. For example, a few years ago I experienced this reality while visiting some relatives of a sister in my community, whom I'll call Carol. My friend Carol's cousin had a few children by different men, and one of these children was asking Carol why she and her sister had the same last name. The child and her half-siblings all had different last names, and this was so normal to her that she couldn't fathom why people would have the same last name. As Carol patiently explained that she and her sister had the same mother *and* father, I saw in that child's face a puzzled look as she tried to grasp this new reality. It made me wonder if our society had already passed a tipping point in regard to marriage and family life.

Christians, too, are affected by the trends in the wider society. For example, a recent study commissioned by *Our Sunday Visitor* indicates that marriage rates among Catholics have fallen dramatically:

> The number of marriages celebrated in the Church has fallen from 415,487 in 1972 to 168,400 in 2010 — a decrease of nearly 60 percent — while the U.S. Catholic population has increased by almost 17 million. To put this another way, this is a shift from 8.6 marriages per 1,000 U.S. Catholics in 1972 to 2.6 marriages per 1,000 Catholics in 2010.[4]

It is obvious that marriage is facing a real crisis in our society today. At the same time, many studies have shown the benefits of marriage, both for spouses and for their children. Married people tend to be happier, better off financially and socially, and enjoy greater physical health than the unmarried.[5]

The purpose of this essay, however, is not to do a sociological study of marriage but to consider the example of the Holy Family as a way to

---

3. See, e.g., W. Bradford Wilcox and Elizabeth Marquardt, eds., *When Marriage Disappears: The New Middle America* (Charlottesville, VA: University of Virginia, National Marriage Project, 2010).

4. Mark M. Gray, "Exclusive Analysis: National Catholic Marriage Rate Plummets," Our Sunday Visitor, June 26, 2011, n.p., online: http://www.osv.com/tabid/7621/itemid/8053/Exclusive-analysis-National-Catholic-marriage-rat.aspx.

5. For more on the benefits of marriage, see, e.g., Linda Waite and Maggie Gallagher, *Case for Marriage: Why Married People Are Happier, Healthier, and Better Off Financially* (New York: Doubleday, 2000); Steven Nock et al., *Why Marriage Matters: Twenty-One Conclusions from the Social Sciences* (New York: Institute for American Values, 2002).

strengthen marriage today. Marriage is a human and religious good, one that benefits the human persons who enter into it and live it. Further, it benefits society as a whole, because a stable family life provides a wholesome atmosphere in which to raise children. And this is where Church teaching on marriage comes in.

Marriage is unique among the sacraments in that it is based on a human good that can be shared by all people regardless of their religious beliefs. Yet as a sacrament, Christian marriage has a special dimension that ushers spouses into the mystery of the love Christ has for his Church. As the author of Ephesians states in referring to the marital union, "This is a great mystery, and I am applying it to Christ and the Church" (Eph 5:32). The sacramental dimension of marriage makes Christian marriage a *source of holiness* for the spouses. "Since it signifies and communicates grace, marriage between baptized persons is a true sacrament of the New Covenant."[6] A renewed appreciation of marriage as a sacrament can go a long way toward healing the wounds that afflict marriage today.

The Holy Family's Relevance to Married Relatedness

Catholic tradition has proposed the Holy Family as a model for marriage and family life. This aspect of Catholic life is found not only in many official statements, but in the liturgy. For example, the Church celebrates the feast of the Holy Family shortly after Christmas, emphasizing the virtues that Christian families should emulate.

An awareness of the Holy Family precisely as a family adds an important element to Marian devotion. Other forms of Marian devotion sometimes portray Mary as a solitary figure, or more often, with her son Jesus. But seeing Mary as part of the Holy Family involves another important figure: Joseph. Although he is mentioned only briefly in the Gospels and is not present at all in Jesus' public life, the figure of Joseph as part of the Holy Family is crucial because it helps us see Mary as a married woman. When we see Mary not only in relation to her son Jesus, but to her spouse, Joseph, we can more easily understand the Holy Family as a model of married relatedness. Although we don't know the details of Mary's day-to-day life, we do know that when the angel Gabriel informed her of her cousin Elizabeth's pregnancy, "Mary set out and went with haste to a Judean town in the hill country, where she entered the house of Zechariah and greeted

---

6. CCC §1617.

Elizabeth" (Luke 1:39–40). If she gave of herself with such a willing gift of service to her extended family, certainly she was no less generous and loving with Jesus and Joseph.

At this point, an objection might arise: Doesn't the Catholic Church teach that Mary was a virgin for her whole life? So how can we see her as a model of married relatedness? A later part of this essay will look at this in more detail, but for now a few points can be kept in mind.

First, when we look at the saints as models for our lives, including Mary and Joseph, we are not trying to imitate the particular circumstances in which they lived. It would be impossible to do that since they lived in a completely different era and culture than we do. Imitating the saints, being inspired by their examples, doesn't mean we have to do the same things that they did. Instead, it means that their lives hold a lesson for us, a spiritual lesson that can still inspire us today. That spiritual lesson doesn't concern so much *what* good things they did in their lives as *how* they did them, that is, their actions were inspired by great love of God and other people. Holiness is about virtue, and virtues can be lived in all sorts of ways. Married people are certainly not called to imitate Mary and Joseph in having a *virginal* marriage, but they are called to imitate them in having a *loving* marriage.

Second, the Church's teaching on Mary's perpetual virginity does *not* spring from some kind of negative attitude toward sex. Pope John Paul's lengthy catechesis on the theology of the body, in which he explored the meaning of marriage and sexuality, clearly affirms that the human body and its sexual values are gifts of God. We live in a society where sex is splashed around virtually everywhere, used to sell things from cars to medications. The Internet unfortunately has made pornography more easily available than ever. But all this only serves to cheapen sex, to use it merely as a means to maximize pleasure. The Church, instead, offers a vision of the human person that sees sexuality as a gift of God and in marriage, a means to holiness.

The Theology of the Body

In recent years, this teaching on the goodness of sexuality and marriage has been developed through what is popularly called the theology of the body (TOB). TOB offers us a way of better understanding the greatness of marriage. While there are different approaches to developing a theology of the body, the ideas I am drawing on here come from the catecheses of Pope

John Paul II. From 1979 to 1984, he gave a series of general audiences on this topic.[7] Since then, a huge body of literature has sprung up as authors attempt to unpack this theology of the body (TOB) and make it more accessible. In this essay I will focus on a few concepts from TOB, namely, the concept of gift, the spousal meaning of the body, and how this relates to the Holy Family as a model for married couples.

The Concept of Gift

At the heart of the message of TOB, we find the concept of "the gift." In the introduction to his translation of John Paul's talks, Michael Waldstein quotes Pascal Ide who says, "one can condense the whole argument of TOB in the statement, 'Gift expresses the essential truth of the human body.'" In other words, love is understood in terms of making a gift of self. Because we are bodily beings, we express this gift of self through our body in a wide variety of ways that are appropriate to the relationships we have with others. And this understanding of love as a gift of self is also the foundation of our relationship with God. Waldstein then quotes St. Therese of Lisieux, "To love is to give everything and to give oneself," and he says, "Her axiom can serve as a guiding star for the voyage through TOB."[8]

The gift of self that is fundamental to TOB applies to everyone, whether married or single, religious or laity. The principles of TOB are foundational to living the Christian life. Although Pope John Paul focused on marriage in his talks about TOB, he also spoke of the call to consecrated chastity for the sake of the kingdom. This is how St. Therese lived her gift of self. She was a French Carmelite who lived the ordinary life of a 19th century nun, but she did it with extraordinary love. Therese never heard about the theology of the body. She lived a century before the Pope even talked about it. But though she never formally studied it, she lived it by making a gift of self through her Carmelite vocation. Therese never earned a university degree, but she has been declared a doctor of the Church—a recognition that someone has made a profound contribution to our understanding of the faith. Her insight came from the Holy Spirit, and Therese was so open to the Spirit because of her great love. If TOB is new to you, don't feel like you've somehow been left behind. If you're living your Christian faith,

---

7. John Paul II, *Man and Woman He Created Them: A Theology of the Body*, trans. Michael Waldstein (Boston: Pauline, 2006). [Hereafter: *Man and Woman*].

8. Ibid., 124.

you're living the theology of the body to the extent that you give of yourself to others each day. This concept of the gift of self is at the heart of TOB. It sums up the essence of the two great commandments that Jesus gave us: to love God with all our mind, and heart, and soul, and strength, and to love our neighbor as ourselves (see Matt 22:34–40).

The idea that human beings are meant to give themselves to others is drawn from our understanding of the relations within the Trinity—the God in whose image we are made (Gen 1:26–27). The three Persons—Father, Son, and Holy Spirit—are joined in a dynamic union of love. Each Person pours out love to the others. Although the three Persons of the Trinity did not require more than this communion of interpersonal love, the Triune God created the whole universe out of his infinite generosity, in order to share divine love with created beings.

This communion of Persons in the Trinity is the union of love among them. As Scripture says, "God is love" (1 John 4:8). Love is the very essence of God, and divine love brings forth life. The Trinity itself is the origin of the Gift and of all grace, which is a sharing in divine life. God, literally, loves us into being. God loves us in a way that is entirely different from the way we love. We love because we find goodness in a person and are drawn to it. God instead, loves us first, and by loving us, puts goodness into us. Yes, God literally *loves us into being*. Our vocation, the way we find happiness, is to give love in return: love of God and love of neighbor. Our lives will be happy and fulfilled to the extent that we live this gift of love and share it with others. God put in our hearts an intense yearning for divine love and the life that flows from it, even if we don't recognize it for what it is and seek love in places we'll never find it.

To emphasize this point about the centrality of love, Pope John Paul often quoted this statement from Vatican II: "Man can fully discover his true self only in a sincere giving of himself."[9] In fact, the phrase "sincere gift of self" is a fundamental theme of TOB. It's also called the "law of the gift": the paradox that we can only find happiness when we give ourselves away in love, not when we try to selfishly cling to what we think will bring us happiness. Giving ourselves in love leads to a fuller life. This is evident even in the way we come into the world, through the loving union of our parents. Each one of us is alive because of the gift of love we have received from God through our parents. And even if on the human level love for the

---

9. GS §24.

child conceived is lacking, it is not lacking on God's part, who always loves us no matter what.

Mary and the Gift

When we turn to Mary, we find a real person who perfectly lived out the gift of self. The dogma of the Immaculate Conception reminds us that God first gifted Mary in a very unique way. The dogma states that the "Blessed Virgin Mary, in the first instant of her conception, by a singular grace and privilege granted by Almighty God, in view of the merits of Jesus Christ, the Savior of the human race, was preserved free from all stain of original sin."[10] This definition is careful to state that Mary did not save herself, but was saved through the merits of Jesus Christ, the Redeemer of the whole human race, including Mary. In preserving her from original sin, God filled her with grace, which is a participation in the life and love of God. This grace enabled Mary to love God with her whole heart and soul, a stance from which she never retreated during her whole life. The Trinity loved Mary in such a way as to grace her from the first moment of her existence. And Mary *received* that gift. Because she was loved, she was able to love in return. And that is what we see her doing from the moment we meet her in the Gospel.

She was a young Jewish girl growing up in a culture very different from ours. We don't know what she was doing when the angel Gabriel appeared to her. Perhaps she was praying, perhaps she was doing some household work as women of the time would have been doing. Was she startled? What did she think? The Gospel account says that she was "troubled" by the angel's words (see Luke 1:26–38).

But when she heard what Gabriel was saying, she responded by saying "yes." The future was not clear to her. How would she tell Joseph about this? She was betrothed to him, and now was going to bear a son while remaining a virgin. The amount of faith that this required is incredible to ponder. Yet Mary said "yes" to God, making a complete gift of herself by responding with her whole being to God's invitation.

In his encyclical *Mother of the Redeemer,* Pope John Paul II wrote that at the Annunciation, Mary entrusted herself to God completely in faith. He

---

10. Pius IX, *Defining the Dogma of the Immaculate Conception*, December 8, 1854, as found in M. Jean Frisk and Marianne Lorraine Trouvé, eds., *Mother of Christ, Mother of the Church: Documents on the Blessed Virgin Mary* (Boston: Pauline, 2001), 24.

says, "Mary responded . . . with all her human and feminine 'I.'" In other words, Mary responded from the depths of who she was as a person, completely and wholeheartedly. He goes on to note that her response had two aspects: (1) perfect cooperation with God's grace, and (2) perfect openness to the action of the Holy Spirit.[11] She opened herself to receive the gift of God, and then in turn made a gift of herself. In doing this, Mary had the unique position of uniting in herself two vocations: the vocation to marriage and motherhood, and the vocation to virginity for the sake of the kingdom. The following section will further explore these two aspects.

The Gift Has a Spousal Meaning

The vocations of marriage and virginity are each rooted in the spousal meaning of the body. This is a key term that John Paul defines by saying that the spousal attribute is *"the power to express love: precisely that love in which the human person becomes a gift* and—through this gift—fulfills the very meaning of his being and existence."[12] This giving and receiving of the gift of one's self creates a communion of persons. As mentioned earlier, the Trinity is a communion of Persons grounded in love. Created in the image of God, we too are called to live in love toward each other, thus forming a communion of persons on the human level. Although far from perfect, our communion of persons is a reflection of the Trinitarian love. There are many ways in which we can show love through our bodies, and this is certainly not limited to sexual union. But the most significant bodily expression of this gift of self is found in married love, in the "one flesh" union by which spouses totally give themselves to each other. At this level, the "sincere gift of self" takes on a spousal meaning. As John Paul says, "One can understand this 'spousal' meaning of the human body only in the context of the person. The body has a 'spousal' meaning because the human person, as the Council says, is a creature that God willed for his own sake and that, at the same time cannot fully find himself except through the gift of self."[13]

These ideas lead us to a certain paradox and mystery in regard to Mary. Because of her vocation to be Mother of the Son of God, Mary had a very unique position. She lived both the vocation to marriage and the

---

11. RM §13.
12. *Man and Woman*, 15:1; italics in original.
13. Ibid., 15:5.

vocation to virginity. God called her to live the spousal meaning of the body in a virginal way, as both mother and a virgin. As mentioned above, the spousal meaning of the body has to do with the way we make a gift of ourselves to others. As embodied persons, this gift is lived out in a human, bodily way, and can be done in a great variety of ways. Mary lived her gift of self in a bodily way, but one that was also virginal, yet included Joseph as her husband. (The next section will explore in more detail the relationship of Mary and Joseph.) In these two aspects of Mary, we can see how she sums up in herself in a most unique way what it means to live the theology of the body. Both of these vocations are ways of loving, of making a gift of oneself. Like every mystery of the faith, it is difficult for us to understand the mystery of Mary's virginal motherhood. On the one hand, we need to be clear that it does not denigrate sexual union in marriage. But if sexual union is a good, why did God ask Mary and Joseph to forego it?

The Virginal Marriage of Mary and Joseph

Mary's virginal motherhood ultimately teaches us something about the incarnation of the Son of God. Ultimately, the marriage of Mary and Joseph was virginal in order to safeguard the truth of the incarnation, the divinity of Jesus Christ. Mary's virginity shows that Jesus has only God for his Father. "Mary's virginity manifests God's absolute initiative in the Incarnation. Jesus has only God as Father."[14] As already noted, the Church's teaching about Mary's virginity does not spring from a negative attitude toward human sexuality. Pope John Paul II always taught clearly, especially in TOB, that human sexuality is a gift of God and is to be treasured and used properly in marriage. Mary had such a unique vocation because the incarnation was a very special, unique part of God's plan of salvation. No other person in the history of the human race was called to give birth to the Incarnate Son of God.

As a mother, Mary gave the world the gift of its Lord and Savior, Jesus Christ. He came to us through her. She said "yes," when our first parents, Adam and Eve, had said "no" to God. So Mary is called the new Eve, the beginning of the new creation that Jesus, the new Adam, brought to us through the redemption: "And thus also it was that the knot of Eve's disobedience was loosed by the obedience of Mary. For what the virgin Eve had bound fast through unbelief, this did the virgin Mary set free through

---

14. CCC §503.

faith."[15] In a very simple yet profound way, all that we can say about Mary could be summed up by saying that she gave the Gift to the world—Jesus Christ. As a virgin, Mary also lived out the "law of the gift." In this other aspect of her vocation, her virginity, she gave a gift to God. She gave the gift of her complete and total dedication to the Father. And because of her love and fidelity, salvation came to the world through Jesus Christ. So by giving a gift to God, Mary also gave a gift to all of us.

But there was one person in her life to whom Mary made a gift of herself in a unique way—her husband Joseph. Although Mary maintained her virginity, she loved Joseph with a real human love, which means a love expressed through the body in some way. They trusted their lives to each other. They knew the joy of loving and being loved, accepting each other with mutual trust. In *Guardian of the Redeemer*, Pope John Paul II says that Mary and Joseph had a real marriage, even though they lived in a virginal way. Their marriage was not just a pious fiction in order to somehow legitimize Jesus. The Pope writes, "And while it is important for the Church to profess the virginal conception of Jesus, it is no less important to uphold Mary's marriage to Joseph, because juridically Joseph's fatherhood depends on it." In examining marriage, Christian writers have defined it through the characteristics that were considered to best express its nature. Three characteristics or goods of marriage in particular are noteworthy: (1) the good of children, who are received with love as a gift from God and nurtured and educated; (2) the good of the fidelity of the spouses, which binds them together in love; and (3) the good of the sacrament, that is, marriage as a sacrament is not only a bond of unity between the spouses but a sacramental sign, one that points to the union of Christ and the Church. In upholding the marriage of Mary and Joseph, the Pope is drawing on this Christian tradition concerning marriage. He quotes St. Augustine: "In Christ's parents all the goods of marriage were realized—offspring, fidelity, the sacrament: the offspring being the Lord Jesus himself; fidelity, since there was no adultery: the sacrament, since there was no divorce."[16]

Yet the expression of love shared by Mary and Joseph did not include the "one-flesh" union. How could Mary and Joseph have lived the spousal gift of self in a virginal way? What significance does this have and what can

---

15. Irenaeus, *Adv. Haer.*, 3.22.4, online: http://www.newadvent.org/fathers/0103322.htm.

16. RC §7.

we learn from it? John Paul's thoughts about continence for the sake of the kingdom can shed light on this topic.

In his TOB catechesis, John Paul spoke at some length on the mystery of continence for the sake of the kingdom. The two realities of continence and marriage are like two sides of the same coin, one that expresses the reality of our Christian vocation as being rooted in love. John Paul speaks of marriage as a "primordial sacrament," that is, something present from the very beginning of the human race, and also as the "sacrament of creation." Marriage continues the work of creation through the gift of children. Spouses become co-creators with God when children are born through their loving union. Marriage is also tied up with the salvific work of God, for the children born of it are called to eternal life.

In Ephesians 5, St. Paul speaks of marriage as a "great mystery," adding, "I mean in relation to Christ and to the Church." The "great mystery" refers to God's eternal plan of redemption in Christ. The Father sends the Son into the world in order to redeem it and lead us to union with the Trinity. God poured his love out entirely for humanity through Christ's death on the cross. This total and complete self-giving love is the extreme expression of God's love for us and is the paradigm of spousal love, of giving one's life for one's spouse. The purpose of Christ's death was to lead us to eternal life, when we will enjoy the fullness of union with him.

The marital union on earth is a symbol of the union that we will have with God in heaven. In eternal life, marriage and sexual union will give way to this totally beatifying union with God in love and through him with all the other persons united to him. As Jesus said to the Sadducees who denied the resurrection, "For in the resurrection they neither marry nor are given in marriage, but are like angels in heaven" (Matt 22:30).

On earth, however, there are some whom God calls to sacrifice marriage and embrace continence for the sake of the kingdom of heaven. As John Paul says, the text of Ephesians 5:25–22, which discusses marriage in terms of the union of Christ and the Church, "is equally valid both for the theology of marriage and for the theology of continence 'for the kingdom,' the theology of virginity or celibacy."[17]

The purpose of foregoing marriage for the sake of the kingdom is to witness here on earth to the promise of eternal life. Because continence anticipates that time when God will be "all in all," it has an eschatological quality.

---

17. *Man and Woman*, 79:7.

The meaning of continence flows from the spousal nature of the person. When God calls someone to this vocation, he calls them precisely as persons who, as male or female, are called to make a "sincere gift of themselves" in a spousal way. This gift is realized differently in continence than in marriage.

"Man (male and female) is able to choose the personal gift of self to another person in the conjugal covenant, in which they become 'one flesh,' and he is also able to *renounce freely* such a gift of self to another person, in order that by choosing continence 'for the kingdom of Heaven' he may give himself totally to Christ."[18] So according to John Paul, both vocations, to marriage and to continence, are ways of living the gift of self through the spousal meaning of the body.

As mentioned above, Mary and Joseph were called to both aspects of spousal love because of their unique role in the incarnation. As John Paul II says, "Only Mary and Joseph, who lived the mystery of his birth, became the first witnesses of a fruitfulness different from that of the flesh, i.e., the fruitfulness of the Spirit. 'What is begotten in her comes from the Holy Spirit' (Matt 1:20)."[19]

This idea of the fruitfulness of the Spirit brings us closer to understanding the mystery of Mary and Joseph's virginal marriage. In some mysterious way their marriage joins the reality of everything entailed in what Ephesians calls "the great mystery." The mystery of conjugal love in marriage finds its roots in the love of Christ for the Church. The mystery of continence for the sake of the kingdom also finds its roots there.

To summarize what John Paul has said in detail in TOB, the marriage of Mary and Joseph conceals within itself both mysteries: that of conjugal love, and that of continence for the sake of the kingdom. Their continence had a very special meaning because through it, the incarnation came about. Humanity received the gift of the divine Word. Mary was fruitful through the action of the Holy Spirit.

The "fruitfulness of the Spirit" gave them a Gift which no human being could have ever dreamed of: the Son of God Incarnate. The Holy Spirit, who had come upon Mary, must have given her deep insight into the mystery that both she and Joseph were joined in guarding, and moved them to understand and live out their spousal love in a virginal way. Of course, we are treading on holy ground here, and it is not given us to know the

---

18. Ibid., 80:6.
19. Ibid., 75:2.

precise way the Holy Spirit worked in Mary. But given her fullness of grace and her openness to the will of God, in light of Church teaching about her perpetual virginity it is reasonable to suppose that she cooperated in God's plan with a sound understanding of why God was calling her to virginity.

Mary and Joseph knew that they had received the greatest Gift God could ever give: his own beloved Son. Their vocation was to treasure that Gift and love and care for Jesus in an exclusive way. So through the grace of the Holy Spirit, they discerned that God intended them to live together in a virginal marriage. Mary as Virgin and Mother was filled with that spousal love that flows from making a "sincere gift of self" to another in love.

Some Applications

What lessons might married couples today draw from the example of the marriage of Mary and Joseph? Undoubtedly there are many, but I would like to focus on these:

1. Happy marriages are built on a mutual gift of self.

This may seem obvious, but it's worth stating. Only love can keep a marriage going year after year, through "better or worse." Love that flows from a mutual gift of self can sustain couples through the difficulties that are sure to come. Years ago as a young sister, I spent some time doing door-to-door evangelizing. On Saturdays we would visit people in their homes with our publications, offering them the Word of God, hoping to bring a reminder of God's love. We would always meet some married couples who had been together for a long time, forty or fifty years. It was delightful to meet them and to see how their love had kept them together. Sometimes they would tell us stories of tragic events they had lived through, perhaps the loss of a child, a serious illness, or financial difficulty. I remember one woman in particular who had stuck by her husband as he battled alcoholism and reached sobriety. She said, "I knew that in my marriage I had a sacrament. My husband was Christ to me, and I wasn't going to abandon him." I was very impressed by the witness of their love. They lived in their own way the mutual gift of self that Mary and Joseph lived.

2. Sex is important but it isn't everything in marriage.

On another occasion we met a man who had gone through a divorce. He told us that he and his wife had experienced a great sexual relationship (which he actually put in more colorful terms) but outside of the bedroom things didn't work out. Their relationship didn't go beyond sexual attraction, and when that burned out, they had nothing left. The virginal marriage of Mary and Joseph reminds us that marriage is more than sex. In an age when young people are often pressured into having sexual relationships before they've learned to become friends, this is a counter-cultural message. Yet it is so important. The mutual gift of self is rooted in appreciating the other precisely as a person, not as a sexual object, as the example of Mary shows us.

3. Children are a gift of God.

Mary and Joseph received the child Jesus as a gift—the greatest Gift! Jesus, the Incarnate Son of God, became the child whom they raised. They received this gift with gratitude and love, and in so doing became a model for all parents. Each child is a gift of God, and parents are called to receive that child with love and respect for the person that he or she is. One aspect of this is to realize that the child is not a means to fulfill the needs of the parents. Trying to force one's children into a profession or career that the parents want—and the child doesn't—is one way this sometimes happens. Respecting each child as the unique gift that he or she is will make for happier families. In the Holy Family, Mary and Joseph welcomed Jesus, "the image of the invisible God" (Col 1:15). When parents welcome a new child into their family, they are welcoming a person who is made in the image and likeness of God.

4. A renewal of Christian marriage will bring about a renewal of vocations to the consecrated life.

It's no accident that the decline in the vitality of marriage is paralleled by a decline in vocations to the priesthood and consecrated life in the Church.[20] In many countries, especially in the West, the shortage of priests and religious has reached crisis proportions. While the reasons for this are complex, the vocation to marriage and the vocation to continence for the sake of the kingdom are like two sides of the same coin. Both are vocations to love, rooted in a gift of self. When one suffers, the other suffers, and when one thrives, the other thrives.

---

20. For statistics from 1965 to 2011, see online: http://cara.georgetown.edu/CARA Services/requestedchurchstats.html.

Mary and Joseph lived out the vocation that God called them to live. In doing so, they lived the spousal gift of self that is the secret of happiness. As Pope John Paul II put it,

> At the culmination of the history of salvation, when God reveals his love for humanity through the gift of the Word, it is precisely the marriage of Mary and Joseph that brings to realization in full 'freedom' the 'spousal gift of self' in receiving and expressing such a love.[21]

In an age when marriage is facing many difficulties and family life is often threatened, their example can serve to help families find happiness in sharing their love in a mutual gift of self.

---

21. RC §7.

4

Mary

Mirror of Justice

CHRISTOPHER M. CARR

The evil do not understand justice, but those who seek the Lord understand it completely.[1]

In the mid-twentieth century, Francis Joseph Sheed (March 20, 1897–November 20, 1981), a noted lay Catholic author and publisher, wrote the following comments: "There is an absolute deadliness about questions that never get asked because everybody [supposedly] knows the answer: because if they ever do get asked, no one has an answer ready . . . [and our] modern society is largely living on such unasked questions."[2] Inevitably, of course, someone does ask the unasked. When one raises a question for which everyone presumably has the answer, it turns out that "everybody does not know [the answer], because everybody does not agree: and where people disagree, some of them must be wrong."[3]

---

1. Prov 28:5 NRSV.
2. F. J. Sheed, *Man: The Forgotten* (London: Sheed & Ward, 1943), 13.
3. Ibid., 8. Sheed made these remarks to focus attention on what he thought was the underlying reality of World War II; he believed that the war was really an armed conflict in lieu of arguments over the Nazi and Christian visions of human nature and the social order (ibid., 13–18).

Sheed's point about the danger in taking knowledge of certain, basic concepts for granted is intrinsically related, and equally applicable, to current debates on matters of justice. The word "justice" is frequently invoked by public servants, political activists and media personalities to promote or prevent a variety of activities, such as legalized abortion, capital punishment, and gay marriage, but the continual disagreement over whether these policies are just shows that people living in the West have generally forgotten what justice is. In order to resolve these controversies over policy, the truth about justice must be retrieved and communicated.

A greater awareness of justice can be obtained by turning to Mary. Her role in the task of rediscovering justice will not be as a model for living justly in every situation but as a kind of mirror that reflects what justice generically means and entails through the specific things we know about her from Scripture and Tradition. All the essential characteristics of justice are variously manifested in Marian doctrines or the events from her life.

The Nature of Justice

To thoroughly understand the nature of something, two groups of qualities have to be identified. The first group lists the basic features that define the thing as unique in itself; the second elaborates on the first by noting the actions the thing is capable of doing. The nature of the more dynamic reality called justice can be known in a similar way. One grasps more completely the essence of this virtue by learning both its basic definition and the acts by which a just state of affairs is achieved.

St. Thomas Aquinas provides the essential components for defining justice in his *Summa Theologica*, and when the subjects of the first four questions he asks about this virtue are consolidated, the following definition emerges: the habitual strength of will whereby one affirms another's human dignity by giving him that which is his due.[4] Being a virtue of the will, it is a quality shared with many other virtues, but what makes justice unique are the other elements in Aquinas' definition. First, when considering all four cardinal virtues, only justice is relational. Prudence is the intellectual virtue that seeks the best means of obtaining a genuine good and as such does not

---

4. See ST II-II, q. 58, art. 1–4. These articles are titled "Whether Justice Is Fittingly Defined as Being the Perpetual and Constant Will to Render to Each One His Right?" (art. 1); "Whether Justice Is Always Towards Another?" (art. 2); "Whether Justice Is a Virtue?" (art. 3); and "Whether Justice Is in the Will as Its Subject?" (art. 4).

immediately affect another person. The same lack of immediacy regarding persons holds true for the other cardinal virtues of the will, fortitude and temperance; neither the obstacles demanding courage nor the distractions requiring self-control necessarily have to be one's neighbor. However, "justice is [directly] concerned... about our dealings with others."[5] The second distinctive element is the "due" that is owed another, which arises from different sources. Josef Pieper writes, "A thing might be due to a man on the basis of agreements, treaties, promises, legal decisions, and ... [even] on the nature of him to whom the obligation is due."[6] Thus, rephrasing the definition taken from the *Summa* of St. Thomas with an emphasis on these two distinguishing characteristics, the essence of justice is *the willingness to give another person what he is entitled to have precisely as a person.*

Yet defining justice as giving a person their just due is only the initial step in understanding this virtue; knowledge of justice is incomplete without also identifying the activities that are the proper means to achieve just ends. Over the centuries of Western reflection on justice, the actions that lead to just states of affairs have fallen into three categories. These categories are: (1) acts that are sufficient to meet the demand of rendering another his just due; (2) acts that everyone is continually bound to perform because the obligation of rendering another his just due can never be adequately satisfied; and (3) acts that exceed what justice requires, strictly understood, but nevertheless are essential for maintaining just relations.

Actions sufficient to supply the dues owed another occur in three different kinds of relational circumstances, which in turn are the basis for the traditional "forms" of justice. A just person acknowledges that man, as a social being by nature, will not experience perfection and happiness without being somehow connected to a community. Thus, someone who acts justly takes care to avoid behaving in a manner that is detrimental to the common good, which is "the sum total of social conditions which allow people, either as groups or individuals, to reach their fulfillment more fully

---

5. ST II-II, q. 58, art. 2. The Catholic philosopher Josef Pieper also points out that justice can only be properly directed to beings who are free to advance or harm their own perfection. That is to say, justice is concerned exclusively with persons, while "nothing can be inalienably due to a brute [let alone a plant or an inanimate object]." Pieper, *Justice*, trans. Lawrence E. Lynch (New York: Pantheon, 1955), 19. See also Piper, *Justice*, 43: "Man is the subject of justice to the extent that he is a spiritual being," in other words, a person.

6. Pieper, *Justice*, 17–18.

and more easily."[7] This manner of acting justly with regard to the social whole is called "general" or "legal" justice, insofar as "a man is directed to the common good"[8] with the aid of just laws designed to promote human happiness through a stable and orderly society.[9] The two other kinds of justice are not concerned with common good but the good due immediately to the individual. Distributive justice takes place when a person in position of authority provides necessary human goods to individuals who do not have the ability to acquire these goods for themselves;[10] commutative justice has to do with equity in the variety of private transactions that take place among individual citizens.[11] In all of these relational circumstances, the due or good that someone requires can be successfully achieved.

But the demands of justice are not always able to be met; "there are some obligations which, by their very nature, cannot be acquitted in full, much as the one who is thus indebted may be willing to do so."[12] Again, the relations from which these perpetual demands arise are three in number. The first relationship is between man and God. Human beings receive

---

7. GS §26. See also CCC §1906.

8. ST II-II, q. 58, art. 6.

9. St. Thomas uses the term "legal justice" in ST II-II, q. 58, art. 5. The term has its origins in the description of this form of justice by Aristotle: "Now the laws in their enactments on all subjects aim at the common advantage either of all or of those who hold power, or something of the sort; so that in one sense we call those acts just that tend to produce and preserve happiness and its components for the political society." Aristotle, *Nicomachean Ethics*, V, 1, in *Basic Works of Aristotle*, ed. Richard McKeon (New York: Random House, 1941), 1003.

10. St. Thomas writes, "There is . . . the order of that which belongs to the community in relation to each single person . . . [which] is directed by distributive justice" (ST II-II, q. 61, art. 1). See also Patience Andrews, *Frederick II of Hohenstaufen* (London: Oxford University Press, 1970), 24: "The king was supposed to be Justice personified. 'His Majesty in the eye of the law is always present in all his courts, though he cannot personally distribute justice.'"

11. See Andrews, *Frederick II*, 24: "[The] order of one private individual to another . . . is directed by commutative justice, which is concerned about the mutual dealings between two persons." This distinction between the two different kinds of "particular justice," which pertains to what is due to particular human beings, is also taken from Aristotle. "Of particular justice and that which is just in the corresponding sense, (A) one kind is that which is manifested in distributions of honor or money or the other things that fall to be divided among those who have a share in the constitution (for in these it is possible for one man to have a share either unequal or equal to that of another), and (B) one is that which plays a rectifying part in transactions between man and man." Aristotle, *Nicomachean Ethics* (V, 2), in *Basic Works*, 1005–6.

12. Pieper, *Justice*, 95.

absolutely everything from God, and the continual effort to somehow acknowledge our infinite debt to him, without ever being able to erase it, is the sub-virtue of justice called *religio*, or religion.[13] Specific acts of religion include devotion to things of God, prayer, adoration, sacrifice, offerings and vows.[14] Not only are human beings not able to fully acquit their debts to God, but the same holds true for certain relationships with other human beings. One set of these purely human relationships involves one's parents and country. *Pietas* is the Latin term St. Thomas uses for attempts at remitting what one owes to parents and country. The word means a "sense of responsibility; . . . due regard; kindness, tenderness; [and] loyalty,"[15] and so refers to any act of "duty and homage."[16] The other set of persons who can never be adequately repaid for what they have given are those "who are distinguished by their office or by some dignity."[17] According to St. Thomas, one must treat such a person with *observantia*, meaning "respect"[18] or "honor,"[19] which might consist "in rendering him service, by obeying his commands, and by repaying him, according to one's faculty, for the benefits we received from him."[20] However, even if some form of payment is offered and deemed sufficient for the assistance rendered, the office and the respect due to the one in it remain.

The last category of behavior relevant to acting justly has to do with giving beyond what justice indicates is another's due.

> [The] man who strives for justice . . . realizes . . . that fulfilling an obligation and doing what he is really obliged to do are not all that is necessary. Something more is required, something over and above, such as liberality, *affabilitas*, kindness, if man's communal

---

13. "[Whatever] man renders to God is due, yet it cannot be equal, as though man rendered to God as much as he owes Him, according to Ps 115:12, 'What shall I render to the Lord for all the things that He hath rendered to me?'" (ST II-II, q. 80, art. 1).

14. After discussing the nature of religion per se as a virtue in ST II-II, q. 81, the specific acts of religion and their relevant vices are explored in ST II-II, qs. 82–100.

15. John C. Traupman, *New College Latin & English Dictionary*, rev. ed. (New York: Bantam, 1995), s.v. "*pietas*."

16. ST II-II, q. 101, art. 3.

17. Pieper, *Justice*, 102. Such persons include government officials, judges, teachers, doctors, police, firemen, etc.

18. *New College Latin & English Dictionary*, s.v. "*observantia*."

19. See ST II-II, q. 102, art. 1–2.

20. ST II-II, q. 102, art. 2.

life is to remain human. Here nothing more . . . is meant than friendliness in our everyday associations.[21]

Friendliness is conduct that exceeds what justice strictly demands in terms of debts to be rendered, but without this "special virtue,"[22] our relationships with others could not be enjoyable. If social relationships are left to sour because of either an apathetic or antipathetic disposition, the willingness to fulfill the proper obligations of justice will deteriorate. Thus, behaving "towards one another in a becoming manner[23] . . . is part of justice."[24]

A review of the Thomistic understanding of justice reveals nine essential characteristics. The first two comprise the virtue's definition, which is the inclination of will to recognize the dignity of another person and so give that person his due. Given the manner in which human beings interact as social creatures, the relational modes in which another's just due is rendered are distinguished according to the three forms of justice: legal, distributive, and commutative. But some debts can never be remitted—namely, those owed to God, parents or country, and other persons in important offices; such creditors therefore become the perpetual objects of justice's three sub-virtues—namely, religion, *pietas,* and respect. The last component of justice is friendliness, which in a way stands outside the formal demands of justice yet is the proper manner to interact with other persons, regardless of their nature or station. Having identified the foundational attributes of justice, one can then turn to Mary for concrete examples of each attribute.

The Essential Characteristics of Justice in Marian Scripture and Doctrine

The attributes that characterize justice are really a series of obligations, and so an effective way of illustrating what justice means is to show how these obligations are fulfilled. Passages in Scripture and the Church's doctrinal statements concerning Mary reveal that every major event in her life illustrates one obligation of justice being either met or ignored. However, the manner of illustration varies. Sometimes she is the one acting; at others, she is the one acted upon. Adoption of both approaches shows that Mary

---

21. Pieper, *Justice*, 105–6.
22. ST II-II, q. 114, art. 1.
23. ST II-II.
24. ST II-II, q. 114, art. 2.

supplies practical examples of the defining principles and activities that constitute justice.

Even though the Jews of Mary's time were obviously not familiar with the classical, Western definition of justice, they did know the fundamental demands imposed by this virtue. Hebrew had "no single . . . word to express . . . justice; what is meant by justice is [instead] contained in the concepts of judgment [*mišpāṭ*] and righteousness [*ṣedek*]."[25] In general, "judgment looks . . . to the vindication or liberation of the righteous . . . and the punishment of the wrongdoer,"[26] while "righteousness" is a quality of anything that "meets a standard"—for example, laws, legal actions, legislators, executors of the law, and persons who act according to the law, as well as the salvation or deliverance that comes from God.[27] These two Hebraic terms cover the essentials of justice, insofar as the words focus attention on other persons and the existence of an objective standard, in this case human nature, by which a person's needs are recognized. If the Jews had been fully aware of the supernatural role that God had enlisted Mary to play in saving and delivering the human race from sin, they might have seen that pivotal moments in her life conformed to these defining ideals of justice. Such moments involve events or actions directed toward others and their due.

Mary was Jewish and so was taught that just conduct was primarily directed to other human beings. Furthermore, like all Jews, she learned that justice was anthropocentric not by studying *mišpāṭ* and *ṣedek* in the abstract but through illustrations taken from the example of God and the Mosaic law. At key moments in the history of Israel, God intervened using divine judgments and salvific righteousness. The plagues sent against Egypt are described as "acts of judgment" (Exod 7:4; see also 12:12),[28] while the ensuing freedom from slavery and later victories over hostile peoples were in fact God's righteous, "saving deeds" (1 Sam 12:6-8, 11; Mic 6:3-5). Perhaps more importantly for Mary, themes of future divine judgment and deliverance from evil with respect to the human race as a whole were also instilled from prophetic texts. Daniel sees in a vision that "dominion" and "kingship" over "all peoples, nations, and languages" will be given by an enthroned Ancient One to "one like a son of man" (Dan 7:9-14), and the

---

25. John L. McKenzie, *Dictionary of the Bible* (1965; repr., New York: Touchstone, 1995), s.v. "Righteous, Righteousness."

26. *Dictionary of the Bible*, s.v. "Judgment."

27. Ibid., s.v. "Righteous, Righteousness."

28. All Scripture citations in this chapter are from the NRSV.

prophet Isaiah reports God's promises of universal salvation and justice (Isa 51:4–8) will be made possible by contributions from a figure called the Suffering Servant (Isa 42:1–4 and 53:10–12). As for the Mosaic law, its statutes can be arranged in such a manner that entire sections are devoted to the treatment of specific groups of people; these groups include other Jews, the poor, Gentiles, family members, employees, servants, slaves, idolaters, priests, lepers, kings, and Nazirites.[29] Mary's life, too, provides concrete instances of this emphasis on other persons that grounds the principles of justice in the events of human history, especially in the Annunciation and her service to others.

Although the Annunciation is the event in which divine love for the entire human race becomes manifest through the Incarnation of God the Son in Mary, the very announcement process reveals God's concern for her personally. The angel's message seems to be phrased in a manner that suggests Mary is to be a passive instrument: "You will conceive. . . . You will name him Jesus. . . . The Holy Spirit will come upon you" (Luke 1:31 and 35). Yet the Incarnation does not occur without her "*fiat*" (Luke 1:38). God is Justice and so must act justly.[30] As an image of God, Mary has free will, and if God were to override her freedom, he would be acting contrary not

---

29. The individual statutes of the Mosaic law are scattered throughout the Pentateuch, and so for purposes of organization, the traditional procedure is to divide them into the 248 mandates and the 365 prohibitions. Moses Maimonides (Mar 30, 1135–Dec 13, 1204) compiled a list of the 613 commandments, and he classifies them further according to theme. For his list with subheadings, see *Encyclopaedia Judaica*, vol. 5, *Coh–Doz*, 2nd ed. (New York: Thomson Gale, 2007), s.v. "Commandments, The 613."

A Nazarite (Hebrew $n^ez\hat{i}r$—"one set apart or of high rank") is someone who makes a temporary or perpetual vow to serve God by adopting an ascetic way of life. The most well-known obligations of a Nazirite are to abstain "from intoxicating beverages, the use of the razor, and contact with the dead" (*Dictionary of the Bible*, s.v. "Nazirite;" see also Num 6:1–21). Reasons for taking the vow to become a Nazirite varied, such as seeking deliverance from a malady or the fulfillment of a petition. See *Jewish Encyclopedia*, vol. 9, *Morawczyk–Philippson* (1901–1906; repr., New York: Ktav, 1964), s.v. "Nazarite [sic]."

30. When Abraham explores the possibility of God showing mercy to the sinful population of Sodom if fifty righteous persons could be found in the city, Abraham asks, "Shall not the Judge of all the earth do what is just?" (Gen 18:25).

Indeed, God announcing to Abraham the decision to have Sodom destroyed is itself a divine act of just concern shown to Abraham, whom God had established as the foundation of the chosen people. "The Lord said, 'Shall I hide from Abraham what I am about to do, seeing that Abraham shall become a great and mighty nation, and all the nations of the earth shall be blessed in him? No, for I have chosen him that he may charge his children and his household after him to keep the way of the Lord by doing righteousness and justice; so that the Lord may bring about what he has promised him'" (Gen 18:17–19).

only to his nature as Justice but also Love. Thus, God respects Mary's inherent personal dignity by acknowledging her freedom to accept his plan of salvation. "Right from the start, her free consent is an integral part of God's saving plan and decision,"[31] and allowance for Mary's consent to be made freely is an act of just concern for another by God.

But Mary exhibits this concern for others, as well. Aside from the wider horizon of man's universal salvation in which she has agreed to participate, her attention to others is given to specific individuals. First, she and her husband Joseph are said to be in a state of "great anxiety" (Luke 2:48) after the boy Jesus stays behind in Jerusalem following the Passover. Parental worry comes naturally when a child's location is unknown,[32] and her maternal feelings toward her divine Son continue throughout his public ministry.[33] The second and, for us, more important expression of her careful attention toward others is found in her role as intercessor. Beginning with her intervention during the wedding at Cana,[34] Mary undertakes a permanent ministry in which every individual, being the object of her son's

---

31. Hans Urs von Balthasar, *Theo-Drama: Theological Dramatic Theory*, vol. 3, *The Dramatis Personae: The Person in Christ*, trans. Graham Harrison (San Francisco: Ignatius, 1992), 300.

See also Karl Rahner, *Mary, the Mother of the Lord* (New York: Herder and Herder, 1963), 60: "When God gives, ... these things become precisely what is most our own .... If he gives us something, it truly belongs to us; it truly constitutes the actual concrete reality of a human individual.... When God willed the blessed Virgin through her free consent to her motherhood to open the world to the eternal mercy of God, this consent was in its very essence hers, her act. It belongs to her and cannot be taken from her. She is and remains for ever [sic] the person who for us and for our salvation and in this sense in our name, uttered that word of consent through which the Word of God was made flesh."

32. According to a compilation of private revelations concerning Mary, her chief fears were "that Archelaus the King might have taken Him prisoner and be mistreating Him ... [or that] Jesus ... [had] gone to live in the desert with John the Baptist." Raphael Brown, comp., *Life of Mary as Seen by the Mystics* (1951; repr., Rockford, IL: Tan, 1991), 153.

33. Mary's motherly instincts can again be seen in an incident recorded by all of the Synoptic Gospels. As Jesus is teaching a crowd, Mary and other relatives attempt to get in touch with him (Matt 12:46-50; Mark 3:31-35; Luke 8:19-21). No reason is explicitly given for this attempt. However, she had apparently "prepared a meal for Him and His disciples" and intended "to urge Him to come and take some food" (Brown, *Life of Mary*, 188). Only the Gospel of Mark (3:20) suggests that the motive for Mary's behavior was providing Jesus with an opportunity for rest and nourishment.

34. See John 2:1-12, esp. v. 5: "[Mary said,] 'Do whatever He tells you.'" See also Brown, *Life of Mary*, 179: "Then, having done her part as intercessor for others, the Mother of God humbly returned to her place among the women."

infinite love, becomes subject to her affection and aid. The Second Vatican Council's Dogmatic Constitution on the Church states:

> [By] her manifold intercession [she] continues to bring us the gifts of eternal salvation. By her maternal charity, she cares for the brethren of her Son, who still journey on earth surrounded by dangers and difficulties, until they are led into their blessed home. Therefore, the Blessed Virgin is invoked in the Church under the titles of Advocate, Helper, Benefactress, and Mediatrix.[35]

The lesson to be drawn from Mary's role as intercessor regarding justice is that one must always nurture a concern for another's welfare, and this attention to others must be universal in scope but individual in practice. Only by such means will her son's dictum of justice, to love one's neighbor as oneself (Matt 22:39; Mark 12:33; Luke 10:27; see also Lev 19:18),[36] become a living reality.

For this living reality to occur, justice cannot be taken to mean that one is simply obliged to be generally well-disposed toward people; this attitude must be discharged by actually giving another his due, and Mary's Jewish education taught her that such dues arise from two sources. Recall that the Hebrew word *mišpāṭ* refers to a moral judgment, and *ṣedek*, a righteousness based upon a being's objective standard of perfection. Taken together, these terms indicate that the ancient Hebrew sense of justice "[implies] total right order," which includes both the "moral order, [and] order in nature."[37] Thus,

---

35. GS 62, which goes on to say: "This [intercession], however, is so understood that it neither takes away anything from nor adds anything to the dignity and efficacy of Christ the one Mediator." See also CCC 969. The model for Mary's role as intercessor follows a pattern established in ancient Near Eastern kingdoms. Usually, the king could have more than one wife, which meant that a stable position of "first lady" or "queen" in the kingdom could not come from the ranks of potentially competing wives but was instead vested in the king's mother. The royal mother's prestige opened a way to communicate with the king, if approaching the sovereign directly did not seem prudent. This arrangement and practice can be seen in 1 Kgs 2:13-21 regarding King Solomon and his mother, Bathsheba. However, even though Bathsheba is a secular prototype of the supernatural, intercessory position now enjoyed by Mary, it is to be noted that the request made through Bathsheba's intercession did not work out so well for the petitioner (vv. 22-25).

36. "Do nothing from selfish ambition or conceit, but in humility regard others as better than yourselves. Let each of you look not to your own interests, but to the interests of others" (Phil 2:3-4).

37. Dennis J. McCarthy and Roland E. Murphy, "Hosea," ch. 14 in *New Jerome Biblical Commentary*, ed. Raymond E. Brown et al. (Englewood Cliffs, NJ: Prentice Hall, 1990), 226 (Hosea 14:9).

even though the ancient Jews, Mary included, were not aware of "justice" in the later, philosophical sense, the moral and natural dimensions of order signified by *mišpāṭ* and *ṣedeḳ* correspond to what are now accepted as the basis for one's just due—namely, voluntary agreements or a thing's nature. Mary is associated with both sources of dues but in different ways. On the one hand, she enters into an agreement to marry Joseph; on the other, Mary possesses a perfectly just human nature in virtue of being entirely free from sin and its corrosive effects.

Her betrothal to Joseph was like any other arranged marriage of the time in that it was freely entered and entailed certain responsibilities. Marriage, "in Israel, as in all the ancient Orient, was neither a religious nor a public affair, but purely private, between two families."[38] But this practice "did not mean that the bride and the groom had no voice in the matter."[39] When Mary and Joseph were married, the normal process involved "a formal exchange of consent before witnesses and the subsequent taking of the bride to the groom's family home."[40] The bride's arrival at her new home marked the beginning of a new life with its obligations; she was now her husband's property and so placed "herself under his marital authority."[41] Although Scripture is silent on Mary's married life, one may reasonably assume that she dutifully accepted Joseph as head of their household. The early Church Fathers describe Mary "as freely cooperating in the work of man's salvation through faith and obedience,"[42] and given that her marriage to Joseph was integral to God's saving plan, she probably did fulfill her role as wife with loving fidelity and deference.

However, living in conformity with the objective standards of married life merely flowed from a more profound interior justice insofar as Mary's human nature was objectively perfect. In Christian thought, the relationship between justice and human nature is twofold. Justice refers to either the willingness to provide another person the due owed his human nature or a human nature in full possession of its due. Hence, Adam and Eve, the First Parents, are said to have been originally created in a state of "original

---

38. A. van den Born, *Encyclopedic Dictionary of the Bible*, 2nd ed., trans. Louis F. Hartman (New York: McGraw-Hill, 1963), s.v. "Marriage."

39. *Dictionary of the Bible*, s.v. "Marriage."

40. Raymond E. Brown, *Birth of the Messiah* (Garden City, NY: Doubleday, 1977), 123.

41. *Encyclopedic Dictionary of the Bible*, s.v. "Marriage."

42. LG §58.

justice," which the *Catechism of the Catholic Church* describes as "the inner harmony of the human person, the harmony between man and woman, and finally the harmony between the first couple and all creation."[43] Mary, too, enjoys this state of justice, to the extent that such a state is possible to one person in an otherwise fallen world. The doctrines of her Immaculate Conception, perpetual sinlessness and inviolate virginity point to the fact that, through God's grace, she was free from sin and the damage it causes. Her human nature was preserved in its full integrity. The reason why these Marian doctrines are important for teaching justice is because they reveal the way in which God intended human nature to be, the further harm to human nature that personal sins have the power to cause, and the protective, healing power of grace. When these same doctrines are placed within God's salvific plan through Jesus Christ, they also set the stage for the promised state of justice that is pure and sublime within Christ.[44]

What is known about Mary through the Christian faith not only corresponds to the essence of justice regarding attention to others and their due but also the activities that comprise just behavior. Ancient Judaism instilled the importance of action. Among the Mosaic law's 613 statutes, only a small number are restricted to interior dispositions of intellect[45] and will.[46] Hence, the law is essentially a collection of directives for actively implementing the ideals expressed by the terms *mišpāṭ* and *ṣedek*. Mary's

---

43. CCC §376.

44. Mary's concern for the poor and their needs is apparent in her *Magnificat*. Historically, we have reason to believe that this concern translated into almsgiving, a form of supplying another's due that justice demands. See Frederick B. Bird, "Comparative Study of the Work of Charity in Christianity and Judaism," *Journal of Religious Ethics* 10 (1982) 144–69. Examples of her attention to the poor are described in Brown, *Life of Mary*, 40, 48, 69, 70, 81–82, etc.

45. "The Jew is required to believe that God exists" (Exod 20:2; Deut 5:6); "It is forbidden to believe in the existence of any but the one God" (Exod 20:3); "The Jew is required . . . to acknowledge His unity" (Deut 6:4); "It is forbidden . . . to indulge in impure thoughts or sights" (Num 15:39); "You are commanded . . . to remember what . . . [the seven Canaanite nations and Amalek] did to Israel" (Deut 25:17); and "Do not . . . forget the evil done by Amalek" (Deut 25:19). *Encyclopaedia Judaica*, s.v. "Commandments, The 613."

46. "The Jew is required to . . . love . . . Him" (Deut 6:5); "You are required to . . . love your fellow as yourself" (Lev 19:18); "Do not . . . bear hatred in your heart" (Lev 19:17); "Do not . . . bear a grudge" (Lev 19:18); "You are commanded to love the proselyte" (Deut 10:19); "[Honor] your parents" (Exod 20:12); "Do not covet another man's possessions even if you are willing to pay for them" (Exod 20:17); "Even the desire [for another man's possessions] is forbidden" (Deut 5:18); and "You must not . . . love anyone who disseminates idolatry" (Deut 13:9). Ibid.

ethical formation was naturally shaped by these directives and ideals, but the available information about the moral dimensions of what she did and was done to her foreshadows justice in its later, classical sense. A survey of the remaining events in her life as conveyed by Scripture and Tradition provides the examples necessary to illustrate justice's three relational forms and the four specific activities that exceed the virtue's limits.

The legal, distributive, and commutative forms of justice are represented in both the Mosaic law and revelation about Mary, yet these divisions' representation in the law is noticeably uneven. Only two statutes in the entire law of Moses qualify as "legal"—namely, that one should "obey the Sanhedrin," and "[not] to rebel against the transmitters of the tradition."[47] Distributive and commutative rules abound. In Mary's life, each kind of justice is also present but in a much more numerically balanced way, if only because the information from which to draw examples is scarce.

Mary exhibits the sub-virtue of legal justice in her obedience to the Roman authorities' call for a census. The historical accuracy of the "census" in Luke's infancy narrative has been subject to much research and debate. Jesus was born before Herod the Great died in 4 BC, but Quirinius, the governor of Syria under whom the census was to have occurred, served only from AD 6–7. Negative solutions to this problem range from the first and second verses of Luke 2:1–2 being corrupt, to Luke fabricating the census as a literary device to get Jesus born in Bethlehem thereby fulfilling the prophecy that from Bethlehem "shall come a ruler who is to shepherd . . . Israel" (Matt 2:6; Mic 5:1).[48] Without claiming to resolve this controversy, a positive answer that respects the credibility of the text, human author, and Holy Spirit seems more probable, in that Luke is making broad, inaccurate generalizations by which he ingenuously modifies what was presumably "the payment of a poll-tax into a general census."[49] An underlying, historical event most likely does ground Mary's just obedience to public authority.

---

47. Ibid. These statutes are both drawn from Deut 17:11.

48. See "Appendix VII: The Census under Quirinius," in Brown, *Birth of the Messiah*, 547–56.

49. Jean Daniélou, *Infancy Narratives*, trans. Rosemary Sheed (New York: Herder and Herder, 1968), 67. See also Brown, *Life of Mary*, 98: "And then one day St. Joseph, while away from home on an errand, heard that a recently proclaimed Roman edict ordered all heads of families in Palestine to be registered on the tax lists in their native cities." See also ibid., 63.

See also *New Catholic Encyclopedia*, vol. 7, *His–Jub* (New York: McGraw-Hill, 1967), s.v. "Joseph, St.": "Although Joseph was apparently living in Nazareth at the time when he was betrothed to Mary (Luke 1:26–27), he was probably a native of Bethlehem, or at least

Regarding distributive justice, Mary never occupied a position of authority from which to distribute another's due, but based on evidence from Scripture, she was aware that leaders could fail in their obligations or become overtly unjust. Allusions to sins of omission are found in the Magnificat (Luke 1:46–55). After she praises God for what he is accomplishing through her (Luke 1:46–50), Mary then issues warnings to individuals entrusted with leading the community and yet have no fear of the Lord (v. 50). The "proud" (v. 51), "powerful" (v. 52), and "rich" (v. 53) all stand under God's judgment for ignoring the "lowly" and "hungry" (vv. 52–53). Mary later experienced a direct violation of distributive justice by Herod the Great shortly after she gave birth to her son. Herod was obsessively concerned with retaining power, and to protect his throne from what he perceived to be rival claimants within his own family, he had ordered the executions of three sons, a wife, and a mother-in-law. Upon hearing the reports that a "king of the Jews" had been born in Bethlehem (Matt 2:2), Herod further abused his office by murdering perhaps as many as twenty boys under the age of two from that town (Matt 2:16–18). The Holy Family, having received an angelic warning of the impending massacre, escaped that injustice only to endure another; they left Palestine for temporary exile in Egypt until news came of Herod's death (Matt 2:13–15).

Commutative justice is arguably this virtue's most common form, yet a lived example of it in Mary's life is the most difficult to find. This form of justice demands that fairness and transparency be present in every negotiated agreement made between individuals of equal status. In a way, Mary is almost disqualified for acts of commutative justice; given her perfect human nature, she has no true equal among human persons. Furthermore, Scripture is silent about any day-to-day dealings she had with her neighbors while raising Jesus in Nazareth. The only agreement mentioned in revelation with someone of equitable legal standing is that to marry Joseph. However, from the Church's Sacred Tradition, the belief has been passed down over the centuries that Mary and Joseph were celibate spouses, forgoing sexual intercourse for the sake of God and his salvific plan. An arrangement of this kind could not have possibly happened unless the spouses had mutually

---

owned property there. It was primarily for the sake of property taxes that he was obliged to be registered in the Roman census at Bethlehem."

agreed to it.[50] Although such marital arrangements are exceedingly rare,[51] they are the most intimate and personal instances of commutative justice.

> 50. In Brown, *Life of Mary*, 68–69, Mary and Joseph are said to have had the following conversation:
>> [Mary said:] "My lord and spouse, our Creator has manifested His mercy to us in choosing us to serve Him together. I consider myself more indebted to Him than all other creatures, for while meriting less, I have received from His hand more than they. As a child, therefore, being compelled by the force of this truth, which His divine light made known to me, I consecrated myself to God by a solemn vow of perpetual chastity in body and soul. I am His, and I acknowledge Him as my Spouse and Lord, with the firm resolve of preserving my chastity for Him. So I beseech you, my master, to help me in fulfilling this vow, while in all other things I will be your servant, working willingly for your well-being all my life. My dear spouse, yield to this resolution and make a similar one, in order that, offering ourselves as a sacrifice to God, He may accept us and bestow on us the eternal reward for which we hope."
>>
>> St. Joseph was overjoyed, and with true supernatural love he replied:
>> "My heart rejoices in hearing your welcome feelings in this matter. I have not told you my thoughts before knowing your own. But I also consider myself under greater obligation to the Lord than other men, for very early He called me by His enlightenment to love Him with an upright heart. And I want you to know that at the age of twelve I also made a promise to serve Him in perpetual chastity. So now I gladly ratify this vow, and in the presence of God I promise to help you as far as I can in serving Him and loving Him according to your desire. With His grace I will be your faithful servant and companion, and I beg you to accept my chaste love and to consider me your brother."
>
> 51. See Ralph McInerny, *Very Rich Hours of Jacques Maritain* (Notre Dame, IN: University of Notre Dame, 2003), 53–54. Perhaps the most notable contemporary example of a celibate marriage is that of Jacques and Raïssa Maritain. Jacques Maritain, the famous Catholic philosopher (Nov 8, 1882–Apr 28, 1973) married Raïssa (Sept 12, 1883–Nov 4, 1960) on Nov 26, 1904. Eight years later, both committed themselves to refraining from physical intimacy for the remainder of their married life.
>> On October 2, 1912, in the cathedral of Versailles, Jacques and Raïssa took a vow that profoundly altered their life together. They took a vow of chastity, renouncing sexual relations, in order the more surely to bind themselves to God. This extremely private decision was of course kept secret throughout their marriage, but as an old man, Jacques decided to reveal it in the privately circulated *Journal of Raïssa*. The reaction of friends prompted him to remove it from the public edition, but in his *Carnet de notes* he included a long chapter, written in 1962, on love and friendship.
>
> Jacques was thirty years old at the time, Raïssa even younger, and they took this step only after long counsel with Father Clérissac. By common agreement, "they had decided to renounce that which in marriage not only satisfies a profound need of the human being, flesh as well as spirit, but is legitimate and good in itself." Thus they also renounced the possibility of sons or daughters. The vow was not based on any contempt for nature, Jacques adds, but in their course toward the absolute and their desire to follow at any price, while remaining in the world, one of the counsels of the perfect life in order to clear the way for contemplation and union with God.

The second group of activities that characterize justice, and which Mary illustrates, are those acts that surpass the virtue's normal limits—namely, religion, *pietas*, *observantia*, and *affibilitas*. Returning to Mary's Jewish upbringing, Mosaic law lists many "religious" commandments but few of the rest. Four statutes apply to one's parents;[52] none, to Israel as a nation; one each, to the wise, a judge, and a king;[53] and only two that serve to lay the foundation for "friendliness."[54] Again, whether Mary is the agent of just action or its object, all four activities are represented in her life and doctrines.

Religion as the sub-virtue of justice that expresses obedience, sacrifice and gratitude to God permeates the way Mary lived. Her obedience is seen most starkly in the *fiat* by which she accepts the role assigned to her in God's plan of salvation. Mary's submission to God also entailed observing the law of Moses, which was still in force when Jesus was born, and thus she obeyed the commandments that "male children must be circumcised" (see Gen 17:10; Lev 12:3; Luke 2:21), "woman must also bring a sacrifice after childbirth" (Lev 12:5–8; Luke 2:22), and "the firstborn of man must be redeemed" (see Exod 13:13; 22:28; 34:20; Num 18:15; Luke 2:23–24).[55] Both Mary's purification and the Mosaic redeeming of her son took place at the temple in Jerusalem prior to her family's escape to Egypt. Many years after their return from Egypt and now with added personal significance, the Holy Family returned to Jerusalem to celebrate the Passover, after which Jesus stayed behind, went back to the temple and engaged the doctors of the law (Luke 2:41–50).

In the case of *pietas*, Scripture and Tradition say nothing about any loyal or loving behavior Mary might have exhibited toward her parents and nation, but these same sources do indicate that Christ bestowed upon her honor as his mother, which then lays the foundations for a similar response from ourselves. Nowhere in the Bible does Jesus address Mary as "mother." The closest the sacred texts get to expressing the due parental honor he owes her and Joseph is the passing remark that, after being retrieved from

---

52. "[Honor] your parents" (Exod 20:12); "Do not . . . strike a parent." (Exod 21:15); "Do not curse . . . a parent" (Exod 21:17); and "[Fear] your parents" (Lev 19:3). *Encyclopaedia Judaica*, s.v. "Commandments, The 613."

53. "Respect the wise" (Lev 19:32); "Do not curse a judge" (Exod 22:27); and "Do not curse . . . a ruler" (Exod 22:27). Ibid.

54. "You are required to . . . love your fellow as yourself" (Lev 19:18); and "You are commanded to love the proselyte" (Deut 10:19). Ibid.

55. Ibid.

the temple as a youth, Jesus "was obedient to them" (Luke 2:51). However, his perpetual filial reverence toward Mary can be inferred by the doctrine of her Assumption.

> The fact that Christ loved Mary and united her in His [salvific] mysteries makes it proper that the woman He had created sinless, that the virgin whom He had chosen for His mother, be, like Him, completely triumphant over death in her Assumption as He had triumphed over sin and death in His Resurrection.[56]

Proper and due regard for Mary as a mother has also become a just responsibility for Christians. When Jesus called Mary, "Woman," during the wedding in Cana (John 2:4) and at the foot of the Cross (John 19:26–27), he essentially identified her as "the new Eve, mother of all the living."[57] Thus, all of Christ's disciples can justly honor Mary as their spiritual mother, and even though salvation is attainable by focusing solely on the Savior, one can argue that, once a Christian recognizes Mary's supernatural maternal status and function, a duty exists under *pietas* to cultivate some degree of Marian devotion.

Awareness of Mary's standing and role in the salvation achieved by her son explains why Christians, since the Church's earliest centuries, assign to her various titles by which she becomes the recipient of *observantia*. The title *Theotókos*, "Mother of God," seems to cover both *pietas* and *observantia*, but the designation of "Queen" more accurately reflects the respect for an office that *observantia* entails. Mary's queenship derives from her motherhood. In the ancient Near East, where kings could have several wives, the only woman who enjoyed an uncontested relationship with the king was the king's mother. This arrangement is seen in the example of Bathsheba and her son, King Solomon, which establishes the precedent for both Mary's intercessory role and royal dignity.[58] Additionally, because Mary's Son is not merely a king but the King of Heaven and all that pertains to it, Marian titles that respectfully acknowledge her queenship can be particularized according to Christ's subjects and attributes. Traditional

---

56. *New Catholic Encyclopedia*, vol. 1, *A–Azt*, s.v. "Assumption of Mary."
See also Brown, *Life of Mary*, 254: "[Jesus said:] Eternal Father, it is right that to My Mother be given the reward of a Mother. And since during all her life and in all her works she was like to Me as it is possible for a creature to be, let her also be like to Me in glory and on the throne of Our Majesty."

57. Bruce Vawter, *Four Gospels: An Introduction* (Garden City, NY: Doubleday, 1967), 86; see also Gen 3:30; Rev 12:1–6.

58. See GS §62 and CCC §969 as referenced and explained in n35 of this chapter.

Marian litanies affirm that Mary, the Queen of Heaven, enjoys a subsidiary authority over the angels, patriarchs, prophets, apostles, martyrs, confessors, virgins, and the saints, as well as some elemental qualities of holiness—namely, love, mercy and peace.[59]

Affibilitas, or friendliness, by which just, human relationships are made pleasant and enjoyable, is displayed in Mary's Visitation to her cousin Elizabeth (Luke 1:39–56). Upon receiving word from Gabriel that Elizabeth was expecting (Luke 1:36–37), Mary "set out and went with haste" (Luke 1:39) to see her. Nothing in either the Jewish or modern understandings of justice required this journey. "Mary's decision was entirely personal"[60] and was likely motivated by a desire "to aid her kinswoman and to congratulate her on her good fortune . . . [and perhaps] to share her own good news with Elizabeth."[61] Conversations between Mary and Elizabeth about how they were contributing to God's plan of redemption would have intensified their personal bond and so resulted in a welcome sense of mutual support, each now knowing that they were not being asked by God to make their contributions as women alone.

Thus, in one way or another, Mary illustrates every one of justice's essential characteristics. Justice is defined as the willingness to focus attention on another and his due. Just attention to others is seen in God's treatment of Mary at the Annunciation, Mary's concern for the boy Jesus, who had returned to the temple, and her ongoing intercession for others begun at the wedding in Cana. As for the dues owed another, these obligations are established by either agreement or human nature. Mary's betrothal to Joseph is an example of the former, while her Immaculate Conception, perpetual sinlessness, and unending virginity guarantee that her human nature originates and remains in a permanent state of justice. The three activities upon which a just state of affairs depends are also represented. Obeying the call to a "census" is an expression of legal justice; the *Magnificat*, Massacre

---

59. See Judith A. Bauer, "Litany of the Blessed Virgin Mary" and "Litany of the Queenship of Mary," in *Essential Mary Handbook: A Summary of Beliefs, Practices, and Prayers* (Liguori, MO: Liguori, 1999), 138 and 142, respectively.

60. Michael O'Carroll, *Theotokos: A Theological Encyclopedia of the Blessed Virgin Mary* (1982; repr., Eugene, OR: Wipf & Stock, 2000), s.v. "Visitation, The." See also Brown, *Life of Mary*, 81: According to private revelations, "it was God's will that Mary should visit her [Elizabeth] in order that both mother and child might be sanctified by the presence of their Redeemer [in Mary's womb]," but this supernatural motive would remain outside the normal requirements of justice as a cardinal virtue.

61. Bauer, *Essential Mary Handbook*, 44.

of the Innocents, and Flight into Egypt all point to violations of distributive justice; and the vow between Mary and Joseph to remain celibate is a private form of commutative justice. Finally, conduct above and beyond the strict demands of justice covers the remaining important Marian doctrines and events in her life: *religio* by her *Fiat* and commitment to performing Jewish practices and rituals, especially the Passover; *pietas* as expressed in her son's obedience, the honor bestowed by him in having her assumed into Heaven, and the Marian devotion of Christians; *observantia* through the titles *Theotókos* and Queen; and *affibilitas* as the motive for the Visitation. In this comparison between justice and the doctrines or events that pertain to Mary, their correlation is quite thorough. Only one dimension of justice appears to not have a corresponding example. Even though the virtue of justice requires that one behave justly toward others, it also demands that one act justly toward oneself. No one Marian doctrine or incident can be summoned to illustrate this obligation, but in truth, her whole life is such an example. Her Son teaches the paradoxical lesson that, in order to truly possess and perfect oneself, one must give oneself away in love and service to others. In accord with this rule, Mary does in fact act justly towards herself by committing herself totally to the redemptive plan of God being accomplished through her son.

Conclusion

The fact that Mary reflects what justice means and entails can ease the pressing task of retrieving and communicating the truth about justice in Western societies. Without deliberate efforts to recall and implement our intellectual heritage with respect to justice, public policies regarding issues such as abortion, the death penalty, and homosexual relationships cannot be seen as the unjust realities they are. Killing the unborn and those convicted of serious crimes intentionally breaches the right to life due each person in accordance with their nature as human beings, while gay sex inherently puts both partners, who claim to genuinely love each other, at risk of injury, infection, sterilization, and death. In the effort to pass on this information, the person of Mary and the authoritative doctrines about her can be useful in making the abstract principles of justice more concrete. Admittedly, the usefulness of appeals to Mary will be more effective within Christian communities; among people of faith there will already be a presumed appreciation of God's existence, goodness, and action that will provide a canvas against which Mary can be shown to exemplify the qualities of this cardinal virtue.

Yet even Christians need to be on their guard against expecting too much from Mary when teaching justice. In the litanies composed in honor of Mary, she is never called "Queen of Justice." Reticence to employ this title probably emerges from two principles. First, what we know of Mary through Scripture and Tradition does not supply enough information to hold her up as a complete example of just behavior to follow in all circumstances, and secondly, the Church is careful to keep the act of judgment, essential for enacting justice, as Christ's sole prerogative. Thus Mary is best acknowledged to be the "Mirror of Justice," a title that more accurately describes Mary's relationship to justice found in the "Litany of the Blessed Virgin Mary."[62] Given the way that Marian doctrines and the events in Mary's life truly reflect what justice is, this title is entirely appropriate and so can remind teachers how these doctrines and events should be used when working to restore justice in the West.

---

62. Bauer, *Essential Mary Handbook,* 138. See also ibid., 141: In the "Litany of the Queenship of Mary," she is called the "Model of virtue."

5

The Marian Dimension of the Church and the Economic Order

NICHOLAS J. HEALY JR.

Mary is totally dependent on her Son and completely directed towards him by the impulse of her faith; and, at his side, she is the most perfect image of freedom and of the liberation of humanity and of the universe. It is to her as mother and model that the Church must look in order to understand in its completeness the meaning of her own mission.[1]

Perhaps the time has come for a new and deeper reflection on the nature of the economy and its purposes. What seems to be urgently needed is a reconsideration of the concept of "prosperity" itself, to prevent it from being enclosed in a narrow utilitarian perspective which leaves very little space for values such as solidarity. . . . An economy which takes no account of the ethical dimension and does not seek to serve the good of the person—of every person and the whole person—cannot really call itself an "economy."[2]

We are unaccustomed to the idea that Mary or Marian holiness might have something to do with the nature or logic of economic transactions and

---

1. Joseph Ratzinger, *Instruction on Christian Freedom and Liberation*, Congregation for the Doctrine of the Faith, Rome, March 22, 1986, §97.

2. John Paul II, "Message for the Celebration of the World Day of Peace," January 1, 2000.

economic institutions. One reason for the mutual estrangement of Mariology and economics is the ideology of classical liberalism, which conceives the realm of economics as neutral or empty of anthropology and ethics. Liberal economics deliberately avoids the question of the objective good of the person, replacing the idea of the good with the novel concept of efficiency or utility. Thus the science of economics is defined as "the social science concerned with the efficient use of scarce resources to achieve the maximum satisfaction of economic wants."[3] Or, in the words of Thomas Sowell, "the market as a mechanism for the allocation of scarce resources among alternative uses is one thing; what one chooses to do with the resulting wealth is another."[4]

The idea that economic choices and economic institutions such as the market are indifferent to the objective good of the person has been sharply challenged by Pope Benedict XVI in his encyclical letter *Caritas in Veritate*:

> The Church's social doctrine holds that authentically human social relationships of friendship, solidarity and reciprocity can also be conducted within economic activity, and not only outside it or "after" it. The economic sphere is neither ethically neutral, nor inherently inhuman and opposed to society. It is part and parcel of human activity and precisely because it is human, it must be structured and governed in an ethical manner.[5]
>
> Today we can say that economic life must be understood as a multi-layered phenomenon: in every one of these layers, to varying degrees and in ways specifically suited to each, the aspect of fraternal reciprocity must be present. In the global era, economic activity cannot prescind from gratuitousness, which fosters and disseminates solidarity and responsibility for justice and the common good among the different economic players.[6]

---

3. Campbell R. McConnell and Stanley L. Brue, *Economics: Principles, Problems, and Policies*, 15th ed. (Boston: McGraw-Hill, 2002), 3. In the nineteenth century, John Stuart Mill outlined a methodology that continues to shape the modern science of economics. In his essay "On the Definition of Political Economy," *London and Westminster Review* (1836) 1–29, Mill insists that economics is not concerned with "the whole conduct of man in society. It is concerned with him solely as a being who desires to possess wealth, and who is capable of judging the comparative efficacy of means for obtaining that end."

4. Thomas Sowell, *Basic Economics: A Common Sense Guide to the Economy*, 3rd ed. (New York: Basic, 2007), 519.

5. CV §36.

6. CV §38.

"The great challenge before us," writes Benedict, "is to demonstrate, in thinking and behavior . . . that in commercial relationships the principle of gratuitousness and the logic of gift as an expression of fraternity can and must find their place within normal economic activity."[7] There are two key premises underlying Pope Benedict's call for a more human economy marked by gift and reciprocity: (1) a renewed understanding of the human person as created in the image of the Triune God; and (2) an ecclesiology of communion whereby the world itself in all of its dimensions—political, economic, scientific, and cultural—is destined for union with God in Jesus Christ. Both of these premises converge on the figure of Mary, who is, in the words of Joseph Ratzinger (Pope Benedict XVI), "the personal concretization of the Church . . . the Church in person and as a person,"[8] and "the most perfect image of freedom and of the liberation of humanity and of the universe."[9] Through the simplicity of her faith and her total availability to God, Mary is both the archetype of the Church *and* the archetype of human action as such. Insofar as the mysteries of Mary's life exemplify and embody the logic of gift, the theology of Mary can help us (re)discover that the deepest meaning of economic life is communion.

It should be emphasized at the outset that the Church does not have technical competence in the economic or political order. Following the clear teaching of *Gaudium et spes*, Catholic social doctrine acknowledges the "legitimate autonomy of earthly affairs."[10] Or, in the words of John Paul II, "the Church has no models to present."[11] The Christian contribution to economics "is precisely her vision of the dignity of the person revealed in all its fullness in the mystery of the Incarnate Word."[12] Accordingly, my aim in this essay is to explore some of the implications of Mariology for the social order by way of reflecting on the relationship between Mariology, ecclesiology, and anthropology.

---

7. CV §36.

8. Joseph Ratzinger, "Thoughts on the Place of Marian Doctrine and Piety in Faith and Theology as a Whole," in *Mary: The Church at the Source* (San Francisco: Ignatius, 2005), 30.

9. Joseph Ratzinger, *Instruction on Christian Freedom and Liberation*, Congregation for the Doctrine of the Faith, Rome, March 22, 1986, §97.

10. GS §36.

11. John Paul II, *Centesimus Annus*, §43.

12. Ibid., 47.

The Marian Dimension of the Church

In his seminal essay, "Thoughts on the Place of Marian Doctrine and Piety in Faith and Theology as a Whole," Joseph Ratzinger provides the context for the famous debate concerning Mariology at the Second Vatican Council. The question presented to the Council Fathers was whether to issue a separate document on Mary or whether to include a treatment of the Virgin Mother within the Dogmatic Constitution on the Church, *Lumen Gentium*. Ratzinger claims that the contentious debate represented a clash between the two main spiritual movements that preceded the Council: the Marian movement and the liturgical movement, which joined forces with the biblical and ecumenical movements. For representatives of the Marian movement, with its slogan *per Mariam ad Jesum*, Mary's unique privileges and her role in salvation history warranted a separate Conciliar document. On the other side, "the liturgical movement stressed the theocentric character of Christian prayer, which is addressed 'through Christ to the Father' . . . [it] sought a piety governed strictly by the measure of the Bible or, at the most, of the ancient Church."[13] Accordingly, the liturgical movement sought to incorporate the treatise on Mary within the document on the Church. The outcome of the debate was the most closely divided vote of the Council: 1,114 bishops voted in favor of integrating Mary into *Lumen Gentium*, 1,074 bishops voted in favor of a separate schema.

Ratzinger argues that the Council Fathers were essentially correct to incorporate the teaching on Mary within *Lumen Gentium*. However, this decision often has been misinterpreted in roughly the following manner: finally, after centuries of exaggerated Marian piety coupled with papal definitions of the unique privileges of Mary, the Catholic Church has recognized that Mary is a recipient of grace and a member of the Church. In short, Mary's significance has been de-emphasized, and, as a result of this decision, there is new hope for ecumenical dialogue with Protestants. What is missing from this interpretation of Vatican II is an acknowledgment that the decision to include Mary within *Lumen Gentium* does not simply affect the status of Mariology; it also has profound implications for how we conceive the mystery of the Church. As Ratzinger argues, "Mariology, rightly understood, clarifies and deepens the concept of the Church."[14]

In *Lumen Gentium,* Mary is described as

---

13. Ratzinger, "Thoughts on the Place of Marian Doctrine," 20.
14. Ibid., 25.

a type of the Church in the order of faith, charity and perfect union with Christ. For in the mystery of the Church, which is itself rightly called mother and virgin, the Blessed Virgin stands out in eminent and singular fashion as exemplar both of virgin and mother. . . . In the most holy Virgin the Church has already reached that perfection whereby she is without spot or wrinkle.[15]

In *Mulieris Dignitatem*, John Paul II extends this traditional idea that Mary is a type or figure of the Church with a reflection on the relationship between the "Marian" and "Apostolic-Petrine" (hierarchical/clerical) dimensions of the Church:

> This Marian profile is also—even perhaps more so—fundamental and characteristic for the Church as is the apostolic and Petrine profile to which it is profoundly united. . . . The Marian dimension of the Church is antecedent to that of the Petrine, without being in any way divided from it or being less complementary. Mary Immaculate precedes all others, including obviously Peter himself and the apostles. This is so, not only because Peter and the apostles, being born of the human race under the burden of sin, form part of the Church which is 'holy from out of sinners,' but also because their triple function has no other purpose except to form the Church in line with the ideal of sanctity already programmed and prefigured in Mary.[16]

A simple thought experiment can help to clarify this teaching on the priority of the Marian over the Petrine dimension of the Church. When we hear or use this word "Church" or *ecclesia*, what image comes to mind? Many of us immediately think of an institution represented and led by the hierarchy; we think of priests, bishops, and especially the Pope. As founded by Christ, the Church is essentially hierarchical, but the visible hierarchy is not the basic form or innermost nature of the Church. The hierarchy of the Church is in service to something more fundamental—it exists for the sake of the holiness of the members of the Church and Mary is preeminent in the order of holiness:

> In the Church this communion of men with God, in the "love [that] never ends," is the purpose which governs everything in her that is a sacramental means, tied to this passing world. "[The Church's] structure is totally ordered to the holiness of Christ's

---

15. LG §63, 65.
16. John Paul II, *Mulieris Dignitatem*, §27n55.

members. And holiness is measured according to the 'great mystery' in which the Bride responds with the gift of love to the gift of the Bridegroom." Mary goes before us all in the holiness that is the Church's mystery as "the bride without spot or wrinkle." This is why the "Marian" dimension of the Church precedes the "Petrine."[17]

The Church is essentially a mystery of union. The source of this union is God himself communicating his life in Jesus Christ. God wants to gather creation into his life in such a way that it is truly one with him and yet truly other. Love does not want the other to disappear, but seeks an abiding relationship or covenant with the other. This mystery of creation redeemed—which requires a unity and difference of God and creation—is the Church. Through the mediation of the Holy Spirit, the Church is the body of Christ, the extension of his life in time. As a mystery of union, the Church is simultaneously the bride of Christ. The Church is both a divine gift *and* a human response that gives thanks and magnifies the generosity of God.

The ecclesial unity of God and creation is prefigured at the moment of the incarnation, when Mary consents to give birth to the Redeemer. As Aquinas teaches, Mary says "Yes" on behalf of all of humanity.[18] Her motherhood is not simply a biological fact, but a spiritual availability that is the innermost form of the faith of the Church. Mary's consent to God's plan of redemption attains its full maturity at the foot of the Cross when she becomes the mother of Christ in a new way by accepting his sacrifice and by receiving the beloved disciple as her own son (see John 19:26–27).

The "Worldly" Mission of the Church or the Vocation of the Laity

One of the most important but least explored implications of the priority of the Marian dimension of the Church concerns the vocation of the laity. In the years since the Second Vatican Council there has been a flood of books and articles emphasizing the crucial role of the laity in our time. While virtually everyone acknowledges the importance of the lay vocation, there remains some confusion and disagreement over two interrelated questions, "Who is a lay person?" and, "What is the specific contribution of the laity to the mission of the Church?"

17. CCC §773.
18. ST III, q. 30, art. 1.

In *Christifideles Laici*, John Paul II provides an initial answer to both of these questions:

> In giving a response to the question "Who are the lay faithful," the [Second Vatican] Council went beyond previous interpretations which were predominately negative. Instead it opened itself to a decidedly positive vision and displayed a basic intention of asserting *the full belonging of the lay faithful to the Church and to its mystery. At the same time it insisted on the unique character of their vocation*, which is in a special way to "seek the Kingdom of God by engaging in temporal affairs and ordering them according to the plan of God."[19]

The essential or specifying feature of the laity is their secular character. In the words of *Lumen Gentium*, the lay faithful "live in the world, that is, in every one of the secular professions and occupations . . . in the ordinary circumstances of family and social life."

The key issue provoked by this definition of the laity concerns the precise meaning of "secularity." Typically we think of the secular realm as opposed to, or at least in some sense "outside of," the reality of the Church. In his *Letter Concerning Toleration*, John Locke gives expression to one of the basic assumptions of Anglo-American culture:

> The Church itself is a thing absolutely separate and distinct from the Commonwealth. The Boundaries on both sides are fixed and immovable. He jumbles Heaven and earth together, the things most remote and opposite, who mixes these two Societies; which are in their Original, End, Business, and every thing, perfectly distinct, and infinitely different from each other.[20]

One of the consequences of this radical dualism between the ecclesial and the secular orders, is that what is specific to the laity falls completely outside of the mystery of the Church and her mission. This misconception of the nature of "secularity" is the reason why John Paul II writes that in order "to understand properly the lay faithful's position in the Church in a complete, adequate and specific manner it is necessary to come to *a deeper theological understanding of their secular character* in light of God's plan of salvation and in the context of the mystery of the Church."[21] In other words, it is not

---

19. CL §9; italics in original.
20. John Locke, *Letter Concerning Toleration*, ed. James H. Tully (Indianapolis: Hackett, 1983), 33.
21. CL §15.

sufficient simply to define the laity in terms of their secular character, what is needed above all is clarification of the meaning of "secularity" in the context of God's plan to recapitulate all things in Christ.[22] The lay vocation is an essential part of the mission of the Church precisely because the Church's mission extends to every human being, every aspect of human culture, and in a certain sense, the entire cosmos. The universality or catholicity of the Church's mission is grounded in the mystery of Christ in whom "all things hold together" (Col 1:18). "The Incarnation of God the Son," writes John Paul II, "signifies the taking up into unity with God not only of human nature, but in this human nature, in a sense, of everything that is 'flesh': the whole of humanity, the entire visible and material world."[23]

The question of "secularity" is further complicated by the Second Vatican Council's teaching regarding the "rightful autonomy of earthly affairs," which is closely connected to the positive meaning of secularity. As noted above, the laity have a specific vocation which consists in representing and embodying the mystery of the Church within the temporal or secular order. Stated differently, the laity are called to order the world from within to the kingdom of God; to bring the world (or the secular) into communion with the body of Christ. Given their secular character, the lay faithful have a particular responsibility for acknowledging the rightful autonomy of creation in all of its distinct aspects—culture, the economic and political orders, education, the sciences, etc. The challenge for a theology of the laity is to show how this task of ordering the world according to the plan of God confirms and deepens the "rightful autonomy" of the created order.

The bulk of this section of the essay has been devoted to examining a generally overlooked dimension of the theology of the laity. We have seen that properly understanding the lay vocation requires situating this calling within a more comprehensive theological account of secularity. Getting this account right, we have said, requires a double shift from a conventional approach to the Church-world relation. First, it is necessary to see that a Christian vision of secularity extends far beyond the usual claim that the secular world is neutral or an autonomous realm set over and against the mystery of the Church. To speak theologically about the secular is, in the

---

22. During a meeting with representatives of the French government in September of 2008, Pope Benedict XVI highlighted the need for a renewed understanding of secularity: "At this moment in history, when cultures continue to cross paths more frequently, I am firmly convinced that a new reflection on the true meaning and importance of secularity is now necessary."

23. *Dominum et Vivificantem*, §50.

first instance, to speak about the original ordering of creation, as this ordering is discernible to a reason formed by contemplation of the central Christian mysteries. The Church's mission embraces all of humanity and every aspect of culture because the world was created *in, through,* and *for* the Incarnate Logos.

Second, it is important to overcome a deeply entrenched dualism that would see the Church as a community of the saved set over against the world. The Church is destined to include the world or the secular order *precisely as secular*. In the words of Paul VI, the Church herself "has an authentic secular dimension, inherent to her inner nature and mission, which is deeply rooted in the mystery of the Word Incarnate, and which is realized in different forms through her members."[24] To be sure, the Church is not simply the conscience of the world, but is the bearer of a divine gift that comes from beyond the world. Nevertheless, this gift would not originate from the Christian God if it did not come in some sense from within the world at the same time. The creature's reception of the divine gift is included within it by reason of that very gift's generosity. Just here, we return to the first aspect of original ordering, which is most fully revealed precisely at the point within the world where the divine gift is received and transmitted with the greatest purity, which is to say, with the greatest freedom.

The foregoing discussion leads organically to the figure of Mary, whose immaculate humanity embodies the unity of purity and freedom. Thanks to this unity, Mary also represents and enacts the original ordering of creation. By the same token, Mariology is not simply a discourse about the extraordinary graces showered upon Mary of Nazareth. Mariology does, of course, dwell on the mysteries of her unique supernatural elevation. However, in doing so, it also presents Mary as the archetype of the Church. Here, too, Mary's role is not confined simply to the supernatural. Rather, she is the paradigm of the Church, not only as a supernatural reality, but also as the revelation of the original form of creation in its rightful autonomy. "Mariology," writes Joseph Ratzinger, "demonstrates that the doctrine of grace does not revoke creation; rather, it is the definite Yes to creation. In this way, Mariology guarantees the ontological independence of creation."[25] It is important to stress, however, that just as the divine gift proceeds at once from beyond the world and from within the world, the latter's rightful autonomy or ontological independence is fully realized only

---

24. Paul VI, "Talk to Members of the Secular Institutes," February 2, 1972.
25. Ratzinger, "Thoughts on the Place of Marian Doctrine," 31.

in the communion between the divine and the creaturely that this double procession implies.

Mariology, Anthropology, and the Economy of Communion

It may surprise the reader that we have spent so much time discussing topics such as ecclesiology and the theology of secularity in an essay that is supposed to be about economic practice. Why, he or she might ask impatiently, is all of this theological background necessary for talking about what Mary has to do with the business world? A first answer to this question is that the reader needs more than a collection of pointers about how to be a good Christian in the marketplace; he or she probably already knows a good deal about that, if only because there is already an abundance of literature on the subject. What the reader needs is help thinking through the sense in which his or her business life is an expression of the vocation of the laity. But giving such help requires situating the question of business in a rich theological context to which Mariology provides an important key. Admittedly, this goal tilts the focus of the essay more in the direction of theological principle than of detailed discussion of this or that aspect of economic life. Nevertheless, if what we have said about the anti-dualistic thrust of a genuine theology of secularity is true, then this concern for theological principles is intrinsic to the lay vocation itself, which involves *ordering* the realities of work and commercial transactions in light of God's plan to recapitulate all things in Christ (see Eph 1:10). For the upshot of our discussion so far is that Mary reveals what it means to be a human person creatively at work in the world. Given that the whole of concrete economic practice revolves around this issue, it follows that Mariology illuminates *every detail* of life in the business world. In a sense, the goal of this essay is simply to convince the reader of this basic point, in light of which he or she can then—as he or she is best placed to do—think through the details.

In conclusion, then, we would like to suggest three areas in which the Marian illumination of human nature and activity helps us (re)discover that the deepest meaning of economic life is communion: (1) creation as gift; (2) creaturely receptivity; and (3) participating in the good.

(1) The first words of Mary's *Magnificat*, "My soul doth magnify the Lord, and my spirit hath rejoiced in God, my Savior" (Luke 1:46-47), offer a window into her soul, not only at the time of the meeting with her

cousin Elizabeth, but throughout her entire life. Through these words, we see that Mary's basic attitude towards reality is one of acknowledgment that everything she is, does, and experiences is a gift from God that expresses his goodness. Mary does not simply thank, however; she enacts her gratitude by handing on the same gift that she herself has received. One need only think of the incarnation: She participates in giving to the world the supreme Gift, God's Only-Begotten Son.

Mary's never-failing acknowledgment that all is gift may seem to have little to do with the business world. We realize, however, that this is not the case if we reflect for a moment on a concept that is something of a common-place in much talk about entrepreneurship: "possibility." We often hear it said that a successful entrepreneur is one who has a special talent for seeing, and exploiting, possibilities ("opportunities" is another way of saying the same thing) that remain invisible to others. This understanding of entrepreneurship is true as far as it goes, but it risks inducing forgetfulness of the fact that what can be presupposes what is, and that what is—is *good*. But if it is good, it is because it is a gift. In other words, the intrinsic worth and desirability of reality is grounded in the generosity of God who gratuitously communicates something of his own goodness to creation.[26] This does not mean, of course, that the possible is unimportant. Rather, it means that the possible is not a substitute for, or a competitor with, the good of being, but is meant to be its fulfillment. Human work and human creativity always presuppose the givenness of reality. Precisely as a gift the material world is entrusted to human beings, who are called to exercise dominion over creation (see Gen 1:28). At its best, the entrepreneurial spirit involves a creative reception that both acknowledges and brings to fulfillment the original gift of creation. That human persons are entrusted with this fulfillment as a task is itself an overflow of the original gift on which the goodness of being depends. But if we want to know what this fulfillment looks like in the economic realm, our best clue is not the ruthless exploiter who measures possibility by the scope of his own violent projects, but the

---

26. Summing up and surpassing the wisdom of the ancient world, Thomas Aquinas writes: "Divine love did not allow him to 'remain in himself without fruit,' that is, without the production of creatures, but love 'moved him to operate' according to a most excellent mode of operation according as he produced all things in being. For from love of his goodness it proceeded that he willed to pour out and to communicate his goodness to others, insofar as it is possible, namely by way of similitude, and thus his goodness did not remain in him, but flowed out into others" (*Commentary on the De Divinis Nominibus of Pseudo-Dionysius the Areopagite*, ch. 4, lect. 9).

Marian soul, who understands that the beauty of the possible depends on working with the grain of reality and its goodness, rather than against it.

(2) The beauty of working with the grain of reality, rather than against it, leads us to a second feature of true humanity that is embodied by the person of Mary: receptivity. At first sight, receptivity seems to be antithetical to the virtues needed for the business world. But this impression dissipates when we consider that one of the most important settings in which receptivity is expressed is work. One way of thinking about work is to approach it in light of the actualization of latent possibilities discussed in the previous point. To work, especially when this involves what is commonly called "creativity," is to bring into the light of actuality some possibility that has, in one way or another, hitherto lain hidden. But, if the possible has lain hidden, it has done so in some already existing real thing: The possibility of the wall lies hidden, for example, in the stone. Of course, it is human beings who see—and realize—the possibility of the wall. Nevertheless, the possibility itself is not the product of our own decision; on the contrary, our decision (to make the wall) is and remains, in a central respect, the product of the possibility. By the same token, to see the possibility and to understand how to realize it depend not on aggressive self-assertion, but on attentive listening: receptivity. As John Paul II puts it in his encyclical on work, *Laborem Exercens*, "In every phase of the development of his work man comes up against the leading role of the gift made by 'nature,' that is to say, in the final analysis, by the Creator. At the beginning of man's work is the mystery of creation" (12). To be receptive in the way that Mary is receptive, is not to be inactive, like the man in the Parable who fearfully buried the talent with which he had been entrusted. Rather, it is to discover that it was not we who started our action, but that all of our initiative is a gift given by God; not just directly through his creative act, but also indirectly through the world he creates and the natures with which he populates it.

(3) This foregoing account of receptivity suggests that my action is sharing in God's action, and that it is God, not I myself, who initiates this sharing. The discussion of receptivity thus leads, by its own logic, to a third aspect of Marian anthropology that is particularly relevant for the business world, namely communion. For to be in communion ultimately means to share, not just profits, but, even more fundamentally, the action by which they are generated.

This notion of sharing action may seem abstruse, but the fact that the notion captures is quite familiar to all of us. Take the begetting of a child. A new human life is not the effect of the action of one of the parents without the other—that much is obvious—but neither does this life come into being because both parents perform individual actions simultaneously. The act of love from which the child proceeds is a single act in which both parents are engaged, each in his or her own way. The point we are making here is that such shared actions are much more common than we might at first think, indeed, that at its root, even economic exchange is an example of this type of act; each party of course contributes in a characteristic way, but the exchange itself exists only to the extent that the contributions, while distinct, have their meaning in relation to each other.

This is important because it helps identify the purpose of economic activity. This purpose is not, for example, the endless growth of the GNP, but shared action and in this shared action, shared life. Returning to the first of our three points, we could say that the purpose of economic life is communion in the good. Even better: economic life itself *is* communion in the good—or else it is not genuinely economic life. This would be the criterion for deciding whether the economy in which we currently live is authentically economic or not.

Each of the three dimensions of Marian anthropology which we have touched upon is meant to appeal to something already present in the experience of business people, especially of entrepreneurs. At the same time, each of the three points throws down a significant challenge to today's dominant understanding of the nature and purpose of economic life. This double focus is not an inconsistency, but expresses the conviction that the conventional ways of accounting for and organizing economy today are actually at odds with what is, or could be, best in the souls of entrepreneurs. For, we believe, it is not any of the regnant economic theories, with their implicit anthropologies, which provides entrepreneurs with the best framework for their self-understanding and self-correction, but rather, Mary of Nazareth and the anthropology of communion that she embodies. In this sense, it is fitting to conclude these reflections with the words of Chiara Lubich, the recently deceased foundress of the Focolare Movement in the Catholic Church, who did so much to promote what she called an "economics of communion":

> The Magna Carta of Christian social doctrine begins when Mary sings: "He has brought down the powerful from their thrones, and lifted up the lowly; he has filled the hungry with good things, and sent the rich away empty" ([Luke] 1:52–53). The Gospel contains

the highest and most radical revolution. And perhaps it is in God's plans that also in this era, deeply concerned as it is with social problems, Mary should be the one to lend a hand to all of us Christians in founding, strengthening, raising up and displaying to the world a new society in which the power of the Magnificat resounds.[27]

---

27. Chiara Lubich, *Essential Writings: Spirituality, Dialogue, Culture* (Hyde Park, NY: New City, 2007), 269.

6

Mary's Song

The Magnificat *(Luke 1:46–55)*

MARY CATHERINE NOLAN

The hungry he has filled with good things;
the rich he has sent away empty.[1]

Mary's Song, known as the *Magnificat*,[2] is sung each evening during Vespers, the liturgical evening prayer of the Roman Catholic Church. This psalm, attributed to Mary is found in the Gospel of Luke 1:46–55.[3] It is a song of praise, joy, and gratitude to God for the wondrous things that God has done in Mary and for all Israel.[4] The *Magnificat* also contains a

---

1. Luke 1:53 NAB.
2. The title *Magnificat* is taken from the first word of the Latin version of the song, which begins *Magnificat anima mea Domine*. There are many musical versions of the *Magnificat* in Latin.
3. The first two chapters of the Gospel of Luke contain what is known as the Infancy Narrative. Three canticles of the Infancy Narrative are part of the liturgical prayers of the Church. They are: *The Magnificat* (1:46–55), attributed to Mary, the mother of Jesus; *The Benedictus* (1:68–79), attributed to Zechariah, the father of John the Baptist and sung during Matins (morning prayer); *The Nunc Dimittis* (2:29–32), attributed to the prophet, Simeon and sung during Compline (night prayer).
4. The word *wondrous* is a translation of the Greek *megala* (Luke 1:49). It refers to great salvific works done through the power of God. It is used in Deuteronomy 10:21 and 11:7 to denote God's work in rescuing the Israelites from Egypt. The *wondrous* thing

strong social message. It speaks of God's benevolence to the lowly, to the hungry, poor, and powerless. God, mighty and holy, is totally faithful to the promises made to Mary's ancestors and comes to the aid of all people for all generations who seek God's help.

Set in the first chapter of his gospel, Mary's song contains the major themes that Luke will develop in the rest of his writing. Mary has taken a journey from her home in Nazareth of Galilee to her cousin Elizabeth's home in *Ein Karem*, near Jerusalem. Journey is a major theme of Luke. In his gospel, Jesus begins his ministry in Galilee and journeys to Jerusalem, where the temple, the center of Jewish worship, is located. In Luke's second book, the *Acts of the Apostles,* the Good News of salvation is brought from Jerusalem to the center of the political world, Rome. Luke's gospel has also been called, the "Gospel of the Poor." In the *Magnificat,* Mary has positioned herself among the poor and lowly. She praises God on their behalf.[5]

Themes of Mary's Song present truths of who God is and how God acts in history that can guide our lives today. These themes are: gratitude, joy, God's regard, God's wonders, God's holiness, God's mercy, God's might, God's action on behalf of justice, God's remembrance, Israel as servant, and the coming of the Reign of God.[6]

The *Magnificat* is set within the narrative of Mary's visit to her older cousin, Elizabeth, wife of the high priest, Zechariah. The barren Elizabeth has long prayed for a child but is beyond the age to bear children. After the annunciation to Mary by the Angel Gabriel that she has been chosen to bear the Messiah, Mary is informed of Elizabeth's pregnancy and told that "nothing is impossible with God"(Luke 1:26–37). Mary accepts her role in

---

God has done in Mary is the virginal conception of Jesus. For more information, refer to Aristide Serra, *E C'era la Madre di Gesu* (Milano: Edizioni Paoline, 1981), 219–23.

5. Raymond E. Brown, *Birth of the Messiah* (Garden City, NY: Doubleday, 1977), 350–55. Brown suggests that Luke may have found Mary's Song in canticles of the early Jewish-Christian community which he refers to as *anawim,* meaning "Poor Ones." See also James T. Forestell, "Old Testament Background of the Magnificat," *Marian Studies* 12 (1961) 225. In the prophecy of Zephaniah (3:12–15), the community of the afflicted and restored Jerusalem appeared under the literary figure of the Daughter of Sion. Forestell understands Mary in the role of Daughter of Sion praising God from the midst of the poor and lowly.

6. The *Reign of God* is the locus of God's action in overcoming all oppressive forces of evil and gathering people into a situation of love and just relationships. It is spatial as well as dynamic and is, therefore, also translated from the Greek, *basileia,* as the *Kingdom of God*. It is both present now in mystery and is coming in fullness at the end time. A good explanation of the coming of the *Reign of God* is given by Joachim Jeremias, *New Testament Theology,* trans. John Bowden (New York: Charles Scribner's Sons, 1971), 96–108.

God's plan with the words, "Behold, I am the servant of the Lord, be it done to me as you say (Luke 1:38)."[7] She then sets out in haste on a journey to visit her cousin. God's plan of salvation has been revealed to Mary and she acts on the information that Elizabeth is also involved.[8] It was an opportunity to share her experience with a trusted woman who would understand. This event is commonly referred to as the Visitation (Luke 1:39–56).

The meeting is one of joy and welcome. Elizabeth comes out to greet Mary and expresses joy in the visit exclaiming, "For as soon as I heard the sound of your greeting, the child in my womb leaped for joy" (Luke 1:44). The aged Elizabeth and the youthful Mary are both pregnant. As Mary and Elizabeth embrace, the Old Testament symbolized by Elizabeth intersects with the New Testament symbolized by Mary. Elizabeth is carrying a son, John the Baptizer, the last of the great prophets of Israel. Mary is carrying Jesus, the Promised One, in whom the reign of God is breaking into human history. Elizabeth is a wise and older married woman who welcomes and affirms the much younger and unmarried Mary with the words, "Blessed are you among women and blessed is the fruit of your womb. And why has this happened to me, that the mother of my Lord comes to me" (Luke 1:42–43). In response to Elizabeth's greeting, Mary's sings her *Magnificat* (Luke 1:46–55).

Mary's Song is similar in structure to the hymn psalms of the Old Testament. Like Hannah, the mother of Samuel, Mary praises God for the gift of a child.[9] Like Miriam, Deborah, and Judith, Mary sings out God's praises, but unlike these earlier women she is not rejoicing in the defeat of Israel's enemies but in God's graciousness in fulfilling the promise of a Savior.[10]

Luke is an elegant writer. In its poetic structure, the *Magnificat* can be divided into two strophes or sections of meaning. The first strophe, verses 46 to 50, gives the meaning of God's act for Mary. It is her personal praise and thanksgiving for God's graciousness to her. The second strophe,

---

7. Unless otherwise noted, New Testament quotes are taken from the NRSV.

8. Brown, *Birth of the Messiah*, 331. Mary's haste is a reflection of her obedience to the plan revealed to her by the angel, a plan that included the pregnancy of Elizabeth.

9. The Song of Hannah (1 Sam 2:1–10) contains themes of God's action on behalf of the poor and humble, similar to themes found in Mary's Song (Luke 1:46–55).

10. Miriam's Song (Exod 15:21) is sung after the safe passage of the Israelites through the Red Sea. Her song praises God for the miraculous defeat of Pharaoh's army. The Song of Deborah (Judg 5:2–31) praises God for victory against Canaanite oppressors. The Song of Judith (Jdt 16:1–17) is a song of praise and thanksgiving to God for victory over the Assyrians. The songs extol God's power to save those committed to him.

verses 51 to 55 gives the meaning of God's act for Israel as a whole.[11] It is common in the psalms that the psalmist speaks in the first person but is the collective voice of the whole people. In Old Testament thought the great marvels performed by God are always for the people even if they are done for an individual.

Mary's Song: First Strophe

⁴⁷ My soul magnifies the Lord,
and my spirit rejoices in God my Savior,
⁴⁸ For he has looked with favor on the lowliness
of his servant girl.
Surely, from now on all generations will call
me blessed.
⁴⁹ For the Mighty One has done great things for me,
and holy is his name.
⁵⁰ God's mercy is from generation to generation
for those who fear him.[12]

Joy and Gratitude

Joy permeates the encounter of Elizabeth and Mary. Elizabeth responds to Mary's arrival with delight saying, "Blessed are you among women, and blessed is the fruit of your womb! And why is this granted me that the mother of my Lord should come to me?"[13] In turn Mary's joy pours forth in praise of God as she sings, "My spirit rejoices in God my Savior." The cause of Mary's joy is God's intervention in human history. Her joy overflows in the experience of God's regard for her who is poor and of low estate.[14]

---

11. Robert C. Tannehill, "Magnificat as Poem," *Journal of Biblical Literature* 93 (1974) 263–68.

12. This translation is the author's, from the Greek text. See Mary Catherine Nolan, *Mary's Song: Living Her Timeless Message* (Notre Dame, IN: Ave Maria, 2001), 9.

13. Luke 1:42–43.

14. Poverty and lowliness as characteristic of the remnant people of Israel from whose midst the Messiah would come is explained by Albert Gelin, *Poor of Yahweh*, trans. Kathryn Sullivan (Collegeville, MN: Liturgical, 1964). Gelin considers Mary to be the perfect and living expression of the *anawim* ("poor and lowly"). He traces the development of

The reign of God is mysterious and full of surprises. Is joy to be found in a situation of poverty and lowliness? In the Bible, those who are poor and of low estate have a special claim upon God's beneficence.[15] Expectations of happiness being in prestige, power, and wealth are turned upside down by the values of God's reign. Joy is experienced in the recognition of God's dynamic presence in life, in relationships and in the forces that shape human history.

Joy accompanies inner freedom. Thomas Merton in an address to his community at Gethsemane told his fellow monks that our culture induces people to think and act in a way that leads to frustration because its predominant question is "Am I happy?"[16] According to Merton, the real question is not "Am I happy?" but "Am I free?" There is a deep longing in the human heart to experience freedom, which is the essence of personhood. Inner freedom can be limited by fear of losing something that society tells us is important such as wealth, power, and prestige. Mary has made a free choice to risk her life in participating in God's plan. She sings out her joy because God has regarded her lowliness. Perhaps it is the lowly who know the joy of inner freedom because they have no power, prestige, or riches to lose.[17]

Gratitude is Mary's attitude. Gratitude is a stance toward life that anchors one in the hope that whatever suffering the circumstances of life may inflict, all is meaningful in God's regard for his people. All has led to the present moment and life itself is good. An attitude of gratitude and the ability to express it is characteristic of a healthy spiritual life. The antithesis of gratitude is resentment. Resentment is crippling. It shrinks one's capacity to love. Entering into the inner disposition of joy and gratitude expressed by Mary is an antidote to the toxic attitude of resentment.

With joy and gratitude Mary expresses her own blessedness.[18] She sees beyond her own personal blessing of a child, however, to the blessing

---

the term *anawim* to include the notion of pious and faithful by the seventh century BC. See Zeph 3:12–15.

15. Luke 6:20: "Blessed are *you* poor, for the Kingdom of God is yours."

16. Thomas Merton was a monk of the Cistercian Abbey of Gethsemane and an author of many books. For an understanding of his thoughts on the spiritual life, consult his work *Contemplative Prayer* (New York: Image, 1990).

17. The conditions of wealth, power, and prestige are set forth in Mary's Song as being in opposition to God (1:51–53). Consider the beatitudes and woes proclaimed by Jesus in Luke 6:20–26. The Greek for "blessed," *makarios*, can also be translated "happy."

18. Blessing in the biblical sense is thought of as a communication of life from God.

that the child will be for all future generations. Happiness with who one is in one's own giftedness glorifies God. Happiness that others are gifted in ways that are different also glorifies God.[19] Just to be is a blessing and the ultimate goal of life's journey is transforming union with God.[20]

Holy is God's Name

Mary sings out her gratitude because God has regard for her in her lowliness. Another reason for her gratitude is that the Mighty One has done great things for her. Mary praises three attributes of God: God's might,[21] God's holiness, and God's mercy.

In Mary's day there was emphasis on the transcendence of God and out of reverence the proper name of God was avoided.[22] However, "Mighty One" was a way to speak of God. The word in the *Magnificat* used for the great things God has done for Mary is, in the original Greek, *megala*. It is the same word used to express the signs and wonders done by God in rescuing his people from oppression in Egypt and in establishing a covenant with them.[23] The wonderful things that God has done for Mary are to transform her by grace and to give her the child in whom a new covenant is established with God.

With life come vigor, strength, and success, which bring one peace of mind and peace with the world. See John L. McKenzie, *Dictionary of the Bible* (New York: Macmillan, 1965), s.v. "blessing."

19. Consider the exhortation of St. Paul to the Romans on the possession and use of God's gifts: Rom 12:3-8; 1 Cor 12:4-11.

20. Paul describes the transformation and glorification of the person who is in union with God after death in 1 Cor 15:35-58.

21. The title "Mighty One" is used of God in the Septuagint (LXX) version of Zeph 3:17 where God shows his might as a warrior in the battle to save Israel. "The Lord, your God, is in our midst, A Mighty One will save you." It is also found in Ps 89:9: "Mighty are you, O Lord, and your faithfulness surrounds you."

22 The personal name of God, *Yahweh*, is written in Hebrew texts with the consonants YHWH but is pronounced *Adonai*. An excellent explanation of the meaning and use of names for God found in the Hebrew Scriptures is given by John L. McKenzie in "Aspects of Old Testament Thought," in *New Jerome Biblical Commentary*, ed. Raymond Brown et al. (Englewood Cliffs, NJ: Prentice Hall, 1990), 77:5-20.

23. *Megala* is used in the LXX to express the "astonishing beyond understanding" works of God (Deut 10:21; 11:7; Judg 2:7; Jer 40:3). In the *Magnificat*, the "great things" are made more specific by vss. 51-54 and constitute the salvation event. See Douglas Jones, "Background and Character of the Lukan Psalms," *Journal of Theological Studies* 14 (1968) 23.

In her song, Mary calls God "Lord," "Savior," and "Holy One." Elsewhere in Luke's infancy narrative, he uses these same terms for Jesus, Mary's son. Jesus is called "Holy One" by the Angel Gabriel at the time of the Annunciation (Luke 1:35); "Lord" by Elizabeth as she greets Mary (Luke 1:43); and "Savior" by the angel who announces the birth of Jesus to the shepherds (Luke 2:11). The name, person, and works of God are thus inseparably linked by Luke with the name, person, and work of Jesus.

What does it mean to call God, Holy One? The holiness of God is frequently mentioned in the Hebrew Scriptures and there are many references to the "Holy Name of God"—for example, in Psalm 111:9, we read, "Holy and awesome is his name."[24] The holiness of God's name derives from God's covenant claim to be holy (Lev 11:44–45).[25] "Holy" expresses the transcendence of God. God is wholly apart, wholly other. Yet, the all-holy God is present to all people. The prophet Isaiah records God himself claiming to be high and exalted, living eternally, and whose name is the Holy One. Yet, God dwells, also, close to his people "to revive the spirits of the dejected, to revive the hearts of the crushed" (Isa 57:15). Mary, who positions herself among the lowly ones, experiences God's holiness. The Holy One dwells with and within her.

The word "holy" is commonly used of persons who reflect moral goodness, great love and total commitment to God. Thus, saints are deemed holy. Also considered holy are things set apart for worship of God. God, however, abides in mystery beyond that which our minds can comprehend. God, the Holy One, is other.[26] An experience of the otherness of God is an experience of God's holiness. In this experience one sees oneself in relation to God as creature to creator. God is! Creatures are because God chooses that they should be. Upon this truth hangs the mystery of creaturely existence, dependent and limited.

Prayer is a theme of Luke's gospel. Mary, a model of prayer, declares "Holy is God's Name" (Luke 1:49). When the disciples of Jesus ask him to teach them a prayer, Jesus tells them to pray, "Father in heaven, hallowed

---

24. Quotes from the Old Testament are taken from the NAB.

25. See Brown, *Birth of the Messiah*, 361. See also Elio Peretto, "Magnificat," in *Nuovo Dizionario Di Mariologia*, ed. Stefano DeFiores and Salvatore Meo (Milan: Edixioni Paoline, 1981), 859. Peretto parallels Ps 111:9 with Ps 103:1 and 145:2, and with "my name is holy" in Is 57:15; Ezek 20:39; 36:20–22; 39:25; and Mal 1:11. Jones adds Eccl 17:10; 47:10; Wis of Sol 10:20; and Tob 113:18 ("Background and Character," 23–24).

26. *Dictionary of the Bible*, s.v. "holy."

be your name" (Luke 11:2), thus establishing acknowledgement of God's holiness as integral to prayer.

One of the effects of the presence of the Holy One in a person's life is a genuine humility of heart. Humility is truth.[27] An experience of God's holiness and love leads one to see oneself in the light of who God is. This is truly humbling. Harsh judgment, prejudice, and intolerance of others will diminish as one comprehends one's own limitedness and failure to love as God loves. Humility of heart makes one loving and lovable.

Another effect of the presence of the Holy One in one's life is poverty of spirit.[28] God is considered the ultimate good and a yearning for God overrides the desire for material goods, position, power and prestige, and comfort. Security is found in God's love. There is no need to control others or use them for self-gratification. Poverty of spirit makes one trustworthy. The good of others is as desirable as one's own.

Patient endurance is also an effect of the presence of the Holy One in one's life. St. Paul calls this *long-suffering* when he lists the fruits of the Spirit (Gal 5:22). Long-suffering is the ability to make a commitment and continue in fidelity to God over the long haul, through many difficulties. It is the courage to remain faithful to prayer in times of spiritual aridity. To endure suffering in order to achieve a higher good requires spiritual stamina.

Poverty of spirit, humility of heart and long-suffering characterized Mary's life. She is the exemplar of one who has been transformed by the Spirit and in whom the Holy One dwells.[29]

God's Mercy

In the first strophe of her song, Mary refers to God's mercy as being forever. As a woman of the covenant she understands God's mercy as being

---

27. A good explanation of humility as truth is given by Albert Nolan in *Jesus Today: A Spirituality of Radical Freedom* (Maryknoll, NY: Orbis, 2006), 120.

28. For an in-depth discussion of poverty of spirit consult the small classic by Johannes Baptiste Metz, *Poverty of Spirit* (Mahwah, NJ: Paulist, 1998).

29. At the time of the Annunciation (Luke 1:28), Mary is greeted by the Angel Gabriel as *Kecharitomene* which means "one full of grace" or "one already transformed by grace." Mary has received the Holy Spirit (1:35). St. Paul lists the fruits of the Spirit as love, joy, peace, patience, kindness, generosity, faithfulness, gentleness, and self-control (Gal 5:22–23).

a merciful love, totally faithful and enduring.[30] The Hebrew word for this merciful love is *hesed*. *Hesed* is God's covenant love, which extends to those who fear him—that is, those who have a religious and filial attitude of respect for God.[31] Christians are covenanted to God by baptism. Whatever one's own weaknesses and failings, God is eternally faithful. God's righteousness is in his will to save. One can trust it. In wisdom literature, "fear of the Lord" is equated with knowledge and insight (Prov 1:29; 2:5). It is also depicted as the beginning of wisdom (Prov 9:10; Ps 111:10). Gelin equates "those who fear Yahweh" with the *anawim*.[32] The thought of fearing God is frequent in Luke both in the third Gospel and in Acts.[33]

Wisdom is the highest of the gifts of the Holy Spirit. It is the most important stage in the spiritual journey. Once one has entered a serious prayer relationship with God, one is led by the Spirit through stages to wisdom which is a contemplative experience of God. Mary certainly trusted God's love for her. The angel Gabriel had greeted her with the words, "Greetings favored one! The Lord is with you" (Luke 1:28). Mary had already been transformed by grace. She was far advanced on her spiritual journey. In accepting her role as mother of the Messiah, Mary showed profound understanding and trust in God's mercy. She is the model in listening to the Spirit and saying "yes" to wherever God led her.

Consideration of God's mercy sustains hope that God who is absolutely faithful to his promises is acting in the events of one's life and in the events of history. Some of these events are dark indeed. In Elie Wiesel's story, *Night*, an old rabbi cries out in anguish in the midst of the Nazi death camp, "Where is the divine mercy? Where is God?"[34] This question is haunting as one observes the pain of those in the death camp hanging between hope

---

30. As a Jewish woman, Mary is in a special relationship with God. The relationship of God with the Jewish people was established in a solemn ritual agreement known as the covenant. It is described in Exod 19:3-6. McKenzie explains "covenant" in *Dictionary of the Bible*, 153-57. See also *New Jerome Biblical Commentary*, 77:74-94.

31. *Hesed* is God's totally faithful, enduring, merciful love. It is the dominating motive of God's acts. See McKenzie, *New Jerome Biblical Commentary*, 77:95-98.

32. Albert Gelin, *Poor of Yahweh* (Collegeville, MN: Liturgical, 1964), 96. See Ps 21:26-27; 33:18.

33. I. Howard Marshall, *Gospel of Luke: A Commentary on the Greek Text* (Grand Rapids: Eerdmans, 1978), 83. Luke uses the phrase in 12:5; 18:2, 4; 23:40; Acts 10:2, 22, 35; 13:16, 26.

34. Elie Wiesel, *Night* (New York: Bantam, 1986), 73.

and despair. One is led to ponder the deep questions of human existence and to take on the responsibility as agents of God's mercy to others.

"God's mercy is from generation to generation" (Luke 1:50), Mary sings out. Through many centuries of Christian history each generation has mediated God's loving kindness and fidelity to the next generation. Through difficulties and adversities many have kept the faith of their own ancestors and passed on this faith. Mary, transformed by God's gracious love, has been invoked throughout the ages as an agent of God's mercy.

Mary's Song: Second Strophe

> 51 God has shown might with his arm;
> he has confused the arrogant in the conceit of
> of their hearts.
> 52 God has pulled down the powerful from their thrones,
> and lifted up the lowly;
> 53 God has filled the hungry with good things,
> and the rich he has sent away empty.
> 54 God has come to the help of his servant Israel,
> remembering his mercy,
> 55 According to the promise he made to our ancestors,
> to Abraham and to his descendants forever.[35]

The first part of the *Magnificat* (vv. 46–50) expresses Mary's faith in God, her savior, and her response of joy and gratitude for the wondrous things that God has done in her. In the second part (vv. 51–55), we see that Mary's faith is the faith of Israel. Luke puts this canticle on Mary's lips as sung not only for herself as an individual but for the people who yearn and hope for the promise of a Messiah to be fulfilled. Mary has the prophetic vision to foresee the reversal of a situation of social sin (rooted in personal sin) that will be part of the coming reign of God, as she is positioned in the midst of the lowly ones, in Hebrew the *anawim*. This reversal is consistent with the way that God has dealt with his people in the past, especially in the Exodus.[36]

---

35. This translation is the author's. See Nolan, *Mary's Song*, 9.

36. Exod 3:16–17. God expresses concern for the plight of the Israelites in Egypt and instructs Moses to lead them out of slavery and into a land, *flowing with milk and honey*. Exod 19–20 recounts the establishment of the Covenant at Mount Sinai. The Ten

God's Mighty Arm

In verses 51–53 of the *Magnificat*, the forces for those opposed to God, God's clients, Mary, and the *anawim*, are set forth. They are three human *greatnesses* or *self-sufficiencies* that lie at the root of social sin: pride (v. 51), power (v. 52), and riches (v. 53).[37] In a great eschatological act, God is bringing about the reversal of an unjust social situation caused by sinful relationships. In the surprising reign of God our expectations of what makes for happiness are turned upside down. Nothing is impossible to God and all are being drawn into a situation of right relationships that will assure a social situation characterized by peace, justice, and love. The six verbs used for God's actions in verses 51–53 of the original Greek text are in the aorist tense, which can be used for past actions projected into the future. Lagrange's explanation is that the ordinary way God has acted in the past is confirmed by what he is doing in Mary now. It is the time of the in-breaking of the reign of God.[38] This is happening through the power of God's mighty arm (Luke 1:51).[39]

The image of God showing might with his arm is a military one. It is the strong arm of the warrior that draws the bow and wields the sword. The mighty arm of God is a metaphor for God's absolute power over all things. In the exodus, an oppressed people were led out of Egypt by God with "strong hand and outstretched arm" (Deut 4:34).[40] The angel Gabriel has told Mary not to be afraid. She has been told that the power of the Most High will overshadow her (Luke 1:30–35). Mary invokes the image of the warrior God who has called her to be part of the unfolding plan of salvation for all people. She trusts that she dwells overshadowed by God's protective power. Mary's example encourages those who face difficulties and even persecution when working for justice to trust that they are overshadowed by the love and protective power of the Mighty One.[41]

Commandments given there contain instructions on how the people are to relate to God and to each other justly. Injustice in a social situation was considered a breaking of the covenant.

37. Gelin, *Poor of Yahweh*, 97.

38. Marie Joseph LaGrange, *Évangile selon Saint Luc*, Études bibliques (Paris: Librairie Lecoffre, 1948).

39. Attributing a mighty arm to God is "anthropomorphism"—i.e., endowing God who is pure spirit with human traits.

40. See also Deut 7:19; 11:2; Ps 98:1; Jer 21:5; 32:21; Ezek 20:33; 34.

41. Consider Ps 55:23: "Cast your care upon the LORD, who will support you; God will never allow the righteous one to stumble" (NAB). See also Ps 91.

God's Action on Behalf of Justice

Who are the arrogant who are being confused in the conceit of their hearts (Luke 1:51)—that is, in the inner core of their being? In Old Testament antecedents to this verse it is the enemies of Israel who are being scattered by God's arm.[42] In the psalms, the enemies of the righteous ones are called proud, arrogant, or insolent.[43] In the first letter of Peter we read, "God opposes the proud, but gives grace to the humble." (1 Pet 5:5; see also Prov 3:34).

Who are the powerful who are being pulled down from thrones (Luke 1:52)?[44] Are they cruel tyrants who use their authority to enhance themselves and oppress their subjects? We have certainly seen such tyrants in our day. Cruel dictators such as Hitler, Stalin, Saddam Hussein, Quadaffi, and others have been brought down. Yet, unless justice flourishes, others will arise. Are they those who use the power of their authority over others to intimidate and oppress them? Power is dangerous. It is like poison that needs to be spread around in order to dilute it and make it less toxic. Power given to authority is necessary to assure the welfare of others. If not used for the common good it deteriorates into oppressive behavior. Jesus' attitude toward power is put forth by Luke in the account of Jesus' temptation in the desert (Luke 4:1–13). After rejecting self-aggrandizing power, Jesus returns from the desert "filled with the power of the Spirit" (Luke 4:14) to be engaged in his mission of preaching with authority, healing, and forgiving sins.

Who are the rich who are being sent away empty? The well-fed, well-housed, well-clothed, and well-educated of today might feel a pang of uneasiness pondering these questions. Why are there so many poor and hungry in the world today? What are the structures of society that keep people in poverty or make food production and distribution inadequate for all? Surely, God is munificent and generous in giving blessings to all.[45]

---

42. See Num 10:35; Pss 68:1; 89:11.

43. See Pss 17:10; 31:19, 24; 35:12; 59:13; 73:6, etc. God is against pride (Prov 3:34; Isa 2:12; 13:11).

44. Peretto regards the Wisdom of Ben Sirach as a reliable antecedent to v. 52, in "Magnificat," 860. See Sir 10:14: "The thrones of the arrogant God overturns and establishes the lowly in their stead."

45. "Consider the ravens: they neither sow nor reap, they have neither storehouse nor barn, and yet God feeds them. Of how much more value are you than the birds!" (Luke 12:24).

Jesus taught his disciples to pray to a loving Father, "Give us this day our daily bread" (Luke 11:3).[46] Is it those driven by greed who are being addressed here?[47] What is to be thought of God's action against the arrogant, the oppressive, and the greedy?

In contrast to God's action against oppressors is God's action for the oppressed. The powerless are lifted up (Luke 1:52). The hungry are fed (Luke 1:53). God levels the playing field so to speak. All are being called into God's reign. God's loving mercy is being poured out on the fearing ones, the powerless and the poor who are in right covenant relationship with God. The proud, powerful, and greedy cannot be in right relationship with God until they are in a right relationship of justice with the humble, powerless, and poor.

The great eschatological reversal of fortunes, which is a characteristic of the reign of God, begins with the humbling of the proud whose attitude brings them in conflict with the values of the "kingdom." Within the "kingdom" the whole community is blessed by the humble attitude that a person holds toward God in as much as this humility finds its expression in one's attitude toward others. There is an echo here of the "blessings" and "woes" that Luke will set forth in the important "discourse on the plain" (Luke 6:20–24).[48]

God's action in lowering the proud and exalting the humble, dethroning the powerful and empowering the lowly, feeding the hungry and sending the rich away empty is dramatic. It appeals to a sense of distributive justice.[49] The central theme of the preaching of Jesus in the gospel of Luke is the coming of the reign of God. The *Magnificat* is characterized by a strong conviction that God is, indeed, at work bringing about the final victory over all forces that oppress and diminish his people. A sign of the presence of the reign of God is a political and social situation of just relationships in

---

46. According to McKenzie, *bread* in the Bible often signifies food in general, as in the Our Father. To eat bread in the kingdom of God was to partake of the messianic banquet, as in Luke 14:15. Alluding to the Eucharist, Jesus called himself the true bread, the living bread, the bread which comes down from heaven (John 6:34–59). *Dictionary of the Bible*, s.v. "bread."

47. E.g., those who amass wealth by defrauding others.

48. Luke Timothy Johnson, "Mary Visits Elizabeth (1:39–56)," in *Gospel of Luke*, vol. 3, ed. Daniel J. Harrington, Sacra Pagina 3 (Collegeville, MN: Liturgical, 1991), 42n51. The pattern of reversal is fundamental to Luke's narrative.

49. Distributive justice refers to fairness in the giving of judgments without regard to social status or the allocation of resources according to needs.

keeping with God's will, where there is no hunger among the many because of the greed of a few; there is no abasement of the many because of the pride of a few; and, there is no oppression by the powerful.

The term for lowly used in verse 52 is *tapeinos* in Greek. It carries the concept of one who is small, lowly, bowed down, insignificant; in Greek usage, a negative, even contemptuous term. But *tapeinos* is a translation of the Hebrew, *anawim*, which includes a wide range of people who are poor and oppressed whether in material ways or in spirit. In the Scriptures, the oppression might be caused by foreign political or military power (Jdt 16:11; 1 Macc) or by those who are rich and mighty (Amos 2:7; Isa 58:4). Albert Gelin has traced the term through all its scriptural meanings. The vocabulary of poverty evolved and was eventually transposed to a spiritual plane. What began as denoting a sociological reality came to have a religious meaning, expressing a right attitude of soul in relationship to God.[50]

In the seventh century BCE, the prophet Zephaniah described the coming "Day of the Lord" as a day of judgment, desolation, and destruction for the rich, proud, and powerful. The humble were instructed to seek justice and take shelter in the Lord (Zeph 2:3). Those opposed to God were to be removed from the midst of the people (Zeph 3:11). But a remnant people, humble and lowly, would be left in Jerusalem (Zeph 3:12–13). It is these remnant people, called to seek justice and humility—that is, to be faithful to the covenant—that Zephaniah personifies as "daughter of Zion" (Zeph 3:14). These then are the *tapeinos* with whom Mary identifies in the *Magnificat* when she refers to her lowliness, *tapinosin* in Greek (Luke 1:48).[51]

The description of the great eschatological reversal continues in verses 52 and 53. The antitheses between the "fearing ones" (1:50) and the "proud ones" (1:51) is expanded by two antithetical verses. The lowly and the hungry are equated with those who fear the Lord, while the proud are among the powerful and the rich.[52] Antithetical verbs, "pulled down" and "lifted

---

50. Gelin, *Poor of Yahweh*, 26: "The poor one became God's client. Poverty meant the ability to welcome God, an openness to God, a willingness to be used by God."

51. Serra remarks that Mary was nurtured in the faith of her people and embraced the redemption longed for by every genuine Israelite. As "Daughter of Zion" she is bound up with the lot of her people and involved within the tension between the poor and the proud ones" (*E C'era la Madre di Gesu*, 174).

52. Forestell, "Old Testament," 216. Taken together these verses express the piety of the *anawim*. There is a close parallel between vv. 52–53 of the *Magnificat* and the *Song of Hannah* in 1 Sam 2:7–8. See also Ps 113:7–8.

up" (1:52) and "filled" and "sent away empty" (1:53), dramatically depict God's action for and against the two opposing groups.

The psalms are filled with references to spiritual poverty (see Psalms 34; 147). Gelin holds that the term *anawim* is used as a key word to the whole religion of the Old Testament and relates it to the first beatitude, "Blessed are you who are poor, for yours is the kingdom of God" (Luke 6:20).[53]

Raymond Brown asserts that the poverty and hunger of the oppressed in the *Magnificat* are primarily spiritual, yet he points out that the first followers of Jesus were Galileans who knew the oppression of absentee ownership of estates (Luke 20:9), foreign occupation, and the resulting taxation (Acts 5:37). The early Christian Church at Jerusalem knew real poverty. But for the poor, the good news of Mary's song is that wealth, power, and fame are not real values in God's reign and the ultimately blessed are not the famous, the mighty, and the rich.[54] Those who embrace the gospel are called to cooperate with God in bringing about a just social situation in distribution of power and resources. This does not imply a revolution where power and wealth are seized from one group and given to another, creating a new group of oppressed.

Liberation in the *Magnificat* is a religious liberation from a sinful condition characterized by an arrogant attitude toward others, a quest for power over others, and a greed for riches at any cost. Social liberation follows from this. Mary calls herself lowly. She is in solidarity with all who are oppressed. Her *yes* to God puts her in solidarity with God's salvific action. Mary's mission is to bear the Messiah who will bring about God's reign of justice among all peoples. Entering into Mary's interior disposition as evidenced from her song puts one, also, into a stance of cooperation with God's salvific action. To be in right covenant relationship with God one must be in right covenant relationship with others. Today, we are becoming more and more conscious of the need to be in right relationship with all of God's creation, that is, caring for the earth and all its creatures.

---

53. Gelin, *Poor of Yahweh*, 36.

54. Brown, *Birth of the Messiah*, 363–64. "Luke's peculiar and emphatic castigation of wealth (6:24–26; 12:19–20; 16:25; 21:1–4) points to the existence of many poor in the communities to be served by Luke's Gospel" (364).

A Servant Theme

In the final verses of the *Magnificat* (1:54-55), the principal reasons for praise are summarized into one great fact: the salvation event is taking place. Mary is the collective voice of the early Christian *anawim* who see themselves as the faithful remnant of Israel.[55] Just as God's help has been given to Mary, who calls herself *servant girl* (1:48),[56] God's help is extended to all of Israel, who is called *Servant* in the sense of a child servant (1:54).[57] Like a father or mother guides the footsteps of a child, God reaches God's people.

There is an allusion here to the Servant of the LORD in the prophecy of Isaiah. Israel is called *my Servant* by God (Isa 41:8).[58] The mission of the Servant is described in four passages, known as the Servant Songs (Isa 42:1-4; 49:1-7; 50:4-11; 52:13-53).[59] Here a prophetic and suffering figure of a Messiah appears. He is a future person in whom Israel's mission to the world will be accomplished.[60] The early Christians saw Jesus as servant. Jesus told his disciples, "I am in your midst as one who serves" (Luke 24:27).[61]

The coming of Mary's child, the child of promise, is a central event in history. It was not an event that instantaneously cured all ills of the human condition or destroyed all forces of evil in the world. It was the beginning of the end time when the reign of God would come in fullness and all evil would be conquered. The early Christian community of disciples, poor and persecuted, looked forward in hope and longing for this end time, known as the *parousia*, when Jesus would return and gather all into the reign of joy and gladness in God's kingdom. But as time passed they understood that their time was an in-between time, the time between the first and second

---

55. Ibid.

56. The term "servant girl" used by Mary in referring to herself is, in the Greek original, *doules* (Luke 1:48).

57. The Greek word for servant used in Luke 1:54 is *paidos*, which refers to a child servant.

58. "You whom I have called my servant (Greek: *pais mou*), whom I have chosen and will not cast off" (Isa 41:8).

59. The Servant Songs are found in Deutero-Isaiah 42:1-4; 49:1-7; 50:4-11; 52:13—53:12. The identification of the Servant of the Lord with Israel is discussed by McKenzie in *Dictionary of the Bible*, s.v. "servant of the Lord."

60. Forestell, "Old Testament," 221.

61. *Dictionary of the Bible*, s.v. "servant of the Lord": "The identification of Jesus with the Servant is best attributed to Jesus himself."

coming of Jesus. This was a time of mission, a time to be involved in spreading the good news, of carrying on the mission of Jesus.[62]

Mary, who had been transformed by grace, understood herself to be a lowly servant girl. She journeyed to bring the presence of her son to her cousin Elizabeth. Mary is a model of service for us. We live in in-between times and bear within ourselves the presence of the Holy Spirit. Bringing this presence to others in loving service is a holy work.

God's Remembering

There is a connection between God's coming to the help of his servant Israel and God's remembering (Luke 1:54). What God remembers is *hesed*, God's merciful, faithful, and enduring covenant love.[63] In the *Magnificat*, verse 48, Mary calls herself servant. This parallels verse 53 where Israel is called servant. Mary's claim that God's *hesed* is forever (Luke 1:50) parallels God's remembering *hesed* (Luke 1:54). God remembers and fulfills the promises made to Abraham and to his descendents forever (Luke 1:55).

The final verse of the *Magnificat* brings us back to the beginning of the great drama of salvation. The promise made to Abraham was sealed by a covenant of which there are two accounts in Genesis (Gen 15:1–21; 17:14). The promise was that he should have many descendants and they would have a land of their own. All that was asked of Abraham under this covenant was faith in God. Abraham appears frequently in Luke. He is the spiritual father of Israel (Luke 1:73; 3:8; 16:24). The thought of Luke seems to be that the greedy, the arrogant, and the oppressively powerful, or those opposed to God's will for his people, have been eliminated from this spiritual community (Luke 1:51–54). But for the true descendants of Abraham, the faithful remnant people, God's mercy is forever.[64]

---

62. "The Second Coming of Jesus," also known as the "Day of the Lord" or the "*Parousia*," is described in several letters of Paul. See especially 1 Cor 15:23–28; 1 Thess 2:19; 3:13; 4:15–17; 2 Thess 1:7–2:2; 2 Pet 3:4, 12; and 1 John 28. The Christians are exhorted to strive for holiness while waiting patiently for the coming of the Lord.

63. There is no single English word to translate the Hebrew *hesed*. In the LXX the Greek *eleos* (mercy) is used. In the Latin Vulgate translation the Latin word is *misericordia* (mercy). It is often translated *loving kindness*. For the many shades of meaning, see *Dictionary of the Bible*, s.v. "mercy." The *hesed* of God is associated with the covenant and with God's will to save.

64. Marshall, *Gospel of Luke*, 85.

The covenant between God and the people, sealed on Sinai (Exod 19:1—24:18), required more than faith. It required observance of the law. The law dictated justice in human relations. Oppression of the poor and powerless was considered a breaking of the law. In verse 49 of her song, Mary has spoken of the might of God's arm. The image is reminiscent of the Exodus and the covenant sealed on Sinai. Though people might break their agreement under the covenant, God is totally faithful. God remembers mercy.

At the time of the annunciation (Luke 1:31–33), Mary is told by Gabriel that the Lord God will give to her son the throne of David, he will rule over the house Jacob forever and his kingdom will never end. The Davidic covenant is recalled here. God promised David that his house would endure forever (2 Sam 7:16). These words of Gabriel, along with the allusion to the Servant of the Lord in the *Magnificat*, establish the messianic role of Mary's son.[65]

Memory is a powerful thing. Memories move one not only to emotions of joy and gratitude but, also, to emotions of anger and sadness. Memories can lead to healthy attitudes of love and forgiveness toward others. Memories may also lead to dangerous attitudes of crippling anger and a desire for revenge. The Lord's Prayer (Luke 11:2–4) contains a petition for God's forgiveness, asking God to forgive as we forgive others. Forgiveness is healing. Remembrances of grievances and injustices have led to grudges or worse, to devastating violence. God remembers *hesed*. Remembering God's *hesed* leads to gratitude and healing. People who have received God's loving kindness are invited to extend mercy, kindness, and forgiveness to others.

Remembrance of the loving kindness and mercy of God lived in the national memory of Mary's people.[66] When national memory is filled not with memories of God's goodness but with historical grievances, there cannot be peace. Our age has seen violence, devastation, and genocide when one group of people is motivated by past grievances to wreak vengeance upon another. History has taught us that violence begets violence, and once a war has begun it is difficult to end.

The message of Mary's *Magnificat* is that God is acting in our lives and in the events of history to bring about the reign of justice, the reign

---

65. The NRSV reads: "And forgive us our sins, for we ourselves forgive everyone indebted to us."

66. Each year when Passover is celebrated, the Jewish people remember their liberation from slavery in Egypt. Ritual reenactment of a past event brings that event into the present.

of right relationships, and therefore the reign of peace. Those in solidarity with God's action actively resist evil in a way that does not perpetrate more evil. Nonviolent resistance to injustice flows from a spirituality that trusts God is at work bringing about the ultimate victory over all injustice and oppression.

The Coming of the Reign of God

Mary's song has echoed over two thousand years with a message of hope. The reign of God is in our midst now wherever God is acting to bring about a situation of peace and justice. Each evening in churches, monasteries, and convents where the Liturgical Hour of Vespers is celebrated, the *Magnificat* is recited, chanted, or sung.[67] This prayer calls to mind God's goodness and mercy. In the midst of daily life and in the midst of world events, God is present. Mary's song is a proclamation that the reign of God is wherever the hungry are filled, the poor, in body or spirit, are given dignity, the arrogant are confused, and warring parties are reconciled.

---

67. Vespers is the ancient liturgical evening prayer of Christians. It consists of a hymn, antiphons, psalms, a canticle, and a scriptural reading, followed by a period of silent meditation or a short homily, the *Magnificat*, petitions, the Lord's Prayer, a closing prayer, and a final blessing. The selection of items varies in keeping with a liturgical calendar, but the *Magnificat* is always used.

7

The Virgin Mary, a Model of Encounter
The Relevance of the Qur'ānic Mary to Christian-Muslim Dialogue

RAMI WAKIM

We are deeply grateful to His Beatitude Gregorios III, who has encouraged and supported the writing of this book, and to Deacon Rami Wakim, Secretary for the Melkite Greek Catholic Patriarchate, who facilitated and wrote this chapter. We appreciate this participation from those who are directly experiencing the hardest of times in the Near East and the expression of their concern that the West must immediately approach understanding that the Virgin Mary is directly related to world peace. —*M. Hearden and V. Kimball, Editors*

Al – Qur'ān: "O Maryam! Verily, *Allâh* gives you the glad tidings of a Word from Him, his name will be the Messiah *'Îsâ* [Jesus], the son of Maryam [Mary], held in honor in this world and in the Hereafter, and will be one of those who are near to *Allâh*"[1]

1. Surah 3:45. (The word *"surah"* [spelled *"surat"* before a vowel] means chapter.) There is no one standardized English translation of the *Qur'ān*. And there cannot be one, because the *Qur'ān* is the word of God as revealed in Arabic. Therefore, any translation is no more than a mere approximation. The available translations can vary in accordance with the different sects and political powers. The author has used a Saudi-endorsed translation because it is basically a modern version of the famous and widely spread translation of Abdullah Yusuf 'Ali (1872–1952). For more information about English

The Bible: "Behold, you will conceive in your womb and bear a son, and you shall name him Jesus. He will be great and will be called Son of the most High."[2]

Introduction

Living at the dawn of the third millennium, one expects times of war, crisis, and conflict to be long forgotten. However, today people all over the planet share a common feeling of exhaustion because of consecutive disasters like wars, counter-revolutions, the build-up of weapons of mass destruction, and not the least an economic crisis, which has touched everybody's life. One particular factor that seems to impinge predominantly on our contemporary life is the revival of wars in the name of religion.

Historically, Christian dogmas such as the Holy Trinity, the Incarnation, and the divinity of Jesus Christ have always been reasons for debates, conflicts, and even serious countercultural clashes. In our present time, this contentious historical heritage has developed into systematic violence and discord with other religions. Salafism[3] and other forms of fundamentalism are the tragedies of our day. This is not to say that their presence is recent, nor that other religions did not produce similar forces. Their danger today is immense because it affects peace in the whole world and threatens to launch an everlasting series of wars and counter-wars. It should not take a great deal of effort to recognize that these extremist movements do not relate inherently to the heart of religion. And it is of paramount importance to distinguish any faith from its extremist applications. Falling into the game of stereotyping and generalizing is very simple in this respect. Nevertheless, truth does not reside in a partial view but in looking at the whole picture.

In Lebanon, experiences of civil war and different attempts at dialogue, for example, have shown that focusing on what separates people is futile. Solidarity and peace require focusing on common beliefs. Thus, values such as mercy, charity, and faith in God's providence have been the subject of meetings and studies in many dialogue groups, resulting in the

---

translations of the *Qurʾān*, see Khaleel Mohammed, "Assessing English Translations of the *Qurʾān*," *Middle East Quarterly* 2 (2005) 58–71.

2. Luke 1:31–32. All biblical citations in this chapter are taken from the NAB.

3. A militant group of extremist Muslims who believe they are to be the only interpreters of the *Qurʾān*.

realization of how much Christians and Muslims have in common. A remarkable fact is that the Virgin Mary has always been the subject of respect and exaltation in Christian and Muslim milieus. She has emerged as a sign of unity, of common ground, and of coming together by the belief systems of Christianity and Islam.

This study aims at examining the proximity of narratives between the Qur'ānic account of Mary and the Christian Tradition, a proximity that has served the population of the Middle East well in strengthening their bonds. Thus, the chapter will first closely inspect the *Qur'ān*'s views on Mary and their counterparts in the Gospel of Luke. Second, it will show how this convergence of belief was translated into action in Lebanon in an effort to emphasize the dialogue of life.

Virgin Mary in the Qur'ān

The Virgin Mary, a Jewish woman, is the only female mentioned in the *Qur'ān* by name. Her Arabic name, Maryam, is repeated thirty-four times. She is also the only woman to have a whole chapter named after her, chapter 19 (*surah* Maryam). Another place where the Virgin is mentioned is in chapter 3 (*surat* Al Imran) which, always according to the *Qur'ān*, speaks of her family. As will be evident, in many places in the *Qur'ān* the Virgin is called "daughter of Imran" and "sister of Aaron." Now Imran, or following the biblical name Amram, is only mentioned in passing in Exodus and 1 Chronicles. Imran, or Amram, is the father of Moses. The *Qur'ān*, however, reveres Imran and considers him as the patriarch of a prophetic family (*Qur'ān* 3:33). This leads to the question, then, in the *Qur'ān*, what is the relationship of Mary to Aaron and Amram, the father of Aaron, Moses, and their sister Miriam? The bigger problem can be seen in the *Qur'ān*'s account that the husband of Anne is also called Imran (*Qur'ān* 3:35). All this, in fact, has evoked a series of objections about the chronological exactitude of the Qur'ānic account of Mary. There seems to be confusion over Mary (Miriam), who was the daughter of Amram and sister of Moses and Aaron.

Qur'ānic commentators do not have a problem in clarifying the confusion over Miriam. First, they explain that the designation "daughter of Imran" and "sister of Aaron" should not be understood literally but rather symbolically to indicate a general relationship. This conceptual meaning in the *Qur'ān* is meant to relate the Virgin Mary to this prophetic family and thus praise her origins. Does this symbolic designation apply also to Anne being called "wife of Imran"? Yusuf Ali declares, in the footnote of his translation of the *Qurʾān*, that the husband of Anne is another Imran, as do many other modern commentators.

Moreover, there is a third way of looking at this issue of the apparent confusion in the *Qurʾān* over Mary, as developed by Northrop Frye in that he approaches the question from a typological angle. For him, it is perfectly normal to associate the Virgin with Miriam because she was the first woman to cross the Red Sea and to be called "prophet" (Exod 15:20–21). This fact makes Miriam, the sister of Aaron, a female archetype for prophetic tradition on the one hand, and makes the Virgin Mary a symbol of Miriam on the other.[4] Whether we accept this interpretation or not has absolutely nothing to do with the honors and praises of the Virgin Mary in the *Qurʾān*.

The canonical Gospels tell very little about Virgin Mary's life. Byzantine liturgy and iconography refer extensively to apocryphal literature in order to depict Mary's childhood. The *Qurʾān*'s account of Mary's miraculous birth and her dwelling in the temple parallels that of the apocrypha as well. This fact has allowed many Muslim and Christian scholars alike to speak about how much more the *Qurʾān* exalts Mary in comparison to the New Testament's narratives.

The Birth and Childhood of Qurʾānic Mary

As mentioned above, the New Testament does not speak of the birth of the Virgin Mary or her childhood. The *Qurʾān*'s version starts with Anne being pregnant and promising to dedicate to God the fruit of her loins:

> "O my Lord! I have vowed to You what is in my womb [my child] to be dedicated to Your services, so accept this [my vow] from me. Verily, you are the All-Hearer, the All-Knowing." Then when she gave birth to her child Maryam [Mary], she said: "O my Lord! I have given birth to a female child," – and Allâh[5] knew better what she brought forth, – "And the male is not like the female, and I have named her Maryam,[6] and I seek refuge with You [Allâh]

---

4. Northrop Frye, *Great Code: The Bible and Literature* (New York: Mariner Books/ Houghton Mifflin, 2002), 172, as quoted in Husn Abboud, "Qurʾānic Mary's Story and the Motif of the Palm Tree and the Rivulet," *Parole de l'Orient* 30 (2005) 270.

5. The word "*Allah*" is Arabic for God. It is the same word used by Christians and different religions to designate God in Arabic.

6. Muslim commentators claim that Maryam literally means "maidservant of God." However, the name could be of Egyptian origins related to the word for "beloved."

for her and for her offspring from Shaitân [Satan], the outcast" (*Qur'ān* 3:35–36).

If we take a look at the commentary Tafsir al-Jalalayn,[7] it shows that Anne was an elderly infertile woman.[8] This means that Islam views Anne's conception as a matter of divine intervention, which allows many Christian thinkers to see in it an echo of Christian belief in the purity of Mary.[9] In fact, there is a confirmation of this in a Hadith[10] transmitted by two recognized shaykhs (Bukhari and Muslim). Muhammad said that "every newborn is touched by Satan and begins [life] by crying, except for Mary and her son" (al-Jalalayn). In the same chapter, the *Qur'ān* presents, as a context to Anne's conception, another miraculous conception, that of Elizabeth, the relative of Mary. All of this points without doubt to the exceptional birth of Mary and draws a map of her extraordinary calling in giving birth to Jesus Christ.

Here, the reader of verse 36 might wonder why Anne says "the male is not like a female." In Jewish society, only male children could ordinarily be presented to serve in the temple. And this is why the verse shows Anne stating precisely the gender of the newborn and asking for a special grace from God. The answer of God to Anne's prayer is found in the following verse:

> So her Lord [Allâh] accepted her with goodly acceptance. He made her grow in a good manner and put her under the care of Zakariyâ [Zacchary]. Every time he entered Al-Mihrâb[11] to [visit] her, he found her supplied with sustenance. He said: "O Maryam [Mary]! From where have you got this?" She said, "This is from Allâh. Verily, Allâh provides sustenance to whom He wills, without limit" (*Qur'ān* 3:37).

---

7. Tafsir al-Jalalayn is one of the most commonly recognized commentaries of the *Qur'ān*. This commentary follows the verses one by one with easy and accessible interpretation.

8. The reference to al-Jalalayn is very simple because it is enough to have the number of the chapter and verse to be able to find the commentary. There is an English translation available online: http://www.altafsir.com/Al-Jalalayn.asp.

9. In Arabic: Yossuf Durra al-Haddad, "Qur'anic Scenes of Mary," *al-Ma'arej* 50 (2004) 113.

10. The word "Hadith" refers to the sayings and actions of Muhammad. When proven correctly transmitted, Hadith is considered an important tool for understanding the *Qur'ān*.

11. "Al-Mihrâb" means a praying place or a private room.

The text clearly establishes Mary as an exception to the rule excluding females from the temple, and an exceptional person, because God accepted a female child to serve in the temple. Although she was given to Zechariah for her care, daily divine intervention took place not only at the level of physical provision but also at the level of moral and spiritual readiness—that is, she was not only provided with food to strengthen the body but also with moral guidance to strengthen her spirit.[12] In this righteous upbringing in the presence of angels, the angels' call to Mary is very understandable as it shows her place in God's providence when compared with every single woman on earth: "And when the angels said: 'O Maryam (Mary)! Verily, *Allâh* has chosen you, purified you, and chosen you above the women of the *'Âlamîn* (mankind and jinn).'" (*Qur'ân* 3:42).

The repetition of the act of choosing in verse 42 is not at all redundant. Al-Jalalayn, referenced in the above quotation, states that both acts of choosing are expressed by the angels, especially Gabriel: the first one signifies accepting her mother's vow and allowing her to enter the temple, while the second refers to the ability to conceive without a man, in which she is alone of all her sex.[13] As for the act of purification, al-Jalalayn indicates that she was immaculate as untouched by men, while other Islamic sources understand it as delivery from polytheism and disbelief or from the menstrual cycle.[14]

God's favoring Mary from the time of her conception is in keeping with the favor shown to all her ancestors as described in verse 33, which precedes the story of Anne's conception: "Allâh chose Adam, Nûh (Noah), the family of Ibrâhîm (Abraham) and the family of 'Imrân above the *'Âlamîn*" (*Qur'ân* 3:33). This series of preparations reflects God's providential plan to help mankind, which is an echo of the Christian concept of salvific economy. The apogee of God's providence in Mary's life is found in receiving the angel Gabriel and hearing the good news from him.

The Annunciation and the Birth of Jesus Christ

In the same line of miracles, the text reaches its apex with the angel's call to the Virgin Mary:

---

12. Al-Haddad, "Qur'anic," 107.
13. Ibid., 108.
14. In Arabic: Hind Obaydin, "Chapter of Maryam According to the Qur'anic Methods of Interpretation," *al-Ma' arej* 50 (2004) 47–65.

> "O Maryam! Verily, *Allâh* gives you the glad tidings of a Word from Him, his name will be the Messiah ʿÎsâ [Jesus], the son of Maryam [Mary], held in honor in this world and in the Hereafter, and will be one of those who are near to *Allâh*. He will speak to the people in the cradle and in manhood, and he will be one of the righteous." She said: "O my Lord! How shall I have a son when no man has touched me." He said: "So [it will be] for *Allâh* creates what He wills. When He has decreed something, He says to it only: Be! - and it is. And He [*Allâh*] will teach him ʿÎsâ (Jesus)] the Book and Al-Hikmah, [and] the *Taurât* [Torah] and the *Injeel* [Gospel]" (*Qurʾān* 3:45–58).

Here we should highlight a very interesting series of names given to Jesus: (1) a "word" from God because he was created without a father by divine commandment through the word "Be," (2) the "Messiah" because he is the blessed one, (3) "Issa" which is an Arabization of Jesus, and 4) "son of Mary" to affirm that he has no earthly father. Inspecting the meanings of these titles goes beyond the scope of this work. As for the honor in this world, it has to do with being a prophet, while in the hereafter it refers to intercession.[15]

Mary appears in all of this as someone who is in awe yet remains very careful to hear the message. Once again, the order of events is of a divine nature focusing on the fact that God chooses, prepares and does everything He sees as good.

Another account of Gabriel's appearance to Mary is found in chapter 19 of the *Qurʾān*, the one named after her: "Maryam." Verses 16 and 17 tell how Mary has secluded herself and how the angel appears in human form in all respects. At the sight of the angel, Mary is filled with fear and apprehension. Here is the conversation they had:

> She said: "Verily! I seek refuge with the Most Gracious (*Allâh*) from you, if you do fear *Allâh*." [The angel] said: "I am only a messenger from your Lord, [to announce] to you the gift of a righteous son." She said: "How can I have a son, when no man has touched me, nor am I unchaste?" He said: "So [it will be], your Lord said: 'That is easy for Me. And [We wish] to appoint him as a sign to mankind and a mercy from Us, and it is a matter [already] decreed'" (*Qurʾān* 19:18–21).

---

15. Tafsir al-Jalalyan and Tafsir al-Baydawi. The latter commentary is briefer and depends on the reader's prior knowledge of interpretation methods.

The center of attention in this quotation is the revelation of the divine decree showing God's mercy and compassion towards human beings. At the very last words of this verse, we realize that Mary's miraculous conception is a premise for a greater cause that is "already decreed," which is giving birth to a son, without a father, who will be a turning point in the history of mankind's relationship with God.

When we turn to the Gospel of Luke, we find very striking similarities despite the historical dissimilarities. The angel's greeting instills apprehension in the Virgin's mind as to what kind of a greeting this is: "one who has found favor with God"? It is well worthwhile to quote the text at length because it shows a very interesting dynamic. Here it is as Luke describes it:

> "Hail, favored one! The Lord is with you." But she was greatly troubled at what was said and pondered what sort of greeting this might be. Then the angel said to her, "Do not be afraid, Mary, for you have found favor with God. Behold, you will conceive in your womb and bear a son, and you shall name him Jesus. He will be great and will be called Son of the Most High, and the Lord God will give him the throne of David his father, and he will rule over the house of Jacob forever, and of his kingdom there will be no end." But Mary said to the angel, "How can this be, since I have no relations with a man?" And the angel said to her in reply, "The holy Spirit will come upon you, and the power of the Most High will overshadow you. Therefore the child to be born will be called holy, the Son of God" (Luke 1:28–35).

The angel's call to Mary, "O favored one," shows the special place that the Virgin holds in the salvific plan of God. It shows how she has been chosen, given a particular grace, and prepared for this very day. It is then very similar to God's choosing Mary and endowing her with a particular blessing in the *Qurʾān*. In Luke, the Virgin is taken by fear and wonderment, which is quite normal before a supernatural appearance. The titles of Jesus Christ are not all preserved by the *Qurʾān*. Particularly, and in comparison, the *Qurʾān*, transforms Jesus' designation as "Son of the Most High," or as in Luke 1:35 "Son of God," into the "son of Mary" (*Qurʾān*, 19:34). As for the Virgin's exclamation about how it is possible to conceive without knowing a man, we find the *Qurʾān* is in the same vein. And the answer of the angel is based upon the power of God that transcends natural norms when fitting. Furthermore, the text goes on to present Elizabeth's miraculous conception as a proof of God's power: "And behold, Elizabeth, your relative, has also conceived a son in her old age, and this is the sixth month for her who was called barren; for nothing will be impossible for God" (Luke 1:36–37).

These last two elements find an echo in the Qur'ānic account of the Annunciation, although verse 38 of the Gospel of Luke in which the Virgin says, "Behold, I am the handmaid of the Lord; let it be to me according to your word" does not appear. It should be noted that for Christian theology, this statement represents the Virgin's voluntary aptitude to cooperate with God's grace and fulfill her vocation. The omission of Mary's response in the *Qur'ān* is consistent with its general direction to emphasize God's eminence and the predestination of the universe.

The significance of the comparison between the two stories cannot be emphasized enough. First, we have undeniable evidence relating to the special position of the Virgin Mary in the salvific economy in both accounts, in the New Testament and in the *Qur'ān*. Second, the stages of both accounts highlight the same aspects of the Virgin's life: (1) the particular grace given to her in the light of the role she is to fulfill, (2) her preparation and readiness to hear the word of God, and in both accounts to receive the Word of God, and finally (3) the purity and innocence of her life that is also preserved during her conception. All these qualities of Mary are directed towards her giving birth to Jesus Christ, the Word of God.

The account of Mary's conception and birth-giving in *surah* 19 ("Maryam") goes like this. First, right after the encounter with the angel, Mary hastens to leave the city: "So she conceived him, and she withdrew with him to a far place (i.e., Bethlehem valley about four to six miles from Jerusalem)" (*Qur'ān* 19:22). Now running away seems to be related to hiding herself from her family because she fears they would not understand how she is with a child without knowing a man. As for the manner of conception, we can deduce from the two accounts set out above that it is by the power of the divine will. The time of conception is not precise because the text does not say anything about it, unlike many interpreters. Al-Jalalayn, for example, goes as far as to speculate that the conception, the formation of the fetus, and delivery took one hour. The story, as told in the *Qur'ān*, has two stages or scenes.

First, there is the delivery as follows:

> And labor[16] drove her to the trunk of a date-palm. She said: "Would that I had died before this, and had been forgotten and

---

16. The original translation has pain of childbirth. The author modified the translation to make it more faithful to the Arabic.

out of sight!" Then cried unto her from below her, saying: "Grieve not: your Lord has provided a water stream under you. And shake the trunk of date-palm towards you, it will let fall fresh ripe-dates upon you. So eat and drink and be glad. And if you see any human being, say: 'Verily! I have vowed a fast unto the Most Gracious (*Allâh*) so I shall not speak to any human being this day'" (*Qurʾān* 19:23–26).

Al-Haddad explains that the word "labor" in Arabic only has the meaning of the embryo kicking out, simply the time of delivery, and does not include the feelings of pain.[17] The wish of Mary to die and be forgotten could mean either she is moved by shame or fear that no one would believe that she could conceive a son without knowing the child's father.[18] As for what calls from underneath her, it is very difficult to decide whether it is an angel or the baby itself. As the Qurʾānic story continues, she is ordered to eat and drink, not to grieve, and to remain silent when asked about the child. In verses 30 to 32 of surah 19, the *Qurʾān* shows the child speaking and defending his mother, thus proving the divine nature of her conception.

The image of Mary next to a date tree and a water stream is an ancient one. Husn Abboud points out that this image has roots in Hellenic culture (the birth of Apollo), and in the Pharaonic culture (drawings in the tomb of Si-Amun in the oasis of Siwa).[19] They are images related to the concept of fertility and the power of life endowed in motherhood. Husn Abboud tells us also that the tree serves as "the miraculous tool that assists her throughout childbirth labor in the wilderness, like the other miraculous tools, that assist the male prophets, such as Solomon's hoopoe,[20] Moses' stick, Jesus' table and Saleh's[21] she-camel."[22] Concerning the place of the birth of Jesus, the *Qurʾān* seems to alter the original New Testament story. The literary analysis shows the place could probably be Egypt. However, the reason to depict Mary in such an iconic image, the palm tree and the stream of water,

---

17. Al-Haddad, "Qur'anic," 102.

18. Ibid., 103.

19. Abboud, "Qur'anic," 266. The author of the article references among others "'Garden,' 'Eden,' 'Female'"; as quoted in Northrop Frye, *Words with Power: Being a Second Study of "The Bible and Literature"* (Toronto: Penguin, 1990).

20. This word refers to an elegant bird from which Solomon learned knowledge.

21. *Saleh* is Arabic for good or pious. He is recognized in the *Qurʾān* as a prophet of a wicked people who were eventually destroyed because of their sin. The she-camel is a sign given as a miracle by God to show the truthfulness of Saleh's message.

22. Abboud, "Qur'anic," 267–68.

the alteration of the place of birth, serve a completely different purpose. As Husn Abboud affirms,

> the Qur'an places the events of the nativity of Jesus in a setting of nature's rejuvenation symbols not because the Qur'an wants to alter the original Christian story, but because the Qur'an wants to say something about female fertility and land fertility, which are very important images for celebrating female fecundity and the power of the maternal.[23]

The second scene tells about the aftermath. We notice a transitional step: the center of attention is being moved from the Virgin to the baby Jesus.

> Then she brought him (the baby) to her people, carrying him. They said: "O Mary! Indeed you have brought a mighty thing [Tafsir Al-Tabari]. O sister of Hârûn (Aaron)! Your father was not a man who used to commit adultery, nor was your mother an unchaste woman." Then she pointed to him. They said: "How can we talk to one who is a child in the cradle?" (*Qur'ān* 19:27–29).

Apparently, they are shocked by the baby and question Mary's purity right away. We can understand here the reference to Aaron as a symbolic reference to the prophetic tradition from which the Qur'ānic Mary takes origin. The *Qur'ān* does not refer to the perplexity of Joseph before the conception of Mary, nor to the escape to Egypt. Rather, the *Qur'ān* alters once more the New Testament story to reinforce an idea: the purity of Mary. Verses 30 to 34 in the *Qur'ān* show the baby Jesus speaking and defending his mother, thus preserving her purity.

Mary at the Center of the Dialogue of Life

In most Middle Eastern cities and towns, where both Christians and Muslims live together, a far more interesting dialogue takes place: it is the dialogue of life. The dialogue of life entails all aspects of daily encounter between people from different religious backgrounds without that difference being an obstacle. Here we can enumerate a number of examples: being neighbors, going to the same schools, creating friendships, and working together. In these milieus, where religious culture is the defining characteristic of a person, a different perspective of life comes to the surface. It is a

23. Ibid., 267–69.

perspective where religion ceases to be only a personal practice of faith but also a people's tradition and way of life regardless of how religiously devout they are. Christian-Muslim religious culture is reflected in all aspects of these people's lives. It is very crucial to understand this and make good use of it.

In one of the biggest schools of Beirut, Notre Dame de Jumhoor which is run by the Jesuit fathers, there is the custom of having *iftar*[24] together and organizing a day of prayers for Muslims and Christians during Ramadan every year. These gatherings inspired Mr. Naji Khoury, the General Secretary of the school's Alumni Association, to go ahead and consult Sheikh Muhammad an-Naqri, former Director General of Dar Fatwa, about possible ways to bring the people of the two religions closer. They settled on the idea that the Virgin Mary could bring them together.[25] And that was how the project of declaring the Feast of the Annunciation as a national holiday for all Lebanese people came into existence. The first meeting was held on March 25, 2007. In 2008, the initiators suggested the project to Muhammad as-Sammak, Secretary General of the Christian-Muslim Committee for Dialogue in Lebanon and Co-President of Religions for Peace. On Annunciation Day in 2009, the dream became reality and both Christians and Muslims have celebrated this day together ever since.

There were some minor objections against celebrating the Annunciation together. The problem arose from the way in which each religion understood this feast. It was thought that only the external aspects of the feast, the angel giving the news to Mary who gives birth to Jesus, are held in common, while the meaning differs from one version of the story to the other: in the New Testament, Mary gives birth to the Son of God who is God, while in the *Qur'ān* she bears the Messiah who is among the greatest prophets of Islam.

According to what we have seen, however, through the examined Qur'ānic verses, the common features of this feast go beyond its external aspects. In both Christianity and Islam, the Annunciation shows the Virgin at the heart of God's plan to save humanity through her aptitude to receive His word. If we take the Virgin as the center of our study, we find evidence that both the Gospels and the *Qur'ān* celebrate God's affirmation of His choice of Mary in the following shared factors: (1) her chastity and

---

24. The daily evening meal when Muslims break their fast during Ramadan.

25. In Arabic: *Hala Homsi*, "Annunciation: The Virgin Mary Has Brought Christians and Muslims in Lebanon Together," *An-Nahar* newspaper, March 14, 2010.

conduct; (2) the account of the appearance of God's messenger, Gabriel, in human shape before her; and (3) her miraculous conception without defilement. Fadlullah rightly points out that the miraculous begetting of Jesus Christ is a turning point in history because it breaks with the ordinary way of procreation. The *Qur'ān* preserves this idea so much because it is related to the creation of Adam and Eve. What is at stake then is a renewal of creation. The exaltation of Mary, the insistence on her purity, and her special place among all women are so highlighted because the first step of this re-creation is accomplished in her.[26]

Certainly, declaring the Annunciation in Lebanon as a national feast commemorates far more than just interfaith proximity. The idea behind this initiative was the fact that the person of the Virgin Mary can indeed bring Muslims and Christians together. And considering this day as a national holiday is an expression of the possibility of encouraging solidarity and living together.

During a trip taken by the Community of Christian Churches in the Canton de Vaud (Switzerland) in October of 2011 to visit the different Christian communities in Lebanon, the group of visitors spoke of their surprise when they saw the great number of Muslim pilgrims who showed up at the sanctuary of Harissa, where an enormous statue of the Virgin was erected.[27] Similarly, many Muslim pilgrims come to visit the Monastery of Our Lady of Saydnaya near Damascus in Syria. The same also happens at Our Lady of Maghdousheh in the south of Lebanon, and at the shrine of Mary the Sultana of Palestine near Jerusalem.

The Swiss pilgrims also spoke of their encounter with the group *Darb Mariam* (path of Mary) which is basically a mixed association of Christians and Muslims, seeking to promote peace between the two communities. Declaring the Feast of the Annunciation as a national holiday has an enormous importance for this association for it represents the core of their endeavors: celebrating common beliefs and values in order to create peace.

---

26. Muhammad Hussein Fadlallah, "Mary's Story as Inspired by the Qur'an," online: http://english.bayynat.org.lb/Messengers/Stories_Mary_Story_1.htm; and: http://english.bayynat.org.lb/Messengers/Stories_Mary_Story_2.htm.

27. Martin Hoegger, "Le Dialogue Interreligieux au Pays de Cèdres," *Dialogue Interreligieux*, online: http://dialogueinterreligieux.eerv.ch/2012/01/17/le-dialogue-inter religieux-au-pays-des-cedres.

Conclusion

Calls for interreligious dialogue are growing all over the world. Many meetings serving this purpose have taken place either under state or religious sponsorship. In regions where different religions have lived together for a long time, these calls take a different shape. In the Middle East for example, there is no lack of places for interreligious dialogue and meeting. From the Christian point of view, all ecclesiastical institutions have a special body in charge of dialogue with Muslims. Similarly, the various Muslim institutions have parallel bodies. In May 2011, the Melkite Greek Catholic Patriarch Gregorios III inaugurated the *Liqaa'* (Encounter) Center for the Dialogue of Civilizations, a center that is cosponsored and financed by His Majesty, Sultan Qaboos of Oman. This fact is very significant since it demonstrates that calls for encounter and dialogue do not exist for superficial reasons but spring from a deep understanding of an eventual common future. Everybody calls for dialogue because it is the only way to safeguard living together, foster spiritual solidarity, and in consequence avoid clashes.

Certainly, the *Qur'ān* draws most of its account of the Virgin Mary from apocryphal literature. Further, in some places, modifications are introduced to the story in order to give a cultural, linguistic, and social significance related to the message of Islam. Looking at these modifications from a historical standpoint could create major problems and give rise to accusations. We have seen that the story of the birth of Jesus in the *Qur'ān* has many Hellenistic and even Pharaonic allusions. As explained, the reason for such modifications is not merely to alter or separate the Qur'ānic from the original Christian story but rather to represent the Virgin Mary as a maternal archetype. All modifications concerning the accounts of the Virgin Mary, then, should be viewed and read mostly from a literary point of view rather than a historical one.[28]

What we need to deduce from studying the Qur'ānic account of the Virgin is to understand how much value she is given. Besides being the only woman mentioned by name, and the only woman to have a chapter named after her, the Virgin is depicted as an iconic mother whose reception of the graces of God meant ultimately the Word of God allowed her to be called "sister of Aaron" so as to designate her prophetic affiliation.

---

28. Abboud, "Qur'anic," 276.

To sum up then, we can say that Mary's entire story in the *Qurʾān* bears the touches of God's providence, from the moment she was born up until the Annunciation, miraculous conception, and begetting of her son.

The Middle East is witnessing a very turbulent time. On one side, there are various uprisings, and on the other there are dangerous conflicts concerning who is to obtain power. It is a highly sensitive time because these conflicts and difficulties can allow the spirit of sectarian separatism and enmity to prevail. And God knows it has already started. What the Middle East needs is a dialogue, one that is based, above all, on the dialogue of life, drawing strength from shared values. We have seen throughout this chapter that the Virgin Mary is indeed an iconic figure whose veneration is almost equal for both Christians and Muslims. She shows us the path of being truly religious, blessed by God, and of bearing the fruit of peace to the world. This is how Sheikh Mahassine sums up the Qurʾānic views of Mary: "She is especially chosen and purified, she is a model of faith in God and natural return to Him, of compliance to His will, of devotion, of modesty, of piety and contemplation, of silence, and of prayer and fasting."[29]

The same measures apply for the entire Western world. If the West does not take refuge in dialogue, which goes beyond organized conferences and sponsored gatherings, i.e. the dialogue of life that touches every person in his or her reality, the whole world will have to prepare for clashes and conflicts of religions and ultimately of civilizations. Let us then learn from the Virgin Mary, from her modesty, silence and listening to God's word, how to become, like her, bearers of the Word and bearers of Good News for the world.

---

29. Omar Mahassine, "La Place de la Vierge Marie dans le Qoran," contribution presented at the Week of Encounters for the Christian-Muslim friendship group, Paris, France, Nov 27–Dec 5, 2004.

8

The Blessed Virgin Mary—Our Educator

DANIELLE M. PETERS

"No human mother can limit her task solely to the procreation of new human beings; she must also undertake the task of nourishing them and educating them."[1]

Introduction

The above citation resonates with every mother. After much longing and anticipation throughout her pregnancy, a mother awaits with trembling and awe the hour of giving birth. Her trepidation may even increase once she holds this gift of God in her arms. "What will become of my child? Will my baby realize how unique he (or she) is to God, unite with God throughout life and see heaven as his (or her) final goal?" Christian mothers ponder these and other questions when faced with the daily joys and challenges implied in the vocation of motherhood. "So it is with the Blessed Virgin Mary,"[2] wrote Paul VI. Like all mothers, Mary longed and prepared for her child Jesus. After his birth "she wrapped him in swaddling clothes" (Luke 2:7). A careful reading of these few words conveys that the young mother did all she could to take care of her son's well-being. Unlike any other mother however, Mary's motherhood included two dimensions: by

---

1. SM §1, online: http://www.vatican.va/holy_father/paul_vi/apost_exhortations/documents/hf_p-vi_exh_19670513_signum-magnum_en.html.
2. Ibid.

accepting to be the mother of Jesus Christ, Mary agreed to a vital role in God's redemptive plan that did not end with her temporal motherly duties. Her being mother of the One blossomed into a new and universal motherhood for all who would become brothers and sisters of Christ. This universal motherhood is referred to as Mary's spiritual maternity, or Mary's motherhood in the order of grace. Vatican II's Dogmatic Constitution on the Church, *Lumen Gentium*, asserts:

> This maternity of Mary in the order of grace began with the consent which she gave in faith at the Annunciation and which she sustained without wavering beneath the cross, and lasts until the eternal fulfillment of all the elect. . . . By her maternal charity, she cares for the brethren of her Son, who still journey on earth . . . until they are led into the happiness of their true home.[3]

It is this "new motherhood of Mary"[4] which constitutes her mission next to her son[5] and which, in the words of Blessed John Paul II belongs to Christ's testament,[6] that is the focus of this chapter. What exactly are we to understand by Our Lady's "motherhood in the order of grace?"[7] At issue is the singular unique cooperation of Mary with the Savior in the entire work of redemption. As spiritual mother, Mary gives birth to Christians and nurtures them spiritually. Her ongoing maternal role includes a formative and educational influence on every child of God. It aims at the fostering of the supernatural life and divine grace received at baptism but cannot be limited to it. According to Vatican II's Declaration on Christian Education, *Gravissimum Educationis*,[8] the overall goal of education is "to help in the Christian formation of the world that takes place when natural powers viewed in the full consideration of man redeemed by Christ contribute to the good of the whole society."

---

3. LG §62, online: http://www.vatican.va/archive/hist_councils/ii_vatican_council/documents/vat-ii_const_19641121_lumen-gentium_en.html.

4. RM §23, online: http://www.vatican.va/holy_father/john_paul_ii/encyclicals/documents/hf_jp-ii_enc_25031987_redemptoris-mater_en.html.

5. See LG §61, RM §22.

6. RM §23. See also, John Paul II, *Jesus, Son and Savior: A Catechesis on the Creed* (Boston: Pauline Book & Media, 1996), 468.

7. LG §61.

8. Paul VI, *Declaration on Christian Education*, October 28, 1965, §2, online: http://www.vatican.va/archive/hist_councils/ii_vatican_council/documents/vat-ii_decl_19651028_gravissimum-educationis_en.html.

Although a crucial component of Mary's role for the Mystical Body of Christ, her educational activity receives only marginal attention in recent magisterial documents.[9] Yet, arguably, the basic anthropological and salvific implications of Mary's motherly role in view of the Mystical Body of Christ meet in her task as educator. As the anthropological paradigm of our vocation to holiness, Our Lady educates us through her example, and as our spiritual mother, she mediates for us the graces needed to grow in holiness. In this chapter we will explore this facet of Mary's ongoing role in the salvation of Christians[10] by highlighting in particular her task as our educator throughout our earthly pilgrimage.[11]

As with any education, the choice of a school and of a teacher for the spiritual life is of crucial importance.[12] Not only must the educator possess the qualities necessary to lead his students to the appointed goal, ideally seen, the teacher should also be the embodiment and transparency of the goal. The Blessed Virgin Mary resembles the teacher *par excellence* who, as "the chosen model of holiness . . . guides the steps of believers on their journey to heaven."[13]

In the first part of our reflections we will shed light on Mary's own life's pilgrimage. In virtue of her receptivity of the will of God she educates us by her example, since "the first stimulus to learning is the nobility of the teacher."[14] Secondly, we will identify the implications of Our Lady's mission as educator on our spiritual journey heavenwards. Finally, Our Lady's example and mission challenge us to enter "Mary's School."[15] This third aspect

---

9. The following magisterial documents offer subtle references to Mary's educational task: John Paul II, *Catechesi Tradendae*, Apostolic Exhortation, October 16, 1979, §73, online: http://www.vatican.va/holy_father/john_paul_ii/apost_exhortations/documents/hf_jp-ii_exh_16101979_catechesi-tradendae_en.html; John Paul II, *The Virgin Mary in Intellectual and Spiritual Formation*, Apostolic Exhortation, March 25, 1988, §7, online: http://campus.udayton.edu/mary/resources/documents/intellec.html; VS 120, online: http://www.vatican.va/holy_father/john_paul_ii/encyclicals/documents/hf_jp-ii_enc_06081993_veritatis-splendor_en.html; CCC §2599.

10. See LG §62.

11. See LG §57, 61.

12. See John Paul II, "Culture and Holiness: A Winning Combination," Address to the Catholic University of the Sacred Heart, November 9, 2000, *L'Osservatore Romano*, Weekly English Ed., November 22, 2000, 7.

13. John Paul II, *Theotókos: Woman, Mother, Disciple* (Boston: Pauline, 2000), 55. [Hereafter: *Theotókos*.]

14. St. Ambrose, *De Virginibus*, bk. 2, ch. 2, 7; PL 16:220, as cited in VS §120.

15. A term repeatedly used by Blessed John Paul II, among others, in RV §1, 3, 14,

of her education attempts to show that her lesson plan draws us into Mary's communion with Christ and as a result we "grow in intimacy with both of them."[16] It is in this rapport of love and trust that the Christian comes to recognize in Christ his own self, his dignity and vocation as image and likeness of God.[17]

Mary's Education through Her Exemplary Pilgrimage of Faith

Our Lady's life journey can be likened to a book that leads heavenward. All Christians are encouraged to frequently page through this book. In doing so, we encounter the realized ideal of a person perfected in Christ whose holiness we are encouraged to emulate. At issue is not some kind of extraordinary existence, possible only for a few uncommon heroes. On the contrary, every Christian is challenged with this high standard of ordinary Christian living.[18] What does Mary's life teach us about our common vocation to holiness?

By a unique and special election of the Father's love, Mary, from the first instant of her existence, enjoyed the intimacy of communion with the Triune God (the Immaculate Conception). Her dignity and nobility as the *Immaculata* (the immaculate concept of the human person) present us with a mirror reflecting our irreplaceable value in the sight of God. Analogous to the privilege of her Immaculate Conception, each human person, no matter his (or her) status in life, is personally loved by God and, in virtue of baptism, graced with supernatural life.

In addition to redemptive grace, God offers us the gift of a free will, thereby inviting us to cooperate like Mary in salvation history. The narrative of the Annunciation depicts this exchange of divine-human interaction

---

43, online: http://www.vatican.va/holy_father/john_paul_ii/apost_letters/documents/hf_jp-ii_apl_20021016_rosarium-virginis-mariae_en.html. See also EE §7, 53, 58, online: http://www.vatican.va/holy_father/special_features/encyclicals/documents/hf_jp-ii_enc_20030417_ecclesia_eucharistia_en.html. Benedict XVI also invites his listeners to enroll in Mary's school; see, e.g., footnote 78.

16. *Theotókos*, 192.

17. See John Paul II, *Mary: A Decisive Moment in the History of Salvation*, Homily in St. Mary Major, Dec 8, 1978, *L'Osservatore Romano*, Weekly English Ed., December 21, 1978, 3.

18. See LG §5. See also NMI §31, online: http://www.vatican.va/holy_father/john_paul_ii/apost_letters/documents/hf_jp-ii_apl_20010106_novo-millennio-ineunte_en.html.

most eloquently. The message of the angel and Mary's resulting dialogue with Gabriel constitutes the axis of Mary's life.

Meditating on Mary's journey we discover a 'key' that unlocks for us the innermost reality of Mary. It is her "obedience of faith"[19] through which she discloses "to humanity the mystery of Christ in a discreet yet direct and effective way."[20] Our Lady's obedience of faith is by no means merely a passive acceptance but rather signals her active cooperation with God's plan wherefore "the consent of the predestined Mother should precede the Incarnation."[21] Luke's gospel portrays Mary as a person whose emotions, will and intellect are perfectly harmonized and at the service of grace. Her *fiat* ("Let it be done") uttered in the spirit of obedience of faith signals the degree of generosity and love that enabled her to freely cooperate with God's plan. The Virgin of Nazareth "allows" God to use her in order to become fruitful first *in* her and then *through* her. As she humbly magnifies the Lord, Mary herself is magnified, since from then on all generations will call her blessed (see Luke 1:43)! It is this experience of total and unconditional self-surrender freely given which facilitated God's self-revelation in her life and through which she in return discovers her identity as well as her mission in the service of her son, Jesus Christ. Blessed John Paul II emphasized that

> the particular union of the *Theotókos* with God—which fulfills in the most eminent manner the supernatural predestination to union with the Father granted to every human being (*filii in Filio*)—is a pure grace and, as such, a *gift of the Spirit*. At the same time, however, through her response of faith Mary exercises her free will and thus fully shares with her personal and feminine "I" in the event of the Incarnation. With her *fiat*, Mary becomes the authentic subject of that union with God which was realized in the mystery of the Incarnation of the Word, who is of one substance with the Father. All of God's action in human history at all

---

19. Mary's *obedience of faith*, a term John Paul II adopted from Vatican II's *Dei Verbum* 5 (see Vatican I, *Dei Filius*, Dogmatic Constitution on the Catholic Faith, ch. 3, in DS §3008) is a theme woven through *Redemptoris Mater*. *Dei Verbum* is available online: http://www.vatican.va/archive/hist_councils/ii_vatican_council/documents/vat-ii_const_19651118_dei-verbum_en.html. See also RM §13–16, 18, 26, 29, 33, 36. The term denotes the greatest action a human person can render to God since it requires the engagement of the intellect, heart, and will in recognizing and submitting to the divine plan.

20. RM §19.

21. RM §13. See also LG §56.

times respects the free will of the human "I." And such was the case with the Annunciation at Nazareth.[22]

A crucial and often ignored aspect of Our Lady's *fiat* relates to her humble cooperation with education received from her son. Sacred Scripture describes the encounter with her twelve-year-old son found in the temple (Luke 2:41ff) where we catch a glimpse of one of the most heartrending lessons she endured. Any parent can imagine the anguish of searching for a lost child. Finally, after three days, Joseph and Mary are reunited with their son. Yet, there was no room for parental sentiments and admonishment. Jesus' words to his mother, "Did you not know that I had to be in my Father's House?" changed in an instant her mother's role to that of becoming the first disciple of her son and Savior. The attitude with which the virginal mother accepted Jesus' teaching is as inspiring as it is worthy of our imitation: in the spirit of her loyal *fiat* she "kept all these things, pondering them in her heart" (Luke 2:51 par Luke 2:19). Luke highlighted Mary's pondering twice in order to make sure we understand this lesson. She did not complain, rebel, or seek compensations in "her loneliness and her suffering as a mother."[23] Rather, she silently pondered her son's words in order to discern God's will. She, who cared for her son with selfless motherliness, is now led to respond to His education, which gradually prepared her for her ultimate *fiat* surrender on Golgotha.

Standing beneath the cross, Mary, like no other, participated in her son's life sacrifice freely given for our redemption. With a maternal heart pierced by the sword of compassion (see Luke 2:35) she renounced what she loved most. Jesus' last will penetrated the very heart of Mary's motherhood. He asked her to join him in his own self-offering (*kenosis*) to the Father for the salvation of humanity. In return she received a "new motherhood"

---

22. MD §4, online: http://www.vatican.va/holy_father/john_paul_ii/apost_letters/documents/hf_jp-ii_apl_15081988_mulieris-dignitatem_en.html. See also RM §13. In his philosophical treatise on *The Acting Person*, Karol Wojtyła (John Paul II) wrote that the person as an individual has the experience of being the subject of his action. In other words, the person can say "I" and, in this conscious experience of self, is the efficient cause of his/her action. At the same time we can speak of the person as the object of the act in so far as through self-determination a person determines himself as the primary and nearest object of the action. The person as subject and object is the "I." Through his/her freely willed and chosen action the "I" becomes an individual who takes responsibility for his/her action. See also John Paul II, *Personal Structure of Self-Determination*, in *Person and Community: Selected Essays*, trans. Theresa Sandock (New York: P. Lang, 1993), 187–95.

23. *Theotókos*, 180.

which, generated by faith, was the fruit of a "new" love ripened by aligning herself to the redemptive love of her son.[24] John Paul II highlights this drama in *Redemptoris Mater*:

> How completely she "abandons herself to God" without reserve, "offering the full assent of the intellect and the will" to him whose "ways are inscrutable" (cf. Rom. 11:33)! . . . Through this faith Mary is perfectly united with Christ in his self-emptying. . . . At the foot of the Cross Mary shares through faith in the shocking mystery of this self-emptying. This is perhaps the deepest "kenosis" of faith in human history. Through faith the Mother shares in the death of her Son, in his redeeming death; but in contrast with the faith of the disciples who fled, hers was far more enlightened. On Golgotha, Jesus through the Cross definitively confirmed that he was the "sign of contradiction" foretold by Simeon. At the same time, there were also fulfilled on Golgotha the words which Simeon had addressed to Mary: "and a sword will pierce through your own soul also."[25]

Mary's generous response through her self-gift at the pinnacle of redemption was in perfect harmony with her *fiat* uttered at the Annunciation. Both events accentuate her vocation and mission as educator. While the incarnation initiated her divine, historical maternity, John's assent to taking Mary into his own home (John 19:27) commenced her spiritual maternity. Both dimensions of motherhood naturally include nourishing and educating first her own son, Jesus Christ, and then she fulfills the same task for John and for all who like the beloved disciple offer her a place in their home.

Mary, Educator on Our Pilgrimage Heavenwards

Mary performs her mission as our motherly educator according to the same principles and attitude she assumed while on her own earthly pilgrimage. Two pericopes from John's gospel in particular shed light on the pedagogical dimension of Mary's spiritual maternity: The wedding at Cana (John 2:1–11) and Christ's testament from the cross (John 19:25–27). At both events Jesus addressed his mother as "woman," a term recalling the first woman, Eve. As the new Eve she was to become the "true mother of

---

24. See RM §23.
25. RM §18, citing *Dei Verbum* §5.

the living" who would take care of our material and spiritual needs.[26] At Cana and on Golgotha Mary, the new Eve, interacted with her son, the new Adam. She established contact between her son and the servants of the newlywed couple, thereby alleviating the material needs of the wedding guests. At the foot of the cross it was her dying son who indicated to her the unique place she was to occupy in the whole economy of salvation. Who can even begin to fathom the sorrow this exchange of sons caused this immaculate mother?

Christ's gift of redemption is always transmitted through the Holy Spirit to all who, by receiving supernatural life at baptism, are reborn in Christ (see John 19:30). The incarnation as well as Christ's testament to his mother and the beloved disciple indicate that "two alone are capable of giving birth together, in synergy to the Son of God in the flesh and, in him, to us, too, as children of the Father: namely the Holy Spirit and Mary."[27] Consequently, when Mary conceived her divine son by the power of the Holy Spirit she also conceived spiritually the members of Christ. From this, it follows that the Virgin Mary is actively involved in our rebirth in the Spirit—at least in the objective plan of redemption.[28] In other words, at baptism, according to God's design, the individual simultaneously becomes a child of God the Father, a member of Christ, a temple of the Holy Spirit, and a child of Mary! The thought-provoking question arises, whether the birth of each of the faithful to eternal life is actually "dependent" on Mary's *fiat*?

It is through the sacrament of baptism that we embark on our pilgrimage heavenwards.[29] The degree of our willingness to entrust ourselves to our motherly educator determines the degree of formation she can exert on us. Hence, Mary's efficacy as our spiritual mother and educator depends on the degree of our acceptance of her gift for us, just as it depended initially on John's reaction to Christ's last words spoken to him. Like the beloved disciple, we are to invite our spiritual Mother into our homes and hearts

---

26. RM §37.

27. Piero Coda, "Ecclesial Movements, Gifts of the Spirit: A Theological Reflection," in *Movements in the Church: Proceedings of the World Congress of the Ecclesial Movements, Rome, 27-29 May, 1998* (Vatican City: Vatican Press, 1999), 103. Coda cites Grignion de Montfort. See also CCC §485, 505.

28. In support of this position, see LG §61.

29. See, e.g., *Rites of the Catholic Church as Revised by the Second Vatican Council*. English translation prepared by the International Commission on English in the Liturgy (New York: Pueblo, 1976), 209.

allowing her to unfold her educational mission in us. In the thought of Blessed John Paul II, this means that "the Christian, like the Apostle John, 'welcomes' the Mother of Christ 'into his own home' and brings her into everything that makes up his inner life, that is to say into his human and Christian 'I.'"[30] For the Polish pontiff, the personal "I" in each person avoids the reduction of individuals to the abstract idea of what it means to be human. Respecting and valuing a person as an individual image and likeness of God excludes treating a person as a number or link in a chain, or an impersonal element in some system.[31] In this vein John Paul II underlines Mary's spiritual maternity as Christ's gift to each one personally:

> Mary's motherhood, which becomes man's inheritance, is a gift: a gift which Christ himself makes personally to every individual. The Redeemer entrusts Mary to John because he entrusts John to Mary. At the foot of the Cross there begins that special entrusting of humanity to the Mother of Christ, which in the history of the Church has been practiced and expressed in different ways.[32]

The Church's long tradition is a strong indicator that living with Mary and entrusting ourselves to her care and formation is best secured in an act of consecration[33] since "the more a soul is consecrated to her the more will it be consecrated to Jesus Christ."[34] Every Christian is consecrated to

---

30. RM §45; see footnote 130: Clearly, in the Greek text the expression *eis ta idia* goes beyond the mere acceptance of Mary by the disciple in the sense of material lodging and hospitality in his house; it indicates rather a communion of life established between the two as a result of the words of the dying Christ: see Saint Augustine, *In Iohannis Evangelium tractatus CXXIV*, tract 119, §3, in CCL 36:659: "He took her to himself, not into his own property, for he possessed nothing of his own, but among his own duties, which he attended to with dedication." See also footnote 22 in this chapter.

31. CL §37, online: http://www.vatican.va/holy_father/john_paul_ii/apost_exhortations/documents/hf_jp-ii_exh_30121988_christifideles-laici_en.html.

32. RM §45.

33. Consecration to Mary (also called dedication, alliance, covenant of love, or entrustment) is a well-established practice in the tradition of the spiritual life. The consecration movement was initiated and promoted, among others, by St. Louis Grignion de Montfort, St. John Eudes, and St. Margaret Mary Alacoque. In our time the Marian Sodalities, the Schoenstatt Movement, the Fatima groupings, St. Maximilian Kolbe's Militia of the Immaculate, the Legion of Mary, and the Family of Mary include a consecration to Mary in their formation and pedagogy. For more information, see FAQ 23 online at: http://campus.udayton.edu/mary/questions/faq/faq23.html.

34. RV §15.

God at baptism.[35] If it is true, as we have shown before, that the grace of baptism makes us children of Mary as well, then it is also valid to assert that the sacrament of initiation includes a consecration to the Mother of God. Henceforth, Mary's mission as educator of the spiritual life is likewise initiated at baptism. The free choice to consecrate oneself to Mary simply denotes a conscious choice of the baptized to elect her as our educator towards holiness. Naturally, "such a deep and comprehensive giving of self,"[36] can ultimately only be rendered to God since it "is a perfect exchange of hearts, of interest and of goods."[37] Human persons can also, however, accept such surrender (e.g. that exchanged between spouses) insofar as they nourish each other in a God-pleasing way that leads to Him.[38]

Genuine entrusting of ourselves to Mary includes three elements: love, imitation, and invocation.[39] In this triad, love is the first and most important component of a relationship to endure and yield fruit. It is in this context that Father Kentenich, founder of the Schoenstatt Movement, describes Marian consecration as "a perfect, mutual giving of self for time and eternity, that is, through the consecration we give ourselves perfectly to the Blessed Mother and she gives herself to us in the same manner."[40] In other words, the Marian consecration can be likened to "a perfect exchange of hearts, of interest and of goods. I give myself to her and she gives herself to me."[41] Such a perfect exchange of self with Our Lady is justified because of her position in the order of salvation.

As our Mother and Educator it is clear that Our Lady will never be an obstacle for us on the way to a deeper union with God, nor will she merely be a guide on the way. On the contrary, according to Schoenstatt's founder it is Mary's principal task as our educator "to bear us for God and

---

35. See CCC §1273.

36. Joseph Kentenich, *Mary, Our Mother and Educator: An Applied Mariology*, Lenten Sermons 1954 (Waukesha, WI: Schoenstatt Sisters of Mary, 1987), 318. [Hereafter: MME 1954.]

37. Joseph Kentenich, *Aus dem Glauben Leben*, Sermons at St. Michael's Parish, Milwaukee, WI, 20 vols (Vallendar: Patris, 1969), 7:42.

38. See MME 1954, 318.

39. See MME 1954, 284. Father Kentenich cites in this context Pius XI's *Lux Veritatis*, Encyclical Letter on the Council of Ephesus, December 25, 1931, §43, online: http://www.papalencyclicals.net/Pius11/P11VERIT.HTM.

40. Jonathan Niehaus, *Schoenstatt's Covenant Spirituality* (Waukesha, WI: Schoenstatt Sisters of Mary, 1992), 66. [Hereafter: SCS 1992.]

41. SCS 1992, 63.

to educate us as perfectly as possible into the form of Christ."[42] Thus, our loving attachment to the person of Mary develops into the means, security and guarantee for our love of God and our rapport with Him in the baptismal covenant.[43] It is the continuous concern of our motherly educator to see to it that our consecration to her becomes effective in "all aspects of Christian life [and leads] even to the summit of sanctity."[44] Therefore Father Kentenich insists that an authentic consecration to Mary must be able to inspire a "far-reaching, well-deliberated, and conscious decision to strive for the highest Christian perfection."[45] Echoing this conviction and aspiration it is not surprising that the late Polish pontiff repeatedly consecrated the Church to her whom he recognized as the "Most Holy Educator."

Lessons Learned in Mary's School

As we have already observed, Mary fulfills her mission for her spiritual children in a way that is analogous to the fulfillment of a biological mother's temporal duties: She nourishes, cares for, and educates her children. Ultimately however, Mary's concern as our spiritual mother consists in forming Christ within us.[46] Being totally conformed to Christ herself, Mary conveys with her own life of discipleship the lessons she teaches. Thus, we can rest assured that by enrolling in Our Lady's School of Holiness we are in the company of present day apostles and future saints.

The Experience of Ecclesial Communities

Mary's School of holiness appeals to all who seriously aspire to Christian perfection. In particular the new ecclesial movements who take their point of departure from Vatican II's universal call to holiness[47] and are committed

---

42. MME 1954, 329.
43. See MME 1954, 182.
44. SCS 1992, 62.
45. MME 1954, 170.
46. See LG §60; Gal 4:19.
47. See LG, ch. 5. See also Janusz A. Ihnatowicz, "Consecrated Life among the Laity. A Theological Study of a Vocation in the Church" (PhD diss., Pontifical University of Saint Thomas Aquinas, Rome, 1984), 15. Francis de Sales, *Introduction to the Devout Life* (New York: Doubleday, 1972), pt. 1, ch. 3. Perhaps the strongest appeal to this teaching prior to Vatican II comes from Pius XI: "We cannot accept the belief that this

to a Marian spirituality, devotion, and/or pedagogy enroll in Mary's school of life.[48] They discover in Our Lady the human person *par excellence!* This anthropological approach of Mary as the prototype of the image and likeness of God who is conformed to the will of God in the here and now, aids them in their primary quest to obtain from her a profound understanding and acceptance of the human condition in the world. Enrolled in the school of Mary, these communities learn from her, the bearer and educator of the Christian life, to respond to God's love in all circumstances of life; to consecrate time and relationships; to adopt a Marian style of life encompassing all aspects from arising in the morning to going to bed at the end of the day and including means to stay healthy spiritually, intellectually, physically, and emotionally.

Moreover, several of these charismatic awakenings have discovered in Mary the embodiment of authentic Christian femininity manifested particularly in her relationships to God, self, and others. Thus they strive to emulate Mary's receptive surrender at the Annunciation which unites her with God who can dispose of her in order to become fruitful first *in* her and then *through* her. As she magnifies the Lord, she herself is magnified (see Luke 1:46–48)! Like Mary, every human person is in the image and likeness of God and called to be an "icon" of the Father's love for his or her surroundings. Mary's *Fiat* means for her then and for us now: *where, when, how, and as long as He wants to use me!* In order to nurture her bond with the Holy Spirit, Mary's inner silence marked by freedom from all inner and outer atmospheric disturbances was vital. Correspondingly, times of solitude and spiritual formation are of the essence for the Spirit of God to be heard within the human heart and mind. The Virgin's experience of being inhabited by God awakens her longing of becoming a place of encounter with God for others. Many ecclesial communities regard the Visitation as a new way of evangelizing. Like her, the first disciple and first messenger of Christ and His gospel, we are chosen in our time and age as *christóphoroi*,

---

command of Christ (cf. Mt 5:48) concerns only a select and privileged group of souls and that all others may consider themselves pleasing to Him if they have attained a lower degree of holiness. Quite the contrary is true, as appears from the very generality of His words. The law of holiness embraces all men and admits of no exception." Pius XI, *Rerum Omnium Perturbationem*, Encyclical Letter promulgated on January 26, 1923, §3, online: http://www.vatican.va/holy_father/pius_xi/encyclicals/documents/hf_p-xi_enc_26011923_rerum-omnium-perturbationem_en.html.

48. For a detailed analysis of these movements, see Danielle M. Peters, *Role of Mary in the New Ecclesial Communities (20/21 c)*, presented at International Marian Research Institute, Dayton, OH, 2010, and presently prepared for publication.

i.e. those who bear and bring Christ to all who yearn for salvation. At the Visitation, Mary found Elizabeth open to the mysteries of God. This is the experience of those movements that promote the traveling of an image of Mary.[49] Numerous conversions can happen when we *"not only speak of Christ, but in a certain sense 'show' him to them."*[50]

Loyal perseverance in her *fiat* surrender by necessity included for the handmaid of the Lord *stabat iuxta crucem* ("stood by the cross," see John 19:25). John Paul II highlights the closeness of Mother and Son at the climax of salvation as follows:

> No one has experienced, to the same degree as the Mother of the crucified One, the mystery of the cross. . . . No one has received into his heart, as much as Mary did, that mystery, that truly divine dimension of the redemption effected on Calvary by means of the death of the Son, together with the sacrifice of her maternal heart, together with her definitive 'fiat.'[51]

As our teacher, the *mater dolorosa* accompanies us on our personal way of the cross. With motherly circumspection and empathy she never leaves our side. Rather, she helps us to understand that love needs to be tested and purified through suffering in order to become free *from* selfish desires and free *for* the beloved. This is a crucial lesson in Mary's School.

The Marian Dimension of Life

When the students of Mary's school fully assimilate the lessons she is teaching, then her curriculum eventually imprints a "Marian dimension on the

---

49. E.g., the traveling Fatima statue or the Schoenstatt Pilgrim Shrine; to this category also belongs the so called "Posada" in Hispanic countries or Herbergsuche (shelter seeking), practiced during Advent. A statue of Our Lady is carried from home to home or from church to church whereby the recipient, unlike the innkeeper in the gospel, offers to Mary a place to rest and give birth to her son.

50. Stanisław Ryłko, "Christians, that is christóphoroi at the heart of the world," in *Pontifical Consilium Pro Laicis: The Beauty of Being a Christian – Movements in the Church*, Proceedings of the Second World Congress of the Ecclesial Movements and New Communities, Rocca di Papa, May 31–June 2, 2006 (Libreria Editrice Vaticana, 2006), 179; italics added.

51. John Paul II, *Dives in Misericordia*, Encyclical Letter on the mercy of God, November 30, 1980, §9, online: http://www.vatican.va/holy_father/john_paul_ii/encyclicals/documents/hf_jp-ii_enc_30111980_dives-in-misericordia_en.html.

life of a disciple of Christ"[52] which "has its beginning in Christ but can also be said to be definitively directed towards him."[53] The "Marian dimension of life" refers to the beauty of Mary's person "which mirrors the loftiest sentiments of which the human heart is capable: the totality of the gift of self in love; the strength that is capable of bearing the greatest sorrows; limitless fidelity and tireless devotion to work; the ability to combine penetrating intuition with words, support and encouragement."[54] In imitation of Mary, the Church and all her members are called to impress this Marian dimension on the world.

It becomes apparent that mere intellectual comprehension does not suffice in order to excel in Mary's school. Rather, our teacher wishes to influence our entire being including the natural, rational, emotional, and supernatural life. In fact, we could say that, Our Lady's curriculum is based on the principle that our nature must first become receptive for grace, which in turn will elevate and perfect our nature.[55] That is to say, grace does not exist for itself alone; rather it is directed towards human nature. Conversely, nature determines the direction and goal of grace in no small measure. Hence we come to see the vital connection between nature and grace! Through grace we become fully the human person we are meant to be as child of the Father, member of Christ, and sanctuary of the Holy Spirit.[56] As a result, in Mary's School we increasingly grow in appreciation of the unmerited gift of grace as well as of the role of our educator, the *Mediatrix* of grace (subordinate to Christ's mediation) in the economy of salvation[57] in general and in view of our particular personal formation.

Education Through and for Love

The all-inclusive formation we receive in the school of our educator thus aims at the wholesome development of all human faculties. It is best

---

52. RM §45. For a discussion on this "Marian dimension," see Pontifical International Marian Academy, *Mother of the Lord: Memory, Presence, Hope*, trans. Thomas A. Thompson (Staten Island, NY: St. Paul, 2007), 21n70.

53. RM §46.

54. Ibid.

55. See Thomas Aquinas, *Summa Theologica* I, q. 1; q. 8, art. 2.

56. See LG §53.

57. See LG §55, 62.

achieved in the reciprocity of love between Mary and us.[58] In and through the uniting and assimilating effect of love we are led to a life with Our Lady consisting of shared interests and aspirations, and to our participation in what is good and dear to her. This mutual loving in, with, and for one another constitutes the essence of the Virgin's education, which, supported by grace, leads to a Marian attitude or Marian way of life. It goes without saying that this educational process involves self-sacrifice and self-denial.

At stake is the formation of the heart! Here we touch upon the core of all educational efforts: the human heart with its capacity to love what is noble and beautiful. Yet, at the same time, the human heart is also the seat of vice: of the lust of the flesh and of the pride of life. Thus, whether a person aspires to his or her vocation to holiness depends on the formation of the heart, since we are inclined to associate with whom or what we love. Our hearts must be purified of self-love (self-idolatry) which impedes our love of God. Addressing all those who prepare to be educated by Our Lady, Father Kentenich, the founder of Schoenstatt Work, drew attention to this "cleansing of love" which classical asceticism calls purification:

> My heart must renounce all egocentric self-will; . . . I must give up the stubbornness of wanting to have everything my way, otherwise I cannot . . . abandon myself to the inspiration of the Holy Spirit, cannot be gradually liberated from the enticements of the world, from the attacks of the devil, and the misleading illusions of my own wayward and mercurial drives.[59]

Christian spiritual tradition and humanist psychology teach that the most effective way to forego selfish and complacent distortions of love is a wholesome giving of self to the other, understood as a "personal you." The more the heart is thus consecrated to the love of God and his mother, the more it becomes immersed in the suitable ambience and privileged forum of Mary's school and receptive to the valuable lessons which Our Lady learned in the Savior's school of love.

Mary's Curriculum

Thus in Mary's school, we learn to ponder with and like Mary the mysteries of God's loving providence in our life. Treasuring all these things in and through the heart of Mary we are led to identify and become sensitive to

---

58. See nn37–40 and the related text in n10.
59. SCS §33.

the meaning of God's intervention in the daily circumstances of life and to act accordingly. Like Mary, during our pilgrimage of faith, we will at times contemplate Christ with a questioning look, a penetrating gaze, a look of sorrow, a gaze radiant with joy, and a heart afire.[60] She intercedes for us to obtain the grace of a pure love thereby encouraging us to overcome the obstacles preventing us from performing our ordinary duties extraordinarily well.[61] The goal of each lesson is achieved when we think, act, and react in conformity with Christ thereby becoming authentic witnesses to him in all spheres of life.

Immaculate Concept—Eschatological Icon

In this context the last two defined Marian dogmas, the Immaculate Conception (1854) and the Assumption (1950), constitute a pedagogical event whose lessons are integral to Mary's School. By being the blueprint—*immaculate concept*—of the fully redeemed human person, Mary models for us essential qualities of the dignity and vocation of humankind.[62] In her we can ascertain the inner wealth and personal resources of a person who is unconditionally and freely surrendered to Christ and his kingdom. The Virgin's *fiat* teaches us that "freedom is not realized in decisions made against God. For how could it be an exercise of true freedom to refuse to be open to the very reality which enables our self-realization"[63] and thus spiritual fullness? Since every free choice is immanent to the process of a person's moral becoming, the art of truly free decision-making and abiding by those decisions is at the heart of any lesson taught in Mary's School. By emulating Mary's longing to respond to God's wish and will rather than to her own whims and feelings we learn to ascend to the true freedom of the children of God.[64]

---

60. See RV §10.

61. John Paul II, "Sanctity Is Acquired by Living Ordinary Things Extraordinarily," Angelus Address of September 1, 2002. *L'Osservatore Romano*, Weekly English Ed., September 4, 2002, 1.

62. See MD §11.

63. John Paul II, *Fides et Ratio*, Encyclical Letter on the relationship between Faith and Reason, September 14, 1998, §13, para. 2. See also §75, para. 2, online: http://www.vatican.va/holy_father/john_paul_ii/encyclicals/documents/hf_jp-ii_enc_15101998_fides-et-ratio_en.html.

64. See CCC §1730–48.

A second lesson the immaculate blueprint wishes to convey is God's unconditional love for each human person. Mary's awareness of being "the beloved daughter of the Father"⁶⁵ and her consciousness of being chosen for a mission excluded any type of inferiority and derailment from God's wish and will for her. To the degree that Mary's School initiates this personal commitment to a new beginning with the help of grace, even guilt and sin can pave the way to holiness as in the experience of St. Paul who said "I rejoice in my smallness so that God's greatness can radiate forth in me" (2 Cor 12:9). Our Lady's curriculum which transmits the paradoxical awareness of being greatly valued exactly because of and despite being utterly small, requires humility and mutual trust. The lessons leading to self-recognition and self-evaluation bring about an optimistic realism that God chooses exactly the weak and humble to build His kingdom!

Likewise we can detect pedagogical implications inherent in Mary's Assumption. In her, who is in heaven with body and soul, we honor the fully redeemed person. *The Catechism of the Catholic Church* (article 972) presents her as the "eschatological icon of the Church" who sheds light on the meaning and fulfillment of the Christian life. The dogma sets a seal on the handmaid's victorious battle over nature, including all drives and passions, as well as over the devil and his influence. At the same time it highlights the fact that "taken up to heaven, she did not lay aside her salvific duty.... By her maternal love she cares for the brothers and sisters of her Son who still journey on earth."⁶⁶

The dogma of the Assumption also draws our attention to the Christian understanding of the human body. As dwelling place of the Trinity (see 1 Cor 6:19), our bodies are the instruments of our souls. Since the spiritual soul constitutes the ultimate principle of the human person, our bodies, which include the emotions, are meant to function in subordination to our rational souls. Concern for our physical well-being or for our exterior beauty is therefore not an end in itself; rather the body's beauty and health are meant to be at the service of the soul. In Mary's school we learn to treat our bodies with reverence and discipline, since knowing their needs and not succumbing to their cravings corresponds to the Christian sense of wellness and beauty.

---

65. LG §53.
66. LG §62.

Finally, Mary's Assumption into heaven can teach us important principles concerning the preparation for a Christian death. The lesson plan of our maternal educator reminds us of the transience of all earthly things.

It is consoling that Mary accompanies us on our personal way of the cross. The encounter with her and her son offers us strength and support and reminds us that our Easter morning, i.e. the resurrection of our bodies and souls, needs to be preceded by our personal Good Friday as well.

Domestic Church and Marian Pilgrimage Places

Mary's school is particularly effective in the domestic church (that is, the Christian family which is a reflection of the Holy Family at Nazareth)[67] as well as in Marian shrines and in the religious traditions of societies, cultures, and nations. This worldwide dimension and presence of Mary's school perpetuates her maternal and pedagogical presence throughout time and in all cultures.

It is in the domestic church where Our Lady can unfold her pedagogical solicitude in a most effective way. When a family or an individual invite Mary and her son into their homes and expressly open themselves to her maternal education, then she can create an atmosphere of peace and harmony, purity and joy, prayer, freedom, respect and love similar to that which prevailed in the Holy Family at Nazareth. Mary's formation of the family in turn generates a communal awareness of support and strength where healthy attachments are experienced and grow through reciprocal love of children to their parents and of spouses to each other.[68] In this setting, "an integral vision of the human person and of his or her vocation"[69] to become a gift for the other is possible.

It is in the domestic church and at pilgrimage places where we can most tangibly sense Our Lady's formation and mediation. Just as the guests at the wedding feast at Cana benefitted from Mary's intercession, we too can turn to Mary who will intercede for us with her son and obtain the material and/or spiritual goods that we need.

---

67. See LG §11; CCC §1655–57. See also FC §21, online: http://www.vatican.va/holy_father/john_paul_ii/apost_exhortations/documents/hf_jp-ii_exh_19811122_familiaris-consortio_en.html.

68. See FC §18.

69. FC §32.

Conclusion

Christ's testament to the Church and to each of the faithful is a "Mother, Teacher, and Guide"[70] to accompany us on our pilgrimage of life. Mary exercises this mission in a twofold manner: she educates us through her example and mediates for us the graces necessary for our vocation and mission in life. The Blessed Mother was well prepared for her educational duties towards her spiritual children through the experience gained by raising her own child, our Lord Jesus Christ, as well as through the lessons she was taught by her son. This communion between Mother and Son through whom Mary is also intimately united with the Church,[71] creates the foundation for our conviction that the school of Mary brings forth saints.[72]

Mary's pedagogy of holiness[73] is supported by the self-gift of teacher and student which includes the "commitment to be conformed to Christ, [by] putting ourselves at the school of his Mother and allowing her to accompany us"[74] on the daily pilgrimage heavenwards. Our Lady's lessons signal a gift and challenge for us! At issue is a timely education towards holiness which, in the words of Pope Benedict XVI, Our Lady offers to each one of us adapted to our needs:

> Mary Most Holy, the pure and immaculate Virgin, is for us a school . . . destined to guide us and give us strength on the path that leads us to the Creator of Heaven and Earth. . . . Remain in the school of Mary. Take inspiration from her teachings, seek to welcome and to preserve in your hearts the enlightenment that she, by divine mandate, sends you from on high.[75]

---

70. RV §37.
71. See LG §63; RM §42.
72. See EE §62.
73. NMI §31.
74. EE §57.
75. Benedict XVI, *Address after the Recitation of the Holy Rosary and Meeting with Priests, Members of the Consecrated Life, Seminarians and Deacons*, Basilica of the Shrine of Aparecida, Brazil, May 12, 2007, *L'Osservatore Romano*, Weekly English Ed., May 20, 2007, 11.

9

Currents and Contentions
Authentic Devotion to the God-Bearer at the Dawn of the Third Millennium

KENNETH F. YOSSA

"Know and remember, that the matter of your salvation is always near to the heart of Our Lady, the Mother of God. . . . As the matter of our salvation is near to the Saviour, so likewise it is near to Her. Turn to Her with full faith, trust, and love."[1]

The place of the God-Bearer has undergone clearly identifiable periods of evolution regarding personal devotion, liturgical, and extra-liturgical public worship and other currents within the life of the Church—particularly in the Christian West. The foundational elements of this devotion have their roots in early Medieval practices and perspectives, extending into an early Modern period of Romanticization, the latter continuing more or less unchanged within the Catholic Church until the mid-twentieth century. Like so many other aspects of spirituality and the dimensions of its corporate ecclesial expression, the post-Conciliar (i.e., after Vatican II) Catholic Church has been challenged from within by questions of how and to what extent (if any) authentic devotion to Mary ought to have a place in the life

---

1. St. John of Kronstadt, *My Life in Christ*, trans. E. E. Goulaeff (Jordanville, NY: Holy Trinity Monastery, Printshop of St. Job of Pochaev, 1994), 255.

of Christians. As the earliest years of the third millennium unfold, the contours of this devotion continue to develop, counterpoised with the Catholic Church's received understanding of Marian devotion, social and cultural movements, and the personal convictions of clergy and faithful.

Marian Devotion: A Journey Toward the Nadir

Prior to Vatican II (1962–1965), devotional acts, whether perennial or seasonal, personal or corporate, honoring the Mother of God were for many centuries quite commonplace throughout the Catholic world. However, by the end of the 1960s, particularly in the West, the Church experienced a general decline in devotion to Our Lady. This can at least partially be attributed to a reaction to forms of devotional life in which the Mother of God somehow seemed to displace the preeminent role of Christ in practices of private piety and/or public manifestations.[2] Karl Rahner noted in the early 1980s, "In the religious life of the average educated Catholic in our rational and enlightened world, devotion to Mary is neither intense nor explicit."[3]

The historical record compels us to admit frankly that some forms of piety directed devotion to Mary in such a way that the role of Christ as Redeemer and universal Intercessor before God the Father was in some cases rendered opaque or otherwise marginalized. Even John Henry Newman admits his own difficulties in the latter nineteenth century with the prevailing Marian devotional climate then current among the faithful of the Catholic Restoration in England and Wales. In a letter to fellow Tractarian John Keble, Newman expresses the Marian doctrine of "advocacy" counterpoised with forms of popular devotion as expressed by Suarez and Bernadine of Sienna:

> The former is a theologian, laying down doctrine—the latter is a devotional author—and moreover writes for Italians, for those who already knew and held the doctrine of her Intercession, and

---

2. It cannot be denied that this position is a reprise of the same objections deriving from the Reformation. However, its terminal point, viz. the apparent affirmation of Divine Sovereignty, is not necessarily the same. This issue will be treated later in this chapter.

3. Karl Rahner, "Courage for Devotion to Mary," in *Theological Investigations*, vol. 23, *Final Writings*, trans. Joseph Donceel and Hugh M. Riley (New York: Crossroad, 1992), 130. [The passage was taken from Rahner's *Schriften zur Theologie 16*, published in Cologne in 1984.] It should be noted that in his essay, Father Rahner provides no explanation for this phenomenon.

were in a country where to neglect devotion to her would have been a rejection of a privilege which they *possessed*. I can never deny my belief that the Blessed Virgin prays efficaciously for the Church, and for individual souls in and out of it. Nor can I deny that to be devout to her is a duty *following* on this doctrine—but I will never say, even though St. Bernadine said it, that no one is saved who is not devout to her, and (tho' I don't know St. B's), I do not think he would have said it had he not been in his own Christendom, or had he known the history of the first centuries, or had he seen the religious state of things which we see ourselves.[4]

Medieval Marian devotion frequently reflected the ethos of royal courts in both the Christian East and West wherein Mary was the all-beneficent "Queen Mother," interceding with her son, the *Kyrios/Dominus*.[5] With the onslaught of the Reformation, belief in the total depravity of man and his utter inability to accomplish or merit any good, traditional Marian imagery became even more firmly established on the Catholic side. Through the development and diffusion of Enlightenment ideas in Europe and the New World, authors such as Louis-Marie Grignon de Monfort and Alphonsus Ligouri[6]—the latter whose lifespan was almost exactly that of Voltaire—provided the basis of a new Marian spirituality that would test the limits of its authenticity. Kathleen Coyle observes that in this period, "romanticism, an attitude of mind favorable to irrational influences, to emotional as well as mystical experiences, rejected the Enlightenment program."[7] With

   4. Newman to John Keble, October 8, 1865, *Letters and Diaries of John Henry Newman*, ed. Charles Stephen Dessain (London: Nelson and Sons, 1972) 22:68; italics in original.

   5. See, e.g., the *Akathistos* to Mary (*irmos* of Ode 1), which is a customary translation in English of the phrase *Basilidi Mētri*. "The mother of the king in Jerusalem was known as 'the great Lady' (see for example, 1 Kgs 15:13), where the phrase is usually translated 'queen mother,' and so the royal couple were mother and son." Leslie Brubaker and Mary B. Cunningham, *Cult of the Mother of God in Byzantium: Texts and Images* (Surrey, UK: Ashgate, 2001), 95.

   6. A word of clarification is needed here. Such authors, both considered outstanding authorities of Catholic teaching (Ligouri himself is a Doctor of the Church), were certainly within the bounds of orthodoxy. However, they both tend toward a kind of post-Baroque exaggeration in their treatment of Marian devotion and theology. Such excessiveness, undoubtedly borne of true love and devotion to the Mother of God, was not uncommon in other eras—particularly in the Christian East. Today, however, this early-modern hyperbole (e.g., the admonition to dedicate oneself as a "slave of Mary") would be extremely difficult if not impossible for many Christian faithful to accept, especially given the evolution of modern society.

   7. Kathleen Coyle, *Mary in the Christian Tradition* (Mystic, CT: Twenty-Third Publications, 1996), 104.

the ascendancy of the modern nation-states in Europe following the Napoleonic era, the "Romantic" era of Marian spirituality was increasing in popularity and would continue well into the mid-twentieth century.[8]

Several trends during the twentieth century—including the *Ressourcement* ("a return to the sources") movement's recovery of the Church Fathers, a renewed promotion of critical Scripture study among Catholics and the concept of *aggiornomento* ("bringing up to date") promoted by the Second Vatican Council—were making received Marian spirituality increasingly anachronistic. Although the discoveries emerging from these trends could have been applied to and integrated with public and personal devotion to Our Lady for renewed and enriched practices (without necessarily discarding all traditional forms), Marian devotion throughout North American Roman Catholic communities was severely curtailed or disappeared almost entirely, with notable exceptions. Usages, which included liturgical and extra-liturgical devotions such as the May Crowning, processions with the rosary, novenas, or even votive Masses in honor of Our Lady remained far from universal. Likewise, traditional private devotions such as the rosary or other prayers, as well as a practical Marian spirituality incorporated into Christian living, continued to varying degrees but, again, remained far from common among practicing Catholics.

In chapter 8 of Vatican II's Dogmatic Constitution on the Church (*Lumen Gentium*: hereafter LG), the Council Fathers "strongly urge[d] theologians and preachers of the word of God to be careful to refrain as much from all false exaggeration . . . in considering the special dignity of the Mother of God."[9] Marian public devotion of the traditional style, was perhaps best preserved among various ethnic communities, especially amid Slavs and the Latin peoples. But such preservation was looked upon by many as an expression of an archaic and/or ethnic piety, which had to be tolerated for the sake of diversity. For others, the notion of traditional Marian piety was valid enough, but not particularly helpful, easily understood or even relevant for the greater portion of a North American postmodern society that was moving supposedly toward a strictly "theocentric" framework.

---

8. At least to some extent, this pre-twentieth-century piety continued more or less unchanged because there had been neither a "critical" evaluation of it, nor extensive opposition to it.

9. LG §67. These sentiments are by no means original to Vatican II, and were expressed in earlier decades by Popes Pius XI (see encyclical letter *Ecclesia Dei*) and Pius XII (see encyclical letter *Fulgens Corona*), as indicated in the footnotes of Conciliar texts.

However, the Council Fathers in literally the same sentence cited from LG balanced this corrective by enjoining the Church to be "moved to a filial love toward our mother [the Blessed Virgin] and to the imitation of her virtues,"[10] and especially that the cult (i.e., devotion) of the Blessed Virgin be generously fostered, and that the practices and exercises of devotion towards her, recommended by the teaching authority of the Church in the course of the centuries be highly esteemed, and that those decrees, which were given in the early days regarding the [devotional] images of Christ, the Blessed Virgin, and the saints, be religiously observed.[11]

Such admonitions unfortunately went largely unheeded. This is perhaps no surprise in those comparatively chaotic years for Western European and North American Catholics in which relevant conciliar and post-conciliar interpretive decrees were randomly and selectively promoted to the detriment of others. Certainly, the ostensible lack of generalized, populist and multigenerational devotion to the Mother of God in the decades immediately following Vatican II can by no means be laid at the feet of either the vast majority of the Council Fathers or their conciliar decrees. Even the (arguably) most famous Council Father noted that Vatican II "made great strides forward with regard to Marian doctrine and devotion."[12] During the Council years and immediately beyond, a number of popular movements (particularly the Blue Army and the Legion of Mary) were dedicated to the promotion of Marian devotion and spirituality. Others, such as the Sodality of Our Lady (for girls and young women), common in North American parishes by the 1950s, had virtually disappeared by the end of the following decade.

Within a very few years after Vatican II, it was clear in many places that new forms of Marian devotion were *not* developing alongside more established ones. Indeed, there essentially were no new devotions in that period, and opposition or abandonment of many traditional devotions—along with a genuine and received Marian piety—simply created a vacuum. This development was significant enough so that Pope Paul VI addressed the issue in the Apostolic Exhortation *Marialis Cultus*. While Pope Paul clearly discussed the excesses and misunderstandings present in pre-conciliar Marian devotion, although not dwelling on these, he also issued a call toward promotion of genuine renewal:

10. LG §67.
11. LG.
12. John Paul II, *Crossing the Threshold of Hope* (New York: Knopf, 1994), 13.

> Hence it is that the forms in which this devotion is expressed, being subject to the ravages of time, show the need for a renewal that will permit them to substitute elements that are transient, to emphasize the elements that are ever new and to incorporate the doctrinal data obtained from theological reflection and the proposals of the Church's magisterium. This shows the need for episcopal conferences, local churches, religious families and communities of the faithful to promote a genuine creative activity and at the same time to proceed to a careful revision of expressions and exercises of piety directed towards the Blessed Virgin.[13]

Certainly, new devotionals were produced in this spirit, especially with new emphasis on Scripture, but it can be argued that original widespread popularist movements or prayer forms along this line never really took root.[14] Rather, those practices which have remained on the global or transregional level are mostly the familiar pre-conciliar usages, especially the rosary and various novenas, although these have occasionally undergone some revision along the lines given in *Marialis Cultus*.[15] Certainly, Pope Paul's vision of a world open and ready to receive the authentic Christian faith and life appropriated to "modern" patterns of thought (guided along a secular-Western conduit), proved repeatedly to be overly optimistic.[16]

---

13. AAS 25.

14. One example is found in the anonymously produced devotional booklet (ca. 1967) *Devotions in Honor of Christ and His Mother of Perpetual Help*. It is essentially the same as the pre-Conciliar versions produced under the auspices of the Redemptorist Fathers, but has notable differences reflecting contemporary sensibilities—e.g., pluralizing the prayers, and substitution of terms such as "miserable sinner" with "poor sinner," and "slave" with "servant."

15. In fact, Pope Paul must have realized the utter impossibility of "starting from scratch" and added in the same paragraph of *Marialis Cultus*: "We would like this revision to be respectful of wholesome tradition and open to the legitimate requests of the people of our time. It seems fitting therefore, venerable Brothers, to put forward some principles for action in this field." MC §25.

16. MC §40. Despite its many beautiful and valid exhortations, Pope Paul's writing evidences an almost excessive concern for "a discrepancy existing between some aspects of this [Marian] devotion and modern anthropological discoveries and profound changes in the psycho-sociological field in which modern man lives and works" (§34). While perhaps critiquing the excesses in some forms of Marian devotion discussed in this essay, as they are here, his tone here suggests that the traditional forms of Marian devotion needed to be *completely reframed* in order to be acceptable to modern peoples—i.e., those living in Western, industrialized nations. In reading these words nearly forty years after they were written, it is difficult to envision how the modern social sciences could or should have had a positive influence upon Marian devotion, and in such a relatively uncritical manner.

There is little doubt that what could be described as a "Low Mariology" attained dominance in North American Roman Catholic culture around the time of Vatican II and for years thereafter, although this decreased gradually as the 20th century hastened to a close. This phenomenon was characterized, at least in part, by a belief resembling that of the continental Reformation wherein Marian devotion or spirituality was suspect at best and blasphemous at worst. At the same time, the ongoing (and essentially post-colonial) post-War movements affirming human dignity, from a secularist point of view, also contributed to this new type of Mariological perspective. While a more in-depth discussion is beyond the scope of this present essay, it can be said that such concepts lead ultimately to an eccentric anthropomorphic objectification.[17] Within such a construct, man is rendered a supremely central figure, whose numinal and transcendent aspects of existence are consequently excluded or marginalized. Such a perspective leads, in turn, toward a minimalism which nullifies or re-modulates even traces of traditional Marian devotion and piety. Here, Mary is no longer a transcendental *Genetrix/Theotókos*, a person with whom we have a loving and familial relationship, but is an existential "spokeswoman" for various civil, political, and social causes. As Kathleen Coyle notes, "Mary must clearly call the church to the inclusive, liberating, and prophetic discipleship that Mary embodies."[18] Putting aside the specific valance such terms bear in certain circles as related, say, to postmodern feminism and the theologies of liberation, there seems to be little or no room for a Mary with whom the Western faithful have a filial, personal relationship—whether expressed in corporate services or private worship.[19]

17. Fr. Alexander Schmemann has commented on the secularization of western culture, its erroneous emphasis on the material world and this-worldly concerns, and the detrimental effects that this focus has on anthropology. He has recommended Mariology that is rooted in traditional doctrine emphasizing the transcendent as an antidote. See ch. 2 of *Celebration of Faith*, vol. 3, *Virgin Mary* (New York: St. Vladimir Seminary Press, 1995).

18. Coyle, *Mary*, 104. It should be made clear here that the identification of Our Lady as an active promoter of justice, righteousness, etc. is not to be disparaged. My concern here is that her active and personal role cannot be limited to such objectives, even more so when she is caricatured as an advocate for movements or causes that might even run counter to an authentic Christian ethic.

19. Migliore rightly identifies a crucial and inaccurate postmodern prioritization of Mary in which she "is seen as a *prototype of the liberation struggle of poor people*, and especially of poor women against injustice and oppression." As a result, Mary's *witness* to divine grace (although she provides much more than this in Catholic understanding) risks identification instead with a "revolutionary faith and action in history." See Daniel

It certainly is the case, as George Tavard points out, that despite the prominence of Mary in the infancy narratives of Matthew and Luke, she "is hardly prominent in the following accounts of the life and ministry of Jesus."[20] This fact is often cited as part of a larger movement, which abandons the Marian devotions found in Church tradition as variously superstitious, non/anti-scriptural, and anti-intellectual on the one hand, and in need of reprogramming for "the modern mentality" on the other.[21] Such attitudes have been fueled by a series of positions that became quite apparent certainly by the early 1970s, in which the focus on Mary was "much more as the 'woman of faith,' 'disciple,' and 'model' than as 'spiritual mother' or 'mediatrix.'"[22] By extension, Mary became excluded from devotional life which led ultimately, in a certain sense, to the "absence of woman as God-mediator and even as God-representative."[23] Even the bishops of the United States at the time corporately lamented this trend in a direct but somewhat restrained critique:

> No survey is needed to show that all over the country many forms of Marian devotion have fallen into disuse, and others are taking an uncertain course. In an age avid for symbols . . . the use of [Roman] Catholic Marian symbols, such as the scapular and the Miraculous Medal, has noticeably diminished. . . . The praying of the Rosary has declined. Some [Roman] Catholics feel that there has even been a campaign to strip the churches of statues of Our Lady and the saints.[24]

L. Migliore, "Woman of Faith: Toward a Reformed Understanding of Mary," in *Blessed One: Protestant Perspectives on Mary*, ed. Beverly Roberts Gaventa and Cynthia L. Rigby (Louisville: Westminster John Knox, 2002) 121–22.

20. George H. Tavard, "Genesis of Mariology," in *Feminist Companion to Mariology*, ed. Amy-Jill Levine and Maria Mayo Robbins (Cleveland: Pilgrim, 2005) 108.

21. More specifically, I refer here more to *attitudes* based within the traditional perspectives of devotion.

22. Arthur Burton Calkins, "Mary Co-Redemptrix: The Beloved Associate of Christ," in *Mary: A Guide for Priests, Deacons, Seminarians and Consecrated Persons*, ed. Mark Miravalle (Goleta, CA: Seat of Wisdom / Queenship, 2008) 391.

23. Bonnie J. Miller-McLemore, "Pondering All These Things," in *Blessed One* (Louisville: Westminster John Knox, 2002) 110.

24. National Conference of Catholic Bishops, *Behold Your Mother: Woman of Faith*, pastoral letter (Lackawanna, NY: Our Lady of Victory Homes of Charity, 1973), 92. In the following paragraph of the pastoral, the bishops add—somewhat curiously—that "it is not possible to assess and comment [in the pastoral] on all the individual aspects of concern" with regard to this phenomenon (ibid., 94).

This "campaign" is often supported by many Catholics, especially among those of the "Silent" and "Baby Boomer" generations (respectively, birth year groups 1935–1942 and 1943–1960). The Irish commentator John D. Sheridan quite pointedly decried what was, in the early to mid-1970s, an increasing divide regarding the place of the Mother of God in the life of the Church from the perspective of private revelation:

> Our Lady's periodic appearance and her repeated warnings are discounted by many of our latter-day theologians, who make recurring apologies for their superstitious fellow-Catholics and complain that any mention of apparitions or heavenly messages embarrasses them before the non-Catholic churchmen with whom they hold innocuous dialogues and theological get-togethers at which Catholic apologies are more noticeable than Catholic apologetics.[25]

This diffidence regarding devotion to Our Lady was also present at a public level. In the Roman Catholic Charismatic Renewal, for instance, practical mention of Mary or her inclusion in prayers or teachings was conspicuously absent from its early years in the late 1960s. This undoubtedly reflected an uncritical adoption of many classical Pentecostal/Holiness and Calvinist concepts by the Renewal, which (at least until more recent times) included the traditional notion within such Reformation-based traditions that "devotion" to Mary must be suspect.[26] I alluded to this at the beginning of the essay, but there is also another factor, which has worked against Marian spirituality and devotion, and indeed creates a negative impact on authentic Christian piety generally.

Finding Equilibrium

Much of the apparent discomfort with Marian devotion was already receding within the pontificate of John Paul II. It is difficult to assess how and to what degree the late blessed Pope of Rome directly provided for

---

25. John D. Sheridan, *Hungry Sheep* (Huntington, IN: Our Sunday Visitor, 1974), 109. It must be added that Sheridan's stinging critique on dialogue suggests a certain bias toward the ecumenical enterprise at that period. Nevertheless, his characterization of professional theologians distancing themselves from apparitions "worthy of credence" is even to this day quite accurate in some circles.

26. Fortunately, a significant shift in this situation has occurred with a surge of Marian devotion since the 1990s and is at least acknowledged as not inconsistent with the spirituality of the "Renewal." I will discuss this presently.

what was clearly a renewal of Marian devotion among individuals, families, and in public services developed toward the end of the last century. This renewal continues to gain increasingly widespread (viz. global) acceptance, especially among the laity. To a great extent this could well be attributed to the application of new social media, particularly the Internet. This shift occurred not because of the spiritual *détente* found in the previous generation, but rather in the initiatives of Pope John Paul II.[27] The latter include the proclamation of the 1987–88 "Marian Year" (only the second in history), as well as his bold and unapologetic acknowledgement of the traditions of Christian families or "domestic churches," of parish and missionary communities, religious institutes, and dioceses; through the radiance and attraction of the great shrines where not only individuals or local groups, but sometimes whole nations and societies, even whole continents, seek to meet the Mother of the Lord.[28]

It would still be a few years before these "traditions" would gain new momentum and authentication at the global level, and in that sense his words were prescient. While John Paul noted "that in our own time too, new manifestations of this spirituality and devotion are not lacking" without specifying their nature or type, it was clear that the pendulum was shifting.[29]

This phenomenon of Marian renewal is part of a larger development within the Roman Catholic community particularly, evident in North America and other Western regions, wherein several factors have indicated a more "traditional" turn. Consider, for example, the 2011 English translation of the Roman Missal that more accurately reflects the words and concepts of the Latin-language typical edition. The nearly unrestricted permission by the Holy See given for the use of the last pre-Conciliar typical editions of the so-called "Tridentine" Missal, Ritual, Breviary, and Pontifical[30] is another example, along with the adapted version of the liturgical offices and attendant customs of the *Book of Common Prayer* used among

27. See n14 above, where I discuss very briefly the existential perspective of Pope Paul VI, whose form of modern Christian humanism exhibited a belief that certain aspects of worship and spirituality were essentially irreconcilable with contemporary Western society and needed to be replaced.

28. RM §28, in AAS 79 (1987).

29. RM §48.

30. The "extraordinary" or so-called Tridentine use of the Roman liturgical Rite. See Benedict XVI, *Summorum Pontificum*, "On the celebration of the Roman Rite according to the Missal of 1962," Apostolic Letter (*Motu proprio*—issued on the pope's own intention), in AAS 99 (2007), 777–81. See n42 below.

former Episcopal and Anglican communities which have entered Catholic communion.[31] Likewise, the resurgence of exposition and benediction of the Blessed Sacrament and Forty Hours' (which in some places were literally extinct), and the 2011 revival of mandatory Friday abstinence in England and Wales are indications that traditional practices, established over time, make an ongoing appeal to early twentieth century men and women that would have been virtually impossible to predict less than two decades ago.

These developments, the merits of which can be argued and can only be judged ultimately at a future time, are indicative of the appropriation of structures surrounding devotion and piety which are not necessarily "modern" or "anti-modern," but rather are understandable, comforting, straightforward, and capable of sustaining growth in the Christian life. Within the Marian devotional enterprise, specifically, such developments may or may not be replications of past traditional practices. The root factor, it seems, returns us again to the focus on the transcendent. In a new context, this does not mean that our relationship with Our Lady is removed from the struggles of this world. In appropriating traditional and recognizable forms as a kind of framework, Roman Catholics now can expand the parameters of their Marian devotional life, and truly integrate it as one of many important relationships within the Communion of Saints in this world as well as the next. An example of such integration was cited a decade before Vatican II, in the prescient admonition of Pope Pius XII:

> Let them, besides, supplicate the Divine Mother, asking bread for the hungry, and justice for the oppressed; return to the fatherland for those banished and exiled; a hospitable roof for the homeless; due liberty for those unjustly cast into prison or custody; for those, who, after so many years have elapsed since the last war, still silently languish and sigh in captivity, the long desired homecoming; for those blind in body or soul, the joy of refulgent light. And for all those separated from each other by hatred, envy and discord, let them implore reconciliation through fraternal charity and through that harmony and peaceful industriousness which is founded on truth, justice and mutual friendship.[32]

---

31. See Pope Benedict XVI, *Anglicanorum Cœtibus*, "Providing for personal ordinariates for Anglicans," Apostolic Constitution, in AAS 101 (2009), 985–90.

32. Pius XII, *Fulgens Corona*, "Proclamation of the Marian Year and the Centenary of the Proclamation of the Dogma of the Immaculate Conception", Encyclical Letter, §39, in AAS 45 (1953).

At least since the mid-1990s, demarcation lines regarding Marian devotion and spirituality have emerged among North American Catholic lay faithful, religious, and clergy. Essentially, these are drawn broadly along generational lines, although there is a great deal of overlap between them. Many of those from the "Greatest Generation," the era of the World War II veterans and their contemporaries, who have held a devotional life over the years, retain essentially the Marian devotions of their youth. These include attendance at pilgrimages, shrines, use of the Rosary, and attendance at May devotions, Saturday Marian votive Masses, and novenas to our Lady under various titles.[33] Those who participate are found to hold primarily the more traditional forms of Medieval and post-Medieval piety mentioned earlier, omitting overtly christological and scripturally-reflective themes. Interestingly, many of those moving currently toward mid-life among the "Generation X" (birth years 1961–1983) along with the older early "Millennials" (birth years 1984–2001), share similar views and have to a great extent adopted such forms of piety and spirituality as well. Newer variations on older forms of Marian piety include the use of the new rosary mysteries "of Light" promulgated by John Paul II (although not original to him), and devotions that include prayers that explore Our Lady's role in the economy of salvation. Another Marian devotional trend found primarily among "Silent" and "Baby Boomer" generations in North America retains a deep suspicion with regard to specific services, rituals, etc. that retain Mary as their essential focus, and can be subdivided between those who have little or no interest in cultivating Marian-specific devotion personally and those who have co-opted the Mother of God as a standard bearer or icon for various causes or ideals (which, by the way, are not all necessarily wrong in their appellations).

There remains the difficulty with promotion of the public *cultus* of Mary and/or developing a relationship with Mary as a friend, helper, and intercessor. Trends for and against the promotion of the public *cultus* have been perhaps most easily identifiable among some religious orders for decades.[34] A similar breakdown across the generational divide, again in fairly general terms, can also be found among diocesan priests who are particularly influenced by the seminaries where their formation is received.

33. The Miraculous Medal novena, promulgated with vigor by the Redemptorist Fathers in the past, has remained one of the most popular.

34. Positions on the issue could widely vary, depending on the age range and location of the order's membership, as well as whether an order possesses a particular Marian charism.

Cui Bono?

So, while we have examined the state of the question regarding the "what" and "why" in the progress or devolution of Marian devotion and spirituality, we can now consider the issue of the value and good of it. My fellow essayists in this work are taking up that discussion as it applies to particular issues regarding Mary's crucial place as a Mother for the world. And there is so much work for her here below! But in the final analysis, perhaps one question that must be posed is whether genuine, loving, and heartfelt devotion (which is ultimately an expression of a *relationship*) is an option for our time—or for any other. Strictly speaking, the Church does not *mandate* personal devotion to the God-Bearer, or the saints in heaven, or the righteous souls detained in purgatory. Indeed, while the Church since at least the fifth century has warmly recommended the Christian faithful to the Mother of God, to go beyond a recommendation would run counter to Christian liberty; devotion of this kind is a matter of personal choice, as long as individuals do not reject its legitimacy or efficacy for others. As Rahner observes,

> It is quite legitimate for individuals to modestly admit that they do not possess a certain charism that they discover and admire in another person . . . provided only that they do not, in principle, absolutely reject such a charism if it is offered to them by God's grace in the course of their religious development.[35]

Yet as a truism, the principle was used to promote a "non-mandatory" approach to devotion, public or private, which undermined pious practices, like regular fasting and abstinence, daily attendance at the Holy Liturgy and frequent confession. Marian devotion could be quietly and simply disposed of, as its relevancy was rendered doubtful for truly *modern* Christians who were fine just "as is." Thus rather than affirming positive aspects of already-existent devotion, or allowing for the organic evolution of new ones reflecting the sentiments of the Council, the public *cultus* of Mary was frequently relegated to the haunts of pilgrimage sites and ethnic festivals, allowing formal and existential private devotion to lie fallow, because the truly enlightened supposedly had spiritually and culturally evolved beyond the need of such things. Contrary to these characterizations, Schillebeeckx commented as far back as the mid-1960s that veneration of Our Lady is far from a "pious option." Indeed, devotion to her is not that rendered to an

---

35. Rahner, "Courage for Devotion to Mary," 138.

alien, one being-apart, but rather of one who fulfilled the divine call and will in a particular way—even as we are called to pursue it, as Christ has presented it to us.

> An explicit veneration of Mary is a vitally necessary condition for the full flowing and normal adult maturity of Christian life. Its distinctive quality is, moreover, based on the objective fact of God's having geared the mystery of Mary—as a singular but real structural principle—to the redemptive mystery of Christ and hence to the essential mystery of our religious life. This implies that a task of great importance for all men was assigned by God to Mary in connection with the vocation of mankind given to us in the person of Christ. Her unique place within the plan of salvation is an appeal made by God to all men. We are bound, in faith and love, to recognize this call and to give our assent to it, because we must, in our constantly growing consciousness of faith, enter into the scheme of salvation in accordance with God's objective will.[36]

In discovering the multitude of ways in which this can be done, and to whatever degree, Catholics and other Christians, as well, are expressing the rejection of the false dichotomy created by a "Mary of history" over (or even excluding) the "God-Bearer of faith," adapting Kähler's famous expression in reference to her divine son.[37] Our Lady, whose "intercession has a special place apart, as the direct consequence of her special relation to the Lord of all, who is also her Son,"[38] is gaining a new generation of friends, sons and daughters who have engaged in a wider movement wherein Western Christians acknowledge deliberately and consciously a core truth of the human race since the Fall: it cannot save itself, redeem itself, or be sufficient in itself, individually or collectively. We again look toward this Mother "who gave birth to God the Word"[39] who compels us to seek out the Only-begotten of Mary and the Father who for all humanity

---

36. Edward Schillebeeckx, *Mary: Mother of the Redemption*, trans. N. D. Smith (New York: Sheed and Ward, 1964), 137.

37. I here refer to the oft-quoted expression "the Jesus of history versus the Christ of faith." This is adapted from the title of an 1892 book written by Martin Kähler (1835–1912) entitled *The So-Called Historical Jesus and the Historical Biblical Christ* (*Der Sogenannte historische Jesus und der geschichtliche, biblische Christus*), Fortress Texts in Modern Theology (Minneapolis: Fortress, 1988).

38. O. R. Cassall-Phillips, "Mary, Mother of God," in *Teaching of the Catholic Church*, ed. George D. Smith (New York: Macmillan, 1961), 2:532.

39. The anaphoras in the Byzantine Divine Liturgies of John Chrysostom and St. Basil the Great.

is the way, truth and life. It is a matter for the Christian people of our time to return to the basics of authentic devotion of faith, overcoming what de Lubac trenchantly identifies as

> the most subversive temptation, the one that is ever and insidiously reborn when all the rest are overcome . . . what [has been] the temptation to "worldliness of the mind" . . . the practical relinquishing of other-worldliness, so that mortal and even spiritual standards should be based, not on the glory of the Lord, but on what is the profit of man; an entire anthropocentric outlook would be exactly what we mean by worldliness.[40]

As a mortal sharing in the first fruits of redemption and by virtue of her divine maternity, Mary teaches us how to live for eternal life in her son who "appeared in our mortal nature [and] made us new by the glory of his immortal nature."[41]

Assessment and Conclusion

Almost from the very beginning of the third Christian millennium, the West has found itself enmeshed in a conjunction of crises economic, moral, religious, and social. These are obvious enough, and are perhaps not unique to Western history—except in the manner these play out in an inexorably shrinking planet. (Indeed, comparatively few places on the planet remain beyond the reach of cell phones and social media!) The Pilgrim Church is not entirely immune to the same cycles and variants in history as the societies it serves. The dialectical shifts even in the Catholic Church's disciplinary policies and initiatives in less than half a century are reminders of this.[42] At the same time, she must be a voice of reason and haven of calm, rising

---

40. Henri de Lubac, *Splendor of the Church*, trans. Michael Mason (San Francisco: Ignatius, 1993), 377. Here, Cardinal de Lubac is quoting Abbot Anscar Vonier, OSB, of Buckfast Abbey, England, who served as the abbey's superior from 1906 until his death in 1938.

41. "Preface of the Epiphany of the Lord," in the *Roman Missal*.

42. A well-known contemporary example, alluded to earlier, is provided in the virtual suppression of the pre-Conciliar Roman Liturgy in 1969, which was partially recalled (albeit for comparatively numerical minorities) in favor of a more extended, but still limited, celebration of the 1962 so-called Tridentine usage by John Paul II in 1988, leading eventually to an essentially unlimited (although optional) restoration by Pope Benedict XVI in 2007. This last initiative established it as a parallel "extraordinary" usage of the Roman liturgical Rite alongside the "ordinary" usage of 1969 and its successors.

above the eddies and currents of the *sæculum*. Indeed, Paul VI noted in his *Last Will and Testament* that the Church cannot help the world by "assuming its thoughts, customs, [and] tastes."[43] The Church's success here below as the purveyor for the world's salvation will depend, as it has throughout history, on its corporate and individual fidelity to the Gospel.

Throughout the Church universal, East and West, public devotion to our Lady retains a permanent place in the array of liturgical offices and feasts honoring her, beseeching her unique intercession as "the first and fairest of those redeemed by Jesus Christ."[44] Likewise, perennial devotions such as the Rosary, the *Akathistos* prayer, and pilgrimages to Marian devotional centers around the world will also, presumably, continue for generations to come. With regard to "private" devotion, it is difficult to predict at present (2012) the extent that the turn-of-the-century renewal of Marian devotion and spirituality will fully pervade the "private" lives of the faithful. More specifically, how will Christians continue to engender a relationship of practical, spiritual intimacy with her, and what forms will it take—particularly in an increasingly secularized West, often at odds with an authentic Christian ethos? Even with certain signs of a definite renewal—based more or less on the traditional forms, but still lacking an *entirely* new and authentic expression—this is a question that only time will answer.

As the ages course along toward the *eschaton*, movements and devotions will likewise continue to wax and wane. Christians for their part are called to respond to our common Mother's loving concern by inviting her into our lives, our joys, hopes, sorrows and worries.[45] Whatever their response, Mary is near at hand as the God-Bearer *pro nobis*. She continues to care for the world, in fulfillment of the unique mission entrusted to her from the cross of her son.[46]

> Contemplated in the episodes of the Gospels and in the reality which she already possesses in the City of God, the Blessed Virgin Mary offers a calm vision and a reassuring word to modern man, torn as he often is between anguish and hope, defeated by the sense of his own limitations and assailed by limitless aspirations, troubled in his mind and divided in his heart, uncertain before the

---

43. *Last Will and Testament of Pope Paul VI*, June 30, 1965, online: http://www.papalencyclicals.net/Paulo6/p6will.htm.

44. From the booklet mentioned above, *Devotions in Honor of Christ and His Mother of Perpetual Help*. It is perhaps a quote from St. Alphonsus Liguori.

45. See preface to GS.

46. See John 19:26–27.

riddle of death, oppressed by loneliness while yearning for fellowship, a prey to boredom and disgust. She shows forth the victory of hope over anguish, of fellowship over solitude, of peace over anxiety, of joy and beauty over boredom and disgust, of eternal visions over earthly ones, of life over death.[47]

---

47. MC §57. I would also highly recommend the reflections of Fr. Johann Roten, who provides an outstanding summation of Ratzingerian Mariology—itself a hermeneutic for further authentic development in Marian Devotion. See Mariological Society of America, "Mary—Personal Concretization of the Church," in *Theotokos: Mother of All People*, Marian Studies 16 (Dayton, OH: MSA Secretariat, Marian Library, University of Dayton, 2006), 242–321.

10

Mary and the Communal Nature of Salvation

MAURA HEARDEN

"The world is a fallen world because it has fallen away from awareness that God is all in all . . . even the religion of this fallen world . . . has accepted the all-embracing secularism which attempts to steal the world away from God."[1]

"In the Holy Spirit's union with Mary . . . there is all the love of the Blessed Trinity; in the other, all of creation's love. So it is that in this union heaven and earth are joined."[2]

A traditionally Christian understanding of human relationships is, in many ways, diametrically opposed to secularized American perspectives. Where popular American culture tends to assume the radical autonomy of individuals—separation from God and each other—Christianity holds fast to the conviction that the human race is bonded at the very core of our *being*: in our common origin, existence, and destiny in God. Consequently, where popular American culture thinks in terms of "private sins" and "victimless

---

1. Alexander Schmemann, *For the Life of the World: Sacraments and Orthodoxy* (Crestwood, NY: St. Vladimir's Seminary Press, 1982), 16.

2. H. M. Manteau-Bonamy, *Immaculate Conception and the Holy Spirit: The Marian Teachings of Father Kolbe*, trans. Richard Arnandez (Libertyville, IL: Prow / Franciscan Marytown, 1977), 5.

crimes," assuming that the effects of self-destructive behavior are, indeed, limited to the self, Christianity teaches us that, because we share an intimate bond constituted by God Himself who transcends time and space, heaven and earth, we have no choice but to bear our brother's burdens—spiritually as well as materially. Indeed, the process of transformation required for salvation is itself a communal enterprise.

A traditionally Catholic understanding of Mary, the person through whom the Creator embraces the world and in whom the world opens its heart to its Creator, expresses truths about our communal existence with remarkable clarity. Even a cursory knowledge of Mary's place in the Christmas story shatters the myth of radical individual autonomy as we must consider the fact that the Second Person of the Trinity united Himself to the *entire* human race through the humanity of *one* woman. For this reason, knowledge of Mary can anchor the Christian mind firmly in a Christian worldview as a sea of secular contradictions storms against it. The following pages will illustrate the profoundly communal dimension of traditional Catholic Mariology by explaining how even the so-called "Marian privileges," those gifts that seem to set Mary apart from the rest of the human race, actually depend upon and exemplify our unity with each other and God. First, however, it is necessary to lay the foundations of our conversation with a brief overview of the concept in which Christian discussions of unity are grounded, that is "sacramental communion."

The Mystery of Sacramental Communion

The word "sacramental" is most often associated with particular sacraments such as Baptism and Eucharist. Paragraph 1131 of the *Catechism of the Catholic Church* describes them in this way:

> The sacraments are efficacious signs of grace, instituted by Christ and entrusted to the Church, by which divine life is dispensed to us. The visible rites by which the sacraments are celebrated signify and make present the graces proper to each sacrament. They bear fruit in those who receive them with the required dispositions.

In other words, God chooses to provide graces necessary for salvation through elements found in the material world, such as water, bread, and wine. These material elements become "signs" in that they draw our attention to a more profound reality that is at once contained within them and communicated through them.

Since the close of the Second Vatican Council, our understanding of God's effective immanence (His presence in and distribution of grace through the material world) has deepened so that many Catholic as well as other Christian scholars now speak of a broader concept known as the "sacramental principle," and the Church in particular as a "sacramental communion."[3] While the particular sacraments of the Church (such as Baptism and Eucharist) hold a unique status in God's saving plan, their nature and instrumentality should not be seen as a radical break from God's relationship with the rest of creation, an insertion of divine activity where there once was none. In a broad sense, the entire created order is sacramental of God because He is present in and working through it, making the whole of natural reality an effective sign of heavenly reality.

As Herbert Vorgrimler states,

> The eternal and uncreated God in sovereign freedom, brings into existence that which is utterly different and, by affirming it, keeps it in being. . . . God wishes to be present to the consciousness of human beings. . . . Humans cannot be aware of this utterly different God . . . except by some sensible mediation.[4]

Therefore God, whose presence in creation is that which holds creation in existence, works through creation to make Himself known to mankind. For example, God spoke to Moses through a burning bush (Exod 3:1–15). Similarly, "God is internal to human persons or events in order to approach people in love . . . to move them to advance together with creation on the way home to God."[5] Human persons, who are made in God's image and are therefore "signs" able to freely and rationally participate in God's work, are the recipients of an awesome privilege and responsibility, particularly those who share in the salvific communion of Christ's Mystical Body, the Church.

The Church (which consists of a hierarchical institution as well as a Mystical Body) is often described as a "sacramental communion." It is "sacramental" in the sense that Christ is truly present in and working through

---

3. For a summary of Catholic scholarship regarding scriptural and historical support on this topic, see ch. 1 of Vorgrimler. For a summary of the development of Catholic scholarship relating the sacramental structure of God's relationship with humanity to the issue of salvation including the notion of Christ as the primordial sacrament and the notion of the Church as the fundamental sacrament, see ch. 3 of Herbert Vorgrimler, *Sacramental Theology*, trans. Linda M. Maloney, 3rd ed. (Collegeville, MN: Liturgical, 1992).

4. Ibid., 28–29.

5. Ibid., 9.

it. It is a "communion" because the presence of the Holy Spirit is a bond uniting all the members of the Body. Because Christ lives in us and we in Christ, the communion that is effected by our membership in the Church has two dimensions that deepen simultaneously. The first dimension may be described as a vertical communion because it refers to the believer's relationship with God. The second dimension may be described as a horizontal communion because it refers to the bonds that the Holy Spirit creates between the creaturely members of the Mystical Body.[6]

However, we have already said that God's presence expands beyond the members of Christ's Mystical Body, encompassing all of creation, a fact upon which our very existence depends. Furthermore, our Christian faith tells us that all human beings are ordered toward everlasting communion with the Trinity and that, although communion within Christ's Mystical Body is necessary for salvation, God's activity beyond that which is united within Christ's Mystical Body is also ordered toward salvation. Therefore, the ontological unity effected by our participation in God's existence, even if we are not members of Christ's Body, might also be called a "sacramental communion" with both vertical and horizontal dimensions. It is, after all, by means of this broader communion that humanity received the revelation that prepared the way for the Messiah.

To summarize, the sacramental principle states that God is present in and working through creation for our salvation, making all of creation, in some way, an effective sign of His grace. As a result of this sacramental structure, human persons share, in varying degrees of depth and specificity, a sacramental communion, united by God to God and each other. The term can be applied in a broad sense to the entire human race and in a deeper, more particular sense to those who are united within the Mystical Body of Christ.

The Blessed Virgin Mary provides a striking illustration of the sacramental communion that we share as members of the human race and, more deeply still, as members of the Church. In her, we see the reality of the bonds that unite us, the way in which God uses these bonds to effect His plans, and the therefore inestimable importance of each individual "yes" to God, the Source of all Life. What better place to begin the specifics of

---

6. The late Pope John Paul II explored the social and spiritual consequences of this simultaneously vertical and horizontal communion when he developed the notion of solidarity. For an excellent exploration of the origins and intricacies of John Paul II's development of solidarity, see Kevin P. Doran, *Solidarity: A Synthesis of Personalism and Communalism in the Thought of Karol Wojtyla/Pope John Paul II* (New York: Lang, 1996).

our discussion than with the motherhood through which God effected the miraculous apex of His sacramental presence in creation, the Incarnation.

Mary's Motherly Mediation

The Marian title, *Theotókos* ("God-Bearer" or "Mother of God"), was dogmatically defined at the Council of Ephesus in AD 431. This, the first of the Marian dogmas, proclaims the fact from which all of Mary's religious significance flows. In addition, the very reason for bestowing the title illustrates Mary's role in the Christian faith, for the title was *not* dogmatized for the purpose of exalting Mary. Rather, the title was given to underscore the intimate communion between God and man in Christ, her divine son.[7] As such, *Theotókos* and its Latin counterpart, *Dei Genitrix* ("Mother of God"), are laden with connotations significant for the horizontal as well as the vertical dimensions of communion involving Mary and all of humanity.

Consider some of the implications of Mary's historical motherhood. The incarnation was the apex of God's sacramental self-communication to mankind. The infinite, eternal Second Person of the Trinity united His divinity with our humanity in the womb of a woman, and this woman was no mere vessel through which God entered the world. Mary gave herself body and soul as an active participant in the event so that St. Proclus of Constantinople proclaimed her "the spiritual garden of the second Adam, the workshop of the unity of the natures."[8] Mary's "yes" to God was *effective*; her flesh was Christ's flesh; her nature and heredity were Christ's nature and heredity. Through God's grace, Mary, a mere creature, a single, solitary person, experienced a communion with the divine that, except for

---

7. For an historical summary of the Council of Ephesus in AD 431, see Hilda Graef, *Mary: A History of Doctrine and Devotion*, with a new chapter covering Vatican II and beyond by Thomas A. Thompson (Notre Dame, IN: Christian Classics, 2009), 79–87.

8. Norman Russell, *Cyril of Alexandria* (London: Routledge, 2000), 33. See also LG §56 for commentary on Mary's active participation through obedience; Matthias J. Scheeben, *Mariology*, vols. 1 & 2, trans. Theodore L. M. J. Greukers (St. Louis, MO: Herder, 1946), ch. 5, in which he provides a theological explanation for Mary's graced cooperation in the formation of the hypostatic union. Raniero Cantalamessa, *Mary: Mirror of the Church*, trans. Francis Lonergan Villa (Collegeville, MN: Liturgical, 1992), 58–59, briefly describes early apologetics against gnosticism and docetism which emphasized the belief that Christ was born through and not merely of the Virgin. Christ's humanity was real because Mary was more than a mere vessel of the incarnate Lord.

the divine-human communion existing within Christ (who alone is the hypostatic union),[9] was and always shall be unsurpassed in human history.

Yet, Mary did not enter into this communion as a single, solitary person. She brought all of humanity—all those who had ever lived and ever will live—with her. She represented "all of creation's love. So it is that in this union heaven and earth are joined . . . the totality of eternal love with the totality of created love."[10] The gift that Mary gave of herself, deemed her *fiat* ("Let it be done") because of her response to the angel, Gabriel, included the biological heritage of Israel. It was also the culmination of the faith of Israel, a faith that extended into the future to embrace all of humanity. Karl Rahner offers the following comments on the implications of such an event:

> Her [Mary's] divine motherhood is effected by her faith (Luke 1:43; 2:27 ff.), and so it is not a merely biological occurrence. Nor is this consequence of her faith an event that belongs only to her private life-history. It is . . . the central event of the whole public history of redemption itself. For this divine motherhood occurs, by God's grace, as a freely-willed conception, receiving for the world the grace that the Incarnation brings; it is a true partnership with God's action for mankind.[11]

God chose to communicate Himself to the world through the physical and spiritual aspects of Mary's person. The role that Mary's faith played in receiving the grace of salvation for the world is, in some ways, comparable to the role that the faith of parents, godparents, and the Church play during an infant baptism. The immaculately conceived Mary, who had already been saved from original sin by the future merits of her son, spoke, in faith, on behalf of an as yet unaware humanity providing a means by which all might be saved. Analogously, during an infant baptism, the parents, godparents, and other members of the faithful, speak, in faith, on behalf of an as yet unaware child, providing a means by which he or she might be saved.

While it is true that no one but Mary will ever bear the incarnation as a physical mother, we do bear Christ to each other. At least two observations about the role that individuals play in the salvation of others come to mind. First, Mary was prepared for this moment by having been immaculately

---

9. The term "hypostatic union" refers to the unity of Christ's divine and human natures within the person—"hypostasis"—of the divine Son.

10. Manteau-Bonamy, *Immaculate Conception*, 5.

11. Karl Rahner, *Mary, Mother of the Lord*, trans. W. J. O'Hara (Wheathampstead, UK: Clarke, 1974), 13.

conceived (that is, saved from original sin from the moment of her conception). Absolute sinlessness was necessary if she was to play her role in this process of divine self-communication, uttering her equally absolute "yes." Thus, we are given a startling illustration of the communal consequences of individual holiness. Second, we understand from witnessing God's way of entering the world throughout Scripture and especially through Mary that her and, by extension, our, participation in the fulfillment of God's plan is of critical importance. Yves Congar explains,

> These three subjects [the Church, our Lady, and Christ] are intimately connected, and their connection depends upon a single principle which must be applied, with due qualification, in each of the three cases; the principle, that is, that human nature plays its part in the work of salvation, yet equally clearly the total power of effecting that salvation is from God. . . .The sacred Humanity [of Christ] united to the Divinity . . . is the instrument of our salvation. . . . This is why our Lady, by her intimate association with the sacred Humanity, and the Church in consequence of it, play the part our teaching assigns to them.[12]

The notion that "human nature plays its part in the work of salvation" relies on the doctrinal framework associated with "sacramental communion": God has chosen to communicate Himself *through* creation, involving the entire universe in the mediation of His grace. Human beings, who were created in God's image, mediate His grace in a special way when using free will to cooperate with rather than reject or corrupt it.

Such human mediation is not to be understood as competing in any way with Christ as the One Mediator between God and Man (1 Tim 2:5–6).[13] It is, rather, understood as a manifestation of the magnificent power of a God who "could have saved us without Christ [or] Mary, or with Christ alone" but *chose* to save us via Mary's acceptance of the incarnation.[14] Theologians have often pondered the possible turn of events should Mary have

---

12. Yves Congar, *Christ, Our Lady and the Church: A Study in Eirenic Theology*, trans. Henry St. John (Westminster, MD: Newman, 1957), 31.

13. While more traditional Protestant scholars might interpret this passage in an exclusive sense, using it as evidence that Christ is the only mediator between God and Man, Catholics traditionally understand the context of the passage as one which emphasizes the unique, universal, but not exclusive, nature of Christ's mediation. See, e.g., LG §49, online: http://www.vatican.va/archive/hist_councils/ii_vatican_council/documents/vat-ii_const_19641121_lumen-gentium_en.html.

14. Charles Balic, *Mariology and Ecumenism in Vatican II* (Graymoor, NY: Unity Apostolate, Central Office, 1966), 21.

said "no" to God. Similarly, we must ponder the possible effects of each "no" that we utter for the salvation of souls other than our own.

Mary's historical motherhood is inextricable from another aspect of her motherhood, recognized by the Catholic faith: her motherhood of the Mystical Body in the order of grace. Pope Pius X summarizes the connection, "In the chaste womb of the Virgin, Christ took to himself flesh, and united to himself the spiritual body formed of those who were to believe in him.... [His mother] is Mother of us all."[15]

In his encyclical *Redemptoris Mater*, Blessed Pope John Paul II identifies Mary's faith as the cornerstone of her biological and spiritual motherhood. He argues that, after presenting the Blessed Virgin as the true mother of Christ's humanity in the first chapters of Luke, the Gospel writer adds a new dimension to her maternal role in Luke 8:20-21 and Luke 11:27-28, by recalling that Christ's family consists of those who hear the Word of God and keep it.[16] Mary, whose *fiat* is the preeminent example of such obedience (Luke 1:38) and who is the only person specifically mentioned in Luke as one who "kept" God's word and "pondered it in her heart" (Luke 1:38, 45; 2:19, 51), is an exemplar of faith and therefore a spiritual mother within Christ's Mystical Body (RM §20-21). The Pope continues his discussion, interpreting Mary's intercession at the wedding feast of Cana (John 2:3-5) and the giving of Mary and John to each other as they stood at the foot of the cross (John 19:25-27) as indications of Mary's continuing maternal role within the Church and Christ's confirmation of that role (RM §21-24).

The passages that Pope John Paul II cites also illustrate the interdependence of Mary's "vertical" gift of herself to God and her "horizontal" gift of herself to humanity. When Mary lovingly and faithfully places herself in her son's hands at the wedding feast of Cana by saying to the servants, "Do whatever he tells you," her son responds with graces (literally, free gifts) for all present at the banquet. He turns water into wine, thus responding to physical needs and begins to reveal his identity to his friends, increasing their faith. When Mary abandons herself to the mystery of God's will at the foot of the cross, she receives her universal motherhood from Christ as he tells John, "Behold your mother."

---

15. This quotation is taken from Pope Pius X's encyclical, *Ad Diem Illum Laetissimum*, §10. The Vatican translation is available online: http://www.vatican.va/holy_father/pius_x/encyclicals/documents/hf_p-x_enc_02021904_ad-diem-illum-laetissimum_en.html.

16. RM §20, online: http://www.vatican.va/holy_father/john_paul_ii/encyclicals/documents/hf_jp-ii_enc_25031987_redemptoris-mater_en.html.

Once again, Mary illustrates a principle applicable to the entire human race. Opening the heart in faith and love to the presence of the Holy Spirit deepens the Christian believer's mediation of the Holy Spirit to one another. Hans Urs von Balthasar comments specifically on the multidirectional, unifying nature of love as well as the consequences of such unity:

> The selflessness of Christian love founds a kind of communism of spiritual goods, and the more perfectly a Christian develops this selfless love in himself, the more all others can live on his goods as if they were their own. Not only are individuals transparent to one another, they also radiate what is theirs into the others—although we can speak only in a loose sense of "theirs," because perfect selflessness and transparency are nothing other than the life of God and Christ in creatures. Mary, as the purest of all creatures, irradiates what is her own least of all. Everyone within the communion of saints has something Marian about him.[17]

Thus, for von Balthasar, Mary's mediation is worthy of special attention. Since Mary is most fully conformed to Christ, she is His most effective vehicle for communicating Himself to others. Mary's conformity to Christ, her utter abandonment of self to the universally active power of the Holy Spirit, began at the moment of her conception.

The Immaculate Conception As Means of Communion

The dogma of the Immaculate Conception teaches that Mary, through no merit of her own, was preserved from all "stain of sin" from the moment of her conception in view of the future merits of Christ.[18] It is easily one of the most controversial and misunderstood dogmas of the Catholic faith.

---

17. Joseph Cardinal Ratzinger and Hans Urs von Balthasar, *Mary: The Church at the Source*, trans. Adrian Walker (San Francisco: Ignatius, 2005), 122.

18. The dogma was defined by Pope Pius IX in the 1854 papal bull, *Ineffabilis Deus*, available online: http://www.papalencyclicals.net/Pius09/p9ineff.htm.

Mary's preservation from sin at the moment of conception was a disputed point until John Duns Scotus proposed the notion of preservative redemption. However, belief in Mary's sinless purity has commanded strong testimony since the first centuries of the Church. For historical overviews, see Michael O'Carroll, *Theotókos: A Theological Encyclopedia of the Blessed Virgin Mary* (Eugene, OR: Wipf & Stock Publishers, 2000), 180–82; René Laurentin, *Queen of Heaven: A Short Treatise on Marian Theology*, trans. Gordon Smith (Dublin: Clonmore & Reynolds, 1956), 11–73; and an introduction to *Ineffabilis Deus*, in M. Jean Frisk and Marianne Lorraine Trouvé, eds., *Mother of Christ, Mother of the Church: Documents on the Blessed Virgin Mary* (Boston: Pauline, 2000), 3–6.

Those who question the dogma's content often do so because they believe it necessarily implies that Mary is set apart from the human race, that she is not really human. The root of this sentiment tends to fall into two general categories. The first is comprised of those who mistakenly believe that the dogma declares Mary free from the necessity of redemption. This objection was answered by Blessed John Duns Scotus (1265/66–1308) who paved the way for the dogmatic definition by reminding the world that God, who is not bound by the laws of time, could save His mother in view of the future merits of Christ. (Mary's need of redemption has been thoroughly discussed in nearly every Catholic treatment of the dogma and so will not be further addressed here.)

The second category of objections comes from people who may not be concerned with the issue of Mary's need for redemption *per se*, but still tend to think solely in terms of what the Immaculate Conception did for her as an *individual*. They will often pose questions such as, "Why should God make an exception for this one woman? Was she greater than the rest of us so that she merited some greater privilege?" or "Doesn't this privilege imply that ordinary womanhood is somehow defective? In the end, doesn't the dogma of the Immaculate Conception simply serve the misogynist tendencies of a patriarchal society that has devalued femininity and must therefore elevate the Mother of Christ above all other women?"

Certainly, the Immaculate Conception implies that ordinary womanhood—and manhood—is defective, for both have been damaged by original sin. The privilege was not, however, given to Mary as a reward for her personal superiority or to isolate her from the rest of humanity. Rather, it was given her for the sake of humanity and had the effect of deepening her communion with the other members of her race.

Anglican theologian and ecumenist John MacQuarrie has shed some light on this subject. He once observed that the use of the phrase "stain of sin" within the papal bull that defines the dogma, *Ineffabilis Deus,* is unfortunate because it points the imagination in the direction of a Manichean-styled, substantive sin.[19] However, if sin is understood in the traditional Christian sense as the *absence* or *perversion* of goodness (i.e., alienation from God) and salvation consists in a perfected reception of goodness (i.e., communion with God), then the Immaculate Conception becomes an inevitable condition for the incarnation and exemplifies the heart and soul

---

19. John MacQuarrie, *Mary for All Christians*, 2nd ed. (Edinburgh: T. & T. Clark, 2001), 66.

of vertical and horizontal communion. The dogma teaches us about the source of grace (the Trinity); describes the shared nature of grace (which forms an interdependent bond among human persons as well as a bond with the divine characterized by personal holiness); the way in which grace is distributed (via a process of creaturely reception and mediation); and the ultimate effect of God's grace (the perfected Church of the age-to-come).

Catholic scholars have observed that the phenomenon of the Immaculate Conception is consistent with observable patterns of God's saving activity throughout human history.[20] God chose to effect redemptive communion in continuity with the biological, cultural, and religious heritage of the people of Israel. Their story reveals a God who prepared this community for the coming of the Messiah by gradually bestowing His unmerited grace on (i.e., communicating Himself to) an often flawed and ultimately unworthy people—like us!—purifying their moral condition and strengthening their faith. He was transforming them, making them a holy people and bringing them into ever-deeper communion with Him by giving them Himself. Often, God chose to communicate His grace by means of special, particular people who were called to be mediators between God and mankind (e.g., Abraham, Moses, the prophets), concrete signs who truly embodied (to a certain extent) the grace they shared.

Over time, the continuity of the Chosen People was predicated on a type of communion among individuals that spanned generations—until it reached its zenith in the womb of Mary, the Mother of the God-Man. The Immaculate Conception graced Mary with the perfect, intimate communion necessary to participate in the formation of the hypostatic union—the unity of humanity and divinity in the divine Person of Christ. It was the Creator's crowning touch on an unmerited, grace-filled process, which began with the Old Testament Patriarchs: "In [Mary] the mediation which Israel had exercised, ever since Abraham, in favour of the sinful world (Gen. XVIII, 17–23) attains its highest efficaciousness."[21]

Plainly said, Mary's Immaculate Conception made her historical mediation possible. If sin is alienation from God, then the humanity of Christ,

---

20. The following thoughts combine ideas taken from Rahner, *Mary*, esp. 49, and Laurentin, *Queen of Heaven*, esp. 81–85.

21. Rahner, *Mary*, 85. Please note that Laurentin is speaking of the highest order of mediation among human creatures, which is always subordinate to and dependent upon the redemption effected by the hypostatic union. See also Herman A. Fiolet, *Ecumenical Breakthrough: An Integration of the Catholic and Reformational Faith*, Duquesne Studies Theological Series 9 (Pittsburgh: Duquesne University Press, 1969), 438–51.

which was to be united in the most intimate communion possible with the divinity of Christ, could not be sinful. If Mary was to be the source of that humanity, the one who was overshadowed by the Holy Spirit (Luke 1:35) for the sake of the entire human race, then she too must be free from sin. She could not give herself completely to God and be, even in part, alienated from Him at the same time. Furthermore, insofar as it bespeaks of her communion with the Holy Spirit—the universal bond between God and men and men with each other—Mary's Immaculate Conception makes possible her continuing mediation on behalf of the human race and as exemplar for the Church.

St. Maximillian Kolbe has left us an edifying and inspiring treatment regarding the ongoing and Spirit-filled mediation of Mary. Kolbe devoted his life to contemplation of Our Lady's words to St. Bernadette Soubirous of Lourdes: "I am the Immaculate Conception." He formed a Mariology which in many ways foreshadowed that of the Second Vatican Council, his insights regarding Mary's relationship with the Holy Spirit being arguably his greatest contribution to Marian studies.[22] After many years, Kolbe concluded that the woman who *is* the Immaculate Conception is a creaturely "theophany, a visible manifestation of the Father's infinite love for men, that love which, through the Holy Spirit, accomplishes in the Church the work of the redemption, the mission of the Son, who is also the Son of Mary."[23] Because the work of redemption involves the uniting of all men in Christ, the *Immaculata* is specifically an instrument of communion.

To appreciate Kolbe's conclusions, it is necessary to begin with his meditation on the life of the Trinity:

> And who is the Holy Spirit? The flowering of the love of the Father and the Son. If the fruit of created love is a created conception, then the fruit of divine Love, that prototype of all created love, is necessarily a divine "conception." The Holy Spirit is, therefore, the "uncreated, eternal conception," the prototype of all the conceptions that multiply life throughout the whole universe.[24]

---

22. H. M. Manteau-Bonamy, one of the *periti* involved in drafting ch. 8 of *Lumen Gentium*, provides specific examples of this foreshadowing throughout his study of Kolbe's Mariology, *Immaculate Conception and the Holy Spirit: The Marian Teachings of Father Kolbe*, which has already been cited. The book includes a press conference given by then Cardinal Wojtyla of Cracow, which also comments on the continuity between Kolbe's work and Vatican II Mariology.

23. Manteau-Bonamy, *Immaculate Conception*, 31–32.

24. Ibid., 3.

According to Kolbe's understanding, the *uncreated* Immaculate Conception (the Holy Spirit) dwelt within the Mother of the Lord from the first moment of her existence in a unique communion with her essence (although not in a *hypostatic* union), effecting the greatest of all possible love within a creature: a complete abandonment of the self to the love of God which would join heaven and earth in the birth of Christ. As the *created* Immaculate Conception, the Blessed Virgin represents "all of creation's love. So it is that in this union heaven and earth are joined . . . the totality of eternal love with the totality of created love."[25]

Kolbe goes on to explain three aspects of the deep union between Mary and the Holy Spirit: (1) absolute conformity of her will to His, (2) free and conscious participation in God's will as His instrument, and (3) reception of the Holy Spirit as His dwelling place or sanctuary.[26] By her spousal reception of the Holy Spirit and her obedient service to his will, Mary becomes the visible (sacramental) sign of His presence and a pivotal instrument for the fulfillment of His mission (which is inseparable from that of the Son) to transform and unite souls with the Trinity. As the instrument and sanctuary of the Holy Spirit, Mary brought Christ into the world and as a living creature who even to this day enjoys a perfected version of the mission in which she participated on earth, she continues to function as the unique *Mediatrix* through whom the Holy Spirit pours forth grace.[27]

Such reflections illustrate the communal nature and import of every Christian's openness to receiving divine grace, which is given to concrete individuals, but is never separate from the salvation of the community at large. There is, however, only one Immaculate Conception in Catholic dogma, so defined as to teach of a perfected transparency to the Holy Spirit making Mary a model creaturely mediator. As such, she is a great aid toward and exemplar of the perfection to which the Church is called, for the Church's sole mission is the mediation of God's grace.

In Mary, "the Church has already reached that perfection whereby she exists without spot or wrinkle (cf. Eph 5:27)."[28] In her sinless life, her

25. Ibid., 5.

26. Ibid., 51. The notion of Mary as the Holy Spirit's "sanctuary" is used in LG §53.

27. It is interesting to note that, although eastern Christianity does not recognize the dogma of the Immaculate Conception, it has underscored the Blessed Virgin's intimate association with the Holy Spirit by giving her the title *Panagia* (All holy). This is the feminine version of the title, *Panagion*, which is applied to the Holy Spirit.

28. O'Carroll, *Theotókos*, 346–48 provides an overview of the history of and scriptural arguments for Mary as a type of the Church.

complete and perfect redemption/communion with God, Christians can see the future to which we all aspire. Mary is also, as Rahner observes, a sign of the Church's present, heavenly reality. He underscores the importance of Mary's existence as such a *sign* to the actualization of the Church as a perfect sacramental communion, saying that, although the Church is comprised of sinners, it is also "the tangible presence, in the sacred history of redemption, of the victory of grace."[29] If the latter is true, says Rahner, the Church as a sacrament, in the broad sense of the term, must truly embody grace in a concrete manner:

> If she [the Church] is to be holy in an actual and tangible manner, not only by propounding an abstract postulate, but as a sign set by God among the nations . . . the Church must be able to say at least once, that redemption by the grace of God produced its complete effect, and in such a way that this perfect victory becomes plainly manifest for us pilgrims, as a promise to us that 'God does not give the Spirit by measure' (John 3:34).[30]

The dogma of the Immaculate Conception is intimately related to the notion of the Church as a sacramental communion. Indeed, it would not be necessary or even effective if Mary did not share an ontological communion with the entire human race. In Mary's life we see the powerful reality of God's saving work. As the Immaculate Conception, the Blessed Virgin is a sign and means of God's grace because it is only as the Immaculate Conception that she is able to become the singular sanctuary of the Holy Spirit, receive Christ in her womb, and act as *Mediatrix* within the Body of Christ. Likewise, in the dogma of the Blessed Virgin's Assumption into heaven, the perfect communion to which all are called is truly made manifest.

The Assumption

The dogma of the Assumption was promulgated by Pope Pius XII in the 1950 document *Munificentissimus Deus*.[31] While carefully avoiding the question of Mary's death, *Munificentissimus Deus* tells us that, at the end of Mary's earthly life, she was taken body and soul into Heaven. Once again,

---

29. Rahner, *Mary*, 76.

30. Ibid., 77.

31. For an introduction to the document by Sr. Jean Frisk, as well as the complete text, see Frisk and Trouvé, *Mother of Christ*, 31–53.

the Church proclaims a Marian privilege that, far from isolating the Virgin from the rest of the human race, actually deepens her communion with us.

Mary's status as the sinless *Theotókos* who intercedes for all Christians in heaven was intertwined with belief in her bodily assumption throughout the history of the latter dogma's development.[32] In *Munificentissimus Deus*, Pope Pius XII continued in this line of thought, explicitly uniting the newly defined Marian dogma with that of the Immaculate Conception: "She, by an entirely unique privilege, completely overcame sin by her Immaculate Conception, and as a result she was not subject to the law of remaining in the corruption of the grave" (MD 4). Christ conquered sin and therefore conquered death. His mother, who was preserved from sin, was preserved from the bodily corruption that is a result of sin.[33]

Although Mary's Assumption was a corollary to her exemplary status as the Immaculate Conception, the pope emphasized the event as a precursor of each Christian's eschatological hope: "Finally it is our hope that belief in Mary's bodily Assumption into heaven will make our belief in our own resurrection stronger and render it more effective," (MD, 42). MacQuarrie provides further development of the pope's theme, saying that the Assumption of the Blessed Virgin is a corollary to the Ascension of Christ as the latter's inevitable implication:[34]

> The closeness of Jesus and Mary . . . could not be broken by the end of their companionship on earth. It is the fulfillment of the Lord's promise, made not just to Mary but to all his followers, that 'where I am, there you will be also' ([John] 14:3). Here we see how the Assumption of Mary and eventually of the whole Church is a consequence or corollary of the Ascension of Jesus.[35]

Christ's bodily Ascension demonstrates the "consummation of God's purpose for his creatures . . . to take them up into his presence, to grant the

---

32. O'Carroll's historical summary mentions several arguments like that of Theodosius of Alexandria (d. 566) who justifies Mary's "bodily resurrection . . . from the divine maternity and . . . sees Mary's constant intercession on behalf of all as a direct result of her final glory." See *Theotókos*, 55–58 (quotation is from 57).

33. It should be noted that Pius XII deliberately left the matter of Mary's death open to investigation by stating the dogma in the following way: "The ever Virgin Mary, having completed the course of her earthly life, was assumed body and soul into heavenly glory" (MD §44).

34. MacQuarrie, *Mary for All Christians*, ch. 4.

35. Ibid., 86.

vision of himself and communion with himself."[36] The bodily Assumption of Mary is the first fruit of this eschatological hope for those who follow Christ.

The logic of this teaching, as explained by MacQuarrie, can be summarized as follows: Perfect communion with God (which includes bodily resurrection) is the goal to which all mankind is called. The Blessed Virgin, as the immaculately conceived *Theotókos*, was graced with a singular spiritual and physical communion with God during her earthly life. To deprive Mary of a bodily assumption at the end of her earthly life would be to lessen the bond that she and Christ already shared, and this would be contrary to God's revealed will for human destiny. Mary's Assumption, then, is a visible sign of the Church's eschatological hope—the hope for communion with the Trinity in Christ.

The benefits of meditation on Mary's assumption are not, however, confined to truths about the eschatological Church. Implications drawn from the dogma have significance for the Pilgrim Church here and now. When Pope Pius XII solemnly proclaimed this dogma, he intended "that all the faithful . . . [would] be stirred up to a stronger piety toward their heavenly Mother, and that the souls of all those who glory in the Christian name may be moved by the desire of sharing in the unity of Jesus Christ's Mystical Body" (MD §42). Clearly, the pope associated Mary's Assumption with the concept of mystical communion in the next life, but the above statement was also intended to focus attention on ecclesial communion in this life. By encouraging meditation on the life of Mary, who was completely obedient to God, the pope hoped to underscore the "value of a human life entirely devoted to carrying out the heavenly Father's will and to bringing good to others," (MD §42). His expressed hope assumed that Marian-style obedience to God was intimately connected with service to the human race. Love of God and love of God's children are two dimensions of the same impulse and meditation on Mary's complete obedience to and communion with God ought to increase the virtue of charity exercised within the Church and beyond. So, too, a deepened, more loving relationship with Mary should, according to this logic, positively influence the believer's relationship with God. Thus, the dogma is significant to the day-to-day spiritual life of the Church as she strives to fulfill her mission on earth.

36. Ibid.

Conclusion

The Marian doctrines discussed throughout this essay are ultimately woven into a single truth about Mary's role in salvation history: Mary's mission as the Bearer of God, the *Theotókos*, is made possible by the divinely bestowed bond of the Immaculate Conception and consummated by her glorious Assumption into Heaven. These cosmic events mediated Christ Himself, and thus His grace, to the world—the saving grace of perfect communion with and in God. Mary's life makes strikingly evident the communion that we already share as well as the communion to which we aspire. We are materially and spiritually interdependent creatures, our brothers' keepers in this life and for the next.

www.ingramcontent.com/pod-product-compliance
Lightning Source LLC
Chambersburg PA
CBHW051742230426
43670CB00012B/2119